Predicaments of *Culture*

in South Africa

D1270751

Imagined South Africa

Unisa Press celebrates ten years of democracy in South Africa with a range of books entitled *Imagined South Africa*. To publish is to name reality; it is to mark identity and to confer the status of valid knowledge on the opinions, views and knowledge of a mass of voices once denied a hearing. This series chronicles the multiple ways in which South Africans of all colours and ideological persuasions have been responding, either critically or creatively, to the numerous contradictions in ten years of democracy.

Abebe Zegeye
Director: Unisa Press

Chabani Manganyi (Ed.)
On Becoming a Democracy:
Transition and Transformation in South African Society

Dial Ndima
The Law of Commoners and Kings:
Narratives of a Rural Transkei Magistrate

Reitumetse Mabokela and Zine Magubane (Eds)
Hear Our Voices: Race, Gender and the Status of
Black South African Women in the Academy

Devarakshanam Govinden
'Sister Outsiders': Identity and Difference
in the Writings of South African Indian Women

Peter Stewart
Segregation and Singularity: Politics and Its Context Among White
Middle-Class English-Speakers in Late-Apartheid Johannesburg

Keith Beavon
Johannesburg: The Making and
Shaping of the City

Ari Sitas
Voices that Reason: Theoretical Parables

Leon de Kock, Louise Bethlehem and Sonja Laden (Eds)
South Africa in the Global Imaginary

Michael Titlestad
Making the Changes: Representations of Jazz
in South African Literature and Reportage

Chris Ledochowski
Cape Flats Details: Life and Culture
in the Townships of Cape Town

Andries Oliphant, Peter Delius and Lalou Metzer (Eds)
Democracy X: Marking the Present
and Representing the Past

Predicaments of *Culture* in South Africa

Ashraf Jamal

UNIVERSITY OF SOUTH AFRICA PRESS
PRETORIA

KONINKLIJKE BRILL NV
LEIDEN

© 2005 University of South Africa
First edition, first impression
© Published by arrangement with Koninklijke Brill NV, Plantijnstraat 2, PO Box 9000, 2300 PA Leiden, The Netherlands

ISBN 1-86888-285-3

Published by Unisa Press
University of South Africa
PO Box 392, 0003 UNISA

Book series designer: André Nel
Electronic origination: Compleat, Johannesburg
Printer: ABC Press, Epping
Cover image: *Twilight of the Idols*. Artist: Kendell Geers, 2000. Found object and chevron tape. Reproduced with permission from the artist.

At the time of publication, Unisa Press had been unsuccessful in its efforts to trace the copyright holder for permission to reproduce the material by Wopko Jensma and invites the copyright holder or anyone acting on his behalf to contact Unisa Press at the address stated on this page.

In loving memory of my wife, Christine.

This book of thoughts and passions is dedicated to our daughters, Sahar and Mira Jaan.

CONTENTS

I was attempting to describe the way in which the articulation of cultural differences has to do with what can't be translated; what may be incommensurable in the moment of cultural difference emerges in language as an evacuation of the very signifying and symbolic register that is required, in another moment, for its representation. It is a kind of enunciative disturbance that throws the process of interpretation or identification into flux – which for that very reason makes the need to identify, to interpret, to historicize, all the more intense. As I was working out that concept, there were moments I felt there was something I had to say, something I could mouth without the words, something my hands could sketch in the air, yet something I couldn't get hold of. But I did try.

Homi Bhabha in conversation with W. J. T. Mitchell

PREFACE

imagine . . . dead . . . imagine

similar calls for memorials?

The greatest challenge of the South African revolution is in the search for ways of thinking, ways of perception, that will help to break down the closed epistemological structures of South African oppression, structures which can severely compromise resistance by dominating thinking itself. The challenge is to free the entire social imagination of the oppressed from the laws of perception that have characterized apartheid society. For writers this means freeing the creative process itself from those very laws. It means extending the writer's perceptions of what can be written about, and the means and methods of writing.

Njabulo Ndebele

This challenge, posed in 1986 in 'Redefining Relevance' (*South African Literature and Culture* p. 67), encapsulates the drives and motivations that define this inquiry. Its aim, or yearning, is to think in and through a system of oppression that, in 2004, still dominates and disfigures cultural production and reception in South Africa.

That Ndebele conceives the problem of oppression as epistemic points to the arena in which the ongoing reckoning must be focused: the sphere of representation, of signs. This sphere, however, is not reducible to the sum of its parts. Epistemology is not simply a system of signs, not exclusively a theory of knowledge. Rather, as Homi Bhabha notes in 'The Postcolonial and the Postmodern: The Question of Agency', cultural critique should not accept epistemic systems as given, but conceive critique as a pedagogic exploration into its own limits (*The Location of Culture* p. 181).

With Bhabha – whose thinking serves as the linchpin for this inquiry – I have sought not only to reflexively address the limits of critical and cultural inscription, but also to conceive of this engagement as a means through which to free thought and the creative process from that which dominates it. The following disclaimer and alluring invocation defines the enigmatic terms of engagement which distinguish this inquiry:

> if you seek simply the sententious or the exegetical, you will not grasp the hybrid moment outside the sentence – not quite experience, not yet concept; part dream, part analysis; neither signifier nor signified (ibid.).

This formulation not only defines the edge and the vortex of contemporary critical and cultural inquiry, but also alludes to pre-Socratic and mystical modes of thinking, which have been repressed by secular rationalism. My attempt, then, is not only to address the new, but also to give credence to the old; to rethink and refigure a radical heterogeneity which precedes and exceeds the strategies of containment which have forged a restricted, diminished, and pathological conception of South Africa's history, its present and its future.

Ndebele's call for creative ways of thinking, ways of perception, when flanked with Bhabha's enigmatic and seemingly stupefying logic, begs the approach which defines this undertaking. Its vaunted aim is none other than the decolonisation of the mind and the liberation of the social and cultural imagination. An endeavour of this nature cannot be achieved polemically. After Heraclitus, it must go by a route that is trackless and unexplored, and understand that its quest is necessarily speculative. A journey of this nature – that assumes the 'hybrid moment' as its enigmatic locus – is not for the faint-hearted, nor is it for those who would make a virtue of reason and belief. As Theodor Adorno reminds us, it is a journey whose source is terror and whose promise is happiness (*Prisms* p. 235).

Three conflicting and contiguous drives emerge as claimants upon the South African imaginary: fatalism, positivism, and relativism. My relation to these claimants is non-positional. While I reveal my equivocal relation to these claimants, and construct an alternative strain of thought, I also anticipate the counter claims of those who would read against the grain of hope that distinguishes my own non-position. This hope is no mere wish-fulfilment of a promise of cultural freedom, a promise which, at every turn, is perceived as endangered. It is a hope intimately aware of its fraught adequacy and liminal existence; a hope that finds its objective correlative in the miraculous endurance of the detrivores that survive on the leeward slip-face of the desert dunes and feed on the plant waste blown across the breadth of Africa. Or, in the sphere of culture, it is a hope akin to that exemplified at the close of *Life & Times of Michael K*, where we find K before a bomb-blasted site. The novel's concluding question – how to live in the face of ruin – is answered through the vision of a bent spoon and a length of string that is dropped into the shaft, then delicately withdrawn. In the spoon's shallow bowl there is the promise of water.

It is the little that is precious, then, that gives this inquiry its sustenance. Albie Sachs's 'Preparing Ourselves for Freedom' (*Spring is Rebellious* pp. 19–29) sets the stage and announces this inquiry's recurring theme and question: how to bypass, overwhelm, and ignore oppression, and, in so doing, create an other space for thought and creativity. That Sachs fails to sustain this moment does not diminish the veracity of his quest. What Sachs's failure attests to is precisely the capacity of closed systems to dominate thought and creativity. While I heed Sachs's (and Ndebele's) call I am well aware that it will be sustained only once 'the creative process [has freed] itself from those very laws'. This inquiry marks the attempt to do so.

The framing second chapter examines the epistemic and psychic nature of entrapment, and how this entrapment has disfigured the way the South African imaginary has, in a limited and diminished way, come to understand itself. This understanding is encapsulated in Coetzee's fatal formulation that South Africa is as 'irresistible as it is unlovable' (Jerusalem Prize Acceptance Speech p. 99). By inverting this formulation, by thinking against the pathology that founds it, I promise a way of thinking, a way of perception, which conceives of South Africa as that which is *as resistable as it is lovable*. It is love – the unackowledgeable and repressed desire – which, I argue, needs to be restored. This restoration is no easy feat. However, condemned to hope, I turn to the work of others – theoreticians and cultural practitioners – to locate the sustenance needed to restore the necessity – and not the need – for love.

In the third chapter I shift the focus away from the narrow confines of South Africa, to better situate South Africa's predicament within a global context. In the fourth, I sustain this larger context and focus on the battle between reactive and radical syncretism, and the impact of this battle upon South Africa's cultural imaginary. In the fifth, I conduct a close reading of Ndebele's critical oeuvre and, against his valorisation of the 'ordinary', pit the tropes of sublimity and queerness. In the sixth, I refigure and develop the veracity of a queer conception of South African culture under the sign of Folly. In the seventh, through an examination of South African theatre, I counter the emergent cult of individualism with the ethical necessity of the collective. In the eighth, I address the abiding historiographical dilemma of this inquiry: how to *write* South Africa. Finally, in the inquiry's coda, 'immune', I return to Sachs, whose vision of a liberated cultural imagination forms the seam of this inquiry into the predicament of culture in South Africa.

ONE

Towards a Celebratory Cultural Imagination in an Indifferent Time

To love is to think.

— Alberto Caeiro

In 1989 a paper appeared that would rock the mainframe of South African resistance culture. First presented as a series of provocative asides in Stockholm, it would receive its more controversial and sustained airing at an African National Congress (ANC) in-house seminar in Lusaka. The author was Albie Sachs, an activist in the – then – banned ANC movement. That Sachs's paper was first released abroad was not only fitting given the draconian measures within South Africa to silence all discord and protest, it was doubly fitting given the eccentric nature of its content. Not only was Sachs's message at odds with the censorship laws of the South African state, it was a message that also challenged the received beliefs and objectives of the ANC movement. From the outset, Sachs's paper emerged as an anomaly that, in its challenging of the received tenets of resistance culture, opened the buried and gnawing question: what is the ANC fighting *for*? The paper's very title, 'Preparing Ourselves for Freedom', suggests the heated and anxious scurrying towards a certain *readiness*. By asking the gnawing question regarding the ANC's cultural vision, Sachs wittingly, or unwittingly, revealed the insufficiency, indeed the limit that dogged the ANC's understanding of the role of culture in a society on the verge of transformation.

Sachs's paper and the debates it spawned are collected in a seminal text, *Spring is Rebellious: Arguments About Cultural Freedom*, edited by Ingrid de Kok and Karen Press. The title for the collection comes from the following passage by Pablo Neruda, which serves as its epigraph:

> Life transcends all structures, and there are new
> rules of conduct for the soul. The seed sprouts
> anywhere; all ideas are exotic; we wait for
> enormous changes every day; we live through
> the mutation of human order avidly; spring is
> rebellious.

In pitting life against structure, in rendering ideas strange, in grasping the mutation of humanity, and in signalling the wellspring of a change that owes more to the mystery of nature than the secular imposition of new orders, Neruda intuits the ineluctability of creativity. It is this intuition that the respondents to Sachs's paper have either failed to grasp or consciously harnessed to a revisionist or positivist conception of social and cultural change. Sachs is party to this ideological and utilitarian conscription of culture, but, as I will argue, Sachs also transcends the very constraints he sets up. It is this transcendent dimension to Sachs's cultural vision, a dimension eloquently invoked by Neruda, that is the core of this chapter and the seam of the exploration that follows.

Like Neruda, Sachs defers to the integrity and transcendence of an artwork. Like Neruda, he attempts to harness this distinctly new critical conception of art to the avidity of a society on the verge of discovering what it is and what it must become. As we will discover, this strange fusion of the transcendental and material – which Tony Morphet later in this chapter describes as a fusion of the liberal/formalist and revisionist settlements – is no ordinary feat. Rather, it is a fusion, or epistemological convergence, which attests to the extraordinary historical moment that marked the transition from oppression to liberation. Fifteen years hence it is a moment that remains remarkable, and it is for this reason, if this alone, that Sachs's paper remains an epistemological bridging point in the process of cultural change.

By no means a manifesto or treaty, the paper, rather, is a series of provocations and questions which, at its churning core, challenges all deterministic claims for culture. There Sachs broaches the key proposition: what 'freedom' may or may not mean when applied to cultural transformation. At the historical moment when Sachs conceives of freedom, freedom remains an idea so portentous, so exotic that, if one were Sachs, one could almost taste it. Couched in a language that deftly moderates its challenge with a celebratory air of play, the paper confounded those present at its delivery in Stockholm and London and generated a marked unease.

In his reflection on the impact of his paper 'Afterword: The Taste of an Avocado Pear', Sachs remembers the muted outcry in Stockholm and London that resulted from his rejection of a culture of solidarity: 'A hundred faces tightened in affrontment . . . The somnambulistic sureness of the occasion had been broken' (p. 145). Here Sachs touches upon a key critique of resistance culture: that it was a culture of sleep-walkers, a culture distorted by a reflexive poverty and a failure to understand that creativity knows no consensus; that for culture in its varied forms to make an impact, it needed artists who understood the immanence and wakefulness of being.

Sachs goes on to reiterate his key plea: 'We South Africans fight against real consciousness, apartheid consciousness, we know what we struggle against. It is there for all the world to see. But we don't know who we ourselves are. What does it mean to be a South African?' (Afterword p. 146).

This question, as difficult to pose as it is to answer, reveals a critical binary – between the real and the imagined, the reactive and the active – that forms the seam of Sachs's inquiry into culture. For Sachs, 'real consciousness' supposes a cognitive sphere of contestation. More importantly for Sachs, though, there remains another sphere that is irreducible to this cognitive and reactive fight for change. For Sachs this other sphere remains a mystery, the root of which is a profound ignorance of who 'we' are: what it means to be a South African. That this question persists today should reinforce the depth of the dilemma that confronted Sachs. Moreover, the persistence of this question – what does it mean to be? – should alert us to a discrepancy between what 'we' appear to be and what 'we' are.

By foregrounding this discrepancy Sachs posted a warning that, in a time consumed by positivism and instrumentality, was not satisfactorily heeded. Disregarded as eccentric, as precious and beside the point, the question would not, however, go away. On the contrary, it would spark the flame of inquiry, coax the unsaid and mysterious. The sphere where this flame would burn most brightly would be within the arts. Sachs intuited this: 'The artists, more than anyone, can help us discover ourselves. Culture in the broad sense is our vision of ourselves and our world. This is a huge task facing our writers and dancers and musicians and painters and film-makers. It is something that goes well beyond mobilising people for this or that activity, important though mobilisation might be' (Afterword p. 146).

In retrospect one may wonder how any thinking radical could have challenged Sachs's critique of the instrumental nature of resistance culture. But then one must not forget the stranglehold that the apartheid regime had over the imaginations of all those who resisted it. As Sachs would state at the outset of his paper 'Preparing Ourselves for Freedom', we remain caught in the 'ghetto' of the apartheid imagination – in fact, we have failed to demonstrate a counter-imagination, one not only founded on resistance but which, in its execution and deliverance, could trump the very system we were fighting against and in which we remained trapped.

At its very outset Sachs's paper signalled not only confusion, but a misperception of the perspective, location and agency of resistance culture. The first proposition that Sachs makes is that for culture to become free, it must cede its pathological attachment to the oppressive regime that shaped and constrained its deliverance. Culture, to attain this freedom, needed to be active and not reactive, for while it may be both necessary and worthy, reaction remained the instinct of the slave, of the unfree. The very reactive nature of resistance culture, therefore, ensured that it remained implicated in the very specular and juridical economy that it sought to undo. For Sachs, freedom is not reducible to resistance. In 'Preparing Ourselves for Freedom' he provides a number of illustrations to reinforce this fact. Much has been said on this matter. Sachs's paper and the responses to it, gathered in *Spring is Rebellious*, are easily accessible to those interested in a reactive aesthetics and politics – an aesthetics and politics that, for Sachs, amounts not only to bad culture, but also to a hopelessly limited conception of the agency of culture in social transformation.

What interests me, however, is how Sachs shifts from the limits of resistance culture towards a critical epistemological threshold; one that he intimates rather than accentuates or develops. This epistemological threshold, this glimmer he calls 'freedom', is, I would argue, the post-dialectical moment in cultural expression. This moment, as I have already intimated, lies in Sachs's conception of the agency of culture: how, in a non-teleological or non-deterministic way, culture impacts upon, and transforms, lives. For Sachs this transforming power of culture, in all its forms, achieves a degree of freedom in the instant that it surmounts the inhibiting economy that creates its reactively critical and resistant nature. To my knowledge, this post-dialectical moment in Sachs's paper has not been addressed. If this is indeed so, it is in part because the very domain of critical and cultural inquiry is still caught in the Manichean bind which Sachs contests at the outset of his paper. If this is so, it is because the very cultural imagination that he gestures towards remains a nascent and virtual dimension in cultural practice today.

If I now insist upon a more keen address, one which addresses this unthinkable, playful and radical epistemological goad, it is because without it there will be no advance; without it we will remain unfree; without it there can be no culture that could truly call itself free. That the South African National Arts Coalition should, in a media release in Johannesburg on 24 January 1994, conceptualise its 'Festivals of Laughter' in the following manner as captured by Flora Veit-Wild (*Festivals of Laughter* p. 27) all the more reinforces the derivative and reactive nature of cultural expression that persists today:

> The Braai-the-Sacred-Cow-Monument Sculpture Exhibition.
> The Not-approved-by-the-Publications Board Short Story Competition.
> The Completely Politically Incorrect Stand Up Comedy Festival.
> The Riotous Assembly Street Theatre and Dance Festival.
> The Anything-but-the-Anthem Best Original Song Competition.
> The Oh-Shucks-No-Subsidy-Bucks Short Film Festival.
> The Have-You-Slugged-a-Politician-Today Poster Competition.

Clearly, cultural expression continues to be stalked by the apartheid imagination. Clearly, the seemingly subversive nature of this list of goads remains caught in the specular and juridical economy that it purportedly resists. If there has been any alteration in the conception of cultural production in South Africa today, it has been towards an increased ennui and sense of fatality. The ascendance of this ennui and sense of fatality can be measured by the precise degree to which Sachs's searching question – what it means to be a South African – has been divested of its force. It is only in rare instances that a cultural imaginary that does not pay lip service to a deep psychic oppression or that has not fallen victim to what I have called a certain ennui and fatalism has emerged.

Culture's role, for Sachs, was to invite and to trump this rooted sense of oppression and fatalism. Despite the rejection of this invitation, culture persists with its avid and arduous task. As Sachs's leading question suggests, how can one move forward when one does not know who one is? It is this not knowing – this *resistance to self-knowledge* – that is the root of South Africa's continued ills.

The abandonment of Sachs's leading question in the name of positivism and instrumentality is indicative not of an ongoing quest for freedom, but of the derailment of this quest. That freedom in South Africa was largely ceded and bequeathed, rather than seized, all the more accentuates the diminishment and critical occlusion which marked the process of, and quest for, freedom. Freedom, then, becomes a handout and not a reckoning; a guaranteed idea and not a fraught and avidly awaited actuality.

Absent in the transfer of power — a transfer made in the *name* of freedom — was the inquiry, rooted in the exploration of the imagination, which formed the key to Sachs's paper. This is not to say that the imagination does not form an integral part of South Africa's libidinal economy and cultural imaginary. My view, however, is that the 'imagination' and its cognate, 'freedom', have with a stealthy rapidity become normalised givens; simulacral affects instead of immanent and reflexive descriptors for ongoing change. The National Lottery's slogan 'License to Dream' is an axiomatic indicator for what I perceive to be an autocratic — top-down — arbitration of social fantasy and need, in this case via a statistically improbable probability. More generally, one finds the recurrence of a libidinal economy defined by the redemptive tropes that Sachs attaches to creativity. Parmalat 'feed[s] the imagination'. Castle Lager announces the axis of consumption and pleasure as 'a living thing, a together thing'. What is indisputable is that the tropes of liberty and corporate branding have become indissoluble. It is this very branding of freedom and imagination that distinguishes its delimited and targeted economy and currency.

If Sachs's paper remains pertinent therefore, it is because it contains a critical question that no instrumental or opportunistic vision, including Sachs's own, has successfully been able to suppress. It is a question that pertains as much to the imaginary of nationhood as it does to the silenced majority who huddle under the name *South Africa*. The continued relevance of Sachs's paper lies in its resistance to the traducement and commodification of its liberatory agency. Its relevance, furthermore, is not defined by its ability to define what is good or bad art. The very privative and juridical nature of such comparative evaluation is in itself prohibitive and, for Sachs, inadmissable. While Sachs may dwell in this comparative sphere, his sights are set upon a greater goal that, in levelling a privative evaluative system, potentially unlocks the framing limits affixed to cultural production.

Here, in sentiment and intellectual inclination, Sachs's paper bears a striking affinity to Václav Havel's 'Six Asides About Culture' (1986). In that article Havel similarly challenges the over-determining role of ideology in relation to artistic expression. Indeed, Havel goes so far as to say that it does not matter to what or whom an artist expresses his or her allegiance. What matters is the work. The assumption here is that it is possible to create works of merit irrespective of one's ideological affiliation. Moreover, by overcoming the moral determinism that all too often dogs the evaluation of a work, one can potentially release the ethical nature of a particular artwork. The implicit assumption is that the ethical, unlike the moral, knows no claimants, no received history, no final and purposive vision, which is why Havel and Sachs refute critical judgement as the ruler of taste, and why, in a moment of profound generosity, Havel, like Sachs, foregoes any definitive appraisal in the knowledge that the future fate of a work cannot be determined in the present moment. Havel:

> Who among us would dare to say that he can unerringly distinguish something of value — even though it may be nascent, unfamiliar, as yet only potential — from its counterfeit? Who among us can know whether what may seem today to be marginal graphomania might one day appear

to our descendants as the most substantial thing written in our time? Who among us has the right to deprive them of that pleasure, no matter how incomprehensible it may seem to us? (p. 129)

The remarkable open-mindedness and generosity of Havel's vision is matched, albeit residually, in Sachs's paper. If Sachs finally fails to sustain this ethical openness, the limit lies not in the vision but in its circumscription and containment. Nevertheless, as I have already stated, and what I will now develop, is what I have called the post-dialectical moment in Sachs's vision which, at its core, must, like Havel's, conceive of culture as 'a sphere whose very nature precludes all prognostication . . . [for] the secrets of culture's future are a reflection of the very secrets of the human spirit' (Six Asides About Culture pp. 123–24).

If culture can be said to reflect the human spirit, then what is the spirit of South Africa? This is undoubtedly a great question, a question that Sachs has broached, which has persistently been neglected or rhetorically contained. In South Africa, I would suggest, the 'ghetto' remains the defining characteristic of South Africa's cultural imaginary. The release for which Havel, Neruda and Sachs call for has not yet occurred. South Africa remains afflicted by what Havel describes as a 'Biafra of the spirit' (p. 125).

Something akin to the following anxiety forms the impulse for Sachs's paper. Havel: 'something in me rebels . . . against the claim that history has condemned us to the unenviable role of mere unthinking experts in suffering, poor relations of those in the "free world" who do not have to suffer and have time to think' (p. 126).

If Sachs is well aware of the constraints of an equivalent legacy, he, like Havel, remains compelled to invoke a project – none other than the decolonisation of the imagination. This project cannot be formalised, must not be named; hence Havel and Sachs's critique of criticism's tendency to asphyxiate. Because it is all too often shaped by an *a priori* agenda – even and especially when it appears to venture without foreknowledge – criticism lays claim to meaning and, thereby, closes the agency of a given work. As a discipline, then, criticism is inherently unfree.

In his poem 'Retreat', collected in *A Dead Tree Full of Live Birds*, Lionel Abrahams similarly challenges this threat and invokes the post-dialectical moment – a moment freed from prognosticatory and retrogressive determinism:

Stay quiet a while.
Let words
rinse clean,
dissolve.

Squat amid potsherds,
scrape your scales.
Let opinion
fall away.

Bear to be numb and dumb,
void of judgments.

Allow a waiting emptiness
of which none knows.

Silent a while
on a margin,
give no name or shape
to expectation.

Let indifferent time,
random flickers of the air,
ungathered dust
bring some instruction. (p. 40)

The limits that I affix to criticism also pertain to artistic production. The claim of course is a large one. However, by restricting myself to the domain of critical and cultural production in South Africa I hope not only to dwell upon the inherent limits, but, more significantly, to begin to develop Sachs's key intuition: that what freedom needs – if it is truly desired, which all too often is not the case – is the inclination and perception evinced in the words of Neruda, Havel and Abrahams. These, I believe, are the key to Sachs's vision of what culture must be. In the words of each there is a sphere of expression that accepts the unthinkable: that which has not heretofore been thought; that which in its nature resists thought; that which challenges the prohibition of the unnameable. If Sachs insists upon the desire to know what it means to be a South African, then it is the insistence upon *desire* and not a nominal foreclosure that matters: hence Sachs's deferral to the arts as the surest and most mysterious means through which to unriddle the question.

By entitling his paper 'Preparing Ourselves for Freedom', Sachs effected the first step towards an as yet unbroached drama: the drama of what change might mean and how it could be achieved. Others, it has been argued, preceded Sachs, among them Lewis Nkosi, Es'kia Mphahele, Nadine Gordimer, Njabulo Ndebele and Chris van Zyl. Frank Meintjies's article 'Albie Sachs and the Art of Protest' gives credence to this view (pp. 30–35). Here I demur. On the surface Ndebele and van Zyl – the subjects of Meintjies's article – certainly seem to reproduce Sachs's strident call. Nonetheless, neither tackles the core of Sachs's paper. It is not about the fundamentally punitive debate over what makes for a good or bad resistance culture, but the freedom latent in the critical instant when this very question is surmounted. Lionel Abrahams eloquently phrases this epistemological threshold when he calls upon '. . . indifferent time / random flickers of the air / ungathered dust / [to] bring some instruction' (p. 40). Of particular note is the phrase *indifferent time*. Irrespective of the specular and monumental construction of history, irrespective of the ends to which history is put, there is an implacable indifference that time possesses. An indifference that not only mocks claims upon history but which, in its very indifference, reveals the pathos that dogs the varied though deeply implicated perceptions of what culture is and what it must do. What makes Sachs's paper remarkable, indeed unique, is the courage with which it broaches an intractable pathology and how and to what end it pits its attendant quest for freedom.

The burden of this chapter, however, is not reactively defined by what Sachs describes as the pathological 'ghettoes of the apartheid imagination' (Preparing Ourselves p. 19). Rather, I have chosen to embark upon an exploration of what freedom might mean and how, through the arts, it can be achieved. To undertake such a task I have, necessarily, had to defer to the prevailing Manichean binarism, which, like most, I know is not easily circumvented. The position I wish to advocate is not transgressive or reactive; it is not one that is fuelled by a received – revisionist and positivist – intellectual tradition. On the contrary, it is one that J. M. Coetzee defines under the sign of allegory. I refer here to the doctor's perception of Michael K in *Life & Times of Michael K* as some one, some thing, that 'scandalously . . . outrageously . . . take[s] up residence in a system without becoming a term in it' (p. 228).

The doctor in Coetzee's novel strives to unravel or encode the enigma of K. However, no system of questions will unlock K. Hence the doctor's frustration. Hence the perception of K as an elusive trace. Hence the ontological primacy that Coetzee gives to a figure who in his very muteness, his very stubbornness, breaks down the punitive dialectical system of interrogation. In a deceptively whimsical moment the doctor goes on to describe K as a 'polevaulter', then, qualifying the description, the doctor adds: 'Well, you may not be a polevaulter, Michaels, but you are a great escape artist, one of the great escapees' (p. 228). The qualification is double-edged, suggesting renunciation as well as a miraculous withdrawal from a privative hermeneutic deadlock.

Life & Times of Michael K remains a unique work in a resistance culture dogged by a specular desire for accountability. That the novel stands out as an exception in an otherwise increasingly fatalistic *oeuvre* is another point. Its very existence attests not only to the enabling lacuna within its author's artistic process, but, more importantly, to K's non-reactive and post-dialectical stance – a stance which at no point is defined as self-reflexive or auto-intellective, since it cannot be known to the one who enacts it, but only to the one who exists at the interpretive margins. Here Coetzee's achievement is twofold. Firstly, he marginalises power in the figure of the doctor. Secondly, he intimates though never discloses the nature of the force that, in deactivating the authority of hermeneutic power, issues forth a latent, intractable and ruthlessly enduring otherness. If the doctor defines this position or figuration of alterity as allegorical, this definition, technically, is a non-definition because it attaches itself to nothing. Thoroughly persuasive and theoretically compelling though it may be, the doctor's definition of K amounts to nothing more than a limit-text, the sum of which is interpretive exhaustion.

The deeper core, the root of the doctor's failure, is echoed in Abraham's words: 'Silent a while / on a margin, / give no name or shape / to expectation' (p. 40). Abrahams not only stalls the agency of interpretation but, more important, accounts for the necessity of a silence that is not corrosive and confounding but enabling. It is this silence – which precludes judgement – that the doctor must accept against his will. It is this silence that Sachs perceives as the nature of freedom. By silence here I do not merely mean muteness; I am gesturing towards a silence – unexpected, without received shape –

that is the ethical depth-charge that moves culture irrespective of the form and language it assumes. Without this silence there is no art. Without this silence any attempt to track the perspective, location and agency of culture is doomed to record nothing more than the banter: the self-reflexive hall of mirrors that is the sum of commentary.

With these broad propositions before us, let us return to Sachs's paper and recover its lost or displaced significance, which, today, remains critical to an appraisal of the fate of cultural production in South Africa. To reiterate, Sachs begins with the disarmingly simple statement: 'We all know where South Africa is, but we do not yet know what it is.' From the outset of his paper it is the very sovereignty of nomination that Sachs challenges. For Sachs the country, in particular its germinal and rhizomatic culture, cannot be fixed in a formulated phrase. Rather, Sachs suggests that the advance of life, the will to change, is not the forced and over-determined sum of nomination, but a vision and an inclination defined by the adjectival, by a word or phrase that names an attribute, that modifies and describes a noun. It is through such a process of inflection that understanding becomes possible. This, as I have suggested, is the procedure at work in the allegorical construction of K. This procedure, renounced or most certainly challenged by detractors such as Nadine Gordimer as gratuitously evasive, as politically inappropriate, as threatening the authority of revisionism and positivism, the mainstay of resistance culture (The Idea of Gardening p. 3), is championed by Sachs as the surest inroad into expressing and understanding the mystery of South African culture.

The key word Sachs affixes to the mystery is *imagination*. 'The problem,' Sachs writes, 'is whether we have sufficient cultural imagination to grasp the rich texture of the free and united South Africa that we have done so much to bring about' (Preparing Ourselves p. 19). From the outset Sachs sketches the challenge that awaits the cultural practitioner. Nevertheless, the very word he valorises – imagination – is repeated and negated by the following question: 'Can we say that we have begun to grasp the full dimensions of the new country . . . [the] new people that is struggling to give birth to itself, or are we still trapped in the multiple ghettoes of the apartheid imagination?' Clearly the very agency of imagination is fraught and, potentially, compromised. Caught between the straits of hope and fatality – between a newfangled 'cultural imagination' and an 'apartheid imagination' – Sachs forges ahead. The initial tension recurs, forming a contrapuntal argument: 'What are we fighting for, if not the right to express our humanity in all its forms, including our sense of fun and capacity for love and tenderness and our appreciation of the beauty of the world?'

And then, pell-mell: 'There is nothing that the apartheid rulers would like more than to convince us that because apartheid is ugly, the world is ugly . . . It is as though our rulers stalk every page and haunt every picture; everything is obsessed by the oppressors and the trauma they have imposed, nothing is about us and the new consciousness we are developing' (Preparing Ourselves p. 21).

Rhetorically, the contrapuntal movement is persuasive. Sachs, though, has his sights set upon a more transforming and challenging point. He credits South African music as the apex of the 'new consciousness', a consciousness characterised by 'wit and grace and vitality and intimacy', whereas the visual and literary arts remain compromised by a 'solemnity [that] is overwhelming' (p. 20), a solemnity he associates with the moral weight of revisionism and positivism that has burdened and disfigured these respective art forms. Returning to music – in particular the music of Abdullah Ibrahim, Jonas Gwanga, Miriam Makeba and Hugh Masekela – Sachs writes: 'Their music conveys genuine confidence because it springs from inside the personality and experience of each of them, from popular tradition and the sounds of contemporary life; we respond to it because it tells us something lovely and vivacious about ourselves, not because the lyrics are about how to win a strike or blow up a petrol dump'.

It is at this point that Sachs makes what I have termed *an epistemological leap*. For what matters most to Sachs is how the best in South African music '*bypasses, overwhelms, ignores apartheid, establishes its own space*' (my emphasis). It is in this transforming and questioning negativity that art legislates its freedom.

For Sachs this transforming moment remains dialectical and not, as I have proposed, a post-dialectical moment. A more probing reading, however, suggests that Sachs wills the greater unthinkable freedom implicit in the post-dialectical thought or act. How so? On the surface Sachs counterpoints a purely instrumental and non-dialectical view of culture with one that deepens and synthesises the contradictions of lived experience in South Africa. If we are to accept Sachs's position, then the music he valorises would be a dialectical highpoint in art. But if this is so then how can one synthesise a contradiction and bypass, overwhelm, and establish an other space? My point is that this is impossible. Either one sustains the dialectic or one breaks it. Implicitly, if not explicitly, Sachs favours the latter when it comes to art, hence the parallel I make with Václav Havel. Neither activist nor thinker can accept any constraints upon art-making and cultural production. Consequently, Sachs makes the 'challenging proposition . . . that the Constitutional Guidelines should not be applied to the sphere of culture'. Rather, 'culture must make its input to the Guidelines' (Preparing Ourselves p. 23).

Of course, one could rightly say that while Sachs promotes the freedom of cultural expression, he also – dialectically – constrains and reintegrates culture's impact upon, and instrumentality within, society. In other words, Sachs – finally – would hem in the post-dialectical radicality nascent in cultural expression and production. This is not quite the case. It is the very instrumentality of the Constitutional Guidelines that culture in all its forms must interrogate and surpass. If apartheid 'has closed our society, stifled its voice, prevented the people from speaking', then, all the more, it is the vocation of cultural expression to serve as 'the harbinger of *freedom of conscience*, debate and opinion' (Preparing Ourselves p. 24, my emphasis).

From this point onward Sachs harnesses the power of his argument, adumbrates and contains the diversity and freedom for which he calls. For the purposes of my argument, however, the irruption that I have termed *the epistemological threshold* or *post-dialectical moment* in Sachs's thinking has been unleashed. There is, as Sachs well knows, no freedom that does not activate and liberate conscience. Furthermore, freedom of conscience is not quite akin to debate and opinion. If the former seeks to break and surmount the mirror, then the latter accepts a specular and juridical economy. The constraints of this economy of course make it absurd to expect Sachs to forge the liberatory moment that my own reading courts. Nevertheless, for the purposes of my argument it remains critical that the reader recognise what Sachs intimates and does not wholly say: that over and above the democratic or pluralistic levelling of cultural differences there remains a cultural agency that surpasses boundaries, as well as their nominal erasure, that can potentially invoke a third space which, in the South African cultural economy has not quite been expressed, let alone sustained.

The argument I venture here, which in acknowledging the limits Sachs places on the agency of culture while still invoking an as yet unthinkable other space is addressed in Tony Morphet's essay 'Cultural Imagination and Cultural Settlement: Albie Sachs and Njabulo Ndebele'. I will not be focusing on Morphet's comparative reading of the limits and strengths of the cultural visions of Sachs and Ndebele; for the purposes of my argument, I will restrict myself to Morphet's incisive reading of Sachs's essay. Like Morphet, I am interested in the resurgence and agency of the word *imagination*, that is, its tropological import and its relevance to cultural production in South Africa. Like Morphet I have also noted its contradictory usage. Morphet does not dwell upon this matter. However, he implicitly questions the efficacy and paucity of its usage when he states: 'the paper has to be content with being suggestive because it lacks the means for being definitive' (Cultural Imagination p. 132).

The question I would ask is: what is the basis for this lack? Is it, as Morphet suggests, Sachs's contradiction of himself? Does it arise because Sachs plays fast and loose with a word – imagination – the generative power of which is not sustained? Or because the imagination, when affixed to freedom, cannot possess the means to be definitive? This is the intuition that also drives the thought of Neruda, Havel, and Coetzee's conception of the allegorical. My point is that it is the very suggestiveness of Sachs's use of the word imagination that gives his paper its rich significance, a significance which in the heady year of 1989 when the paper was heatedly discussed in Stockholm, Lusaka, and in the cities and townships of South Africa, was no small feat. Definitiveness is not the *raison d'être* for the inception and reception of the paper. It is the very openness of the issues it raises and the redemptive and celebratory force of its appeals that account for the paper's continued currency.

What makes Morphet's essay compelling, however, is the historical positioning of the critical moment that gave rise to Sachs's paper. Morphet locates two key and distinct phases of cultural criticism in South Africa. The first, which he roughly dates between 1950 to the early 1970s, he calls 'the liberal/formalist period'. The second period, from the mid-1970s through to 1986, he calls 'the revisionist period'. These periods of critical and cultural production that he problematically calls 'settlements', thereby imputing these periods of critical production to be 'times of stability and dominance', Morphet contrasts with a post-1986 period of 'rupture and transition' (Cultural Imagination p. 133). For the purposes of his argument, Morphet needs to establish two conflicting – 'relatively stable, relatively durable' – movements or settlements. Secondly, and of greater relevance here, he needs to show the contradictory conflation of these movements in the third phase of critical and cultural production, a phase he represents through the writings of Sachs and Ndebele.

Before arriving at the epistemologically confusing conflation of these two movements in the writing of Sachs – a conflation that I perceive as enabling rather than problematic – I shall turn to Morphet's first 'liberal/formalist settlement'. Its critical *raison d'être*, according to Morphet, is 'the autonomy of the text' (Cultural Imagination p. 134). Within a liberal/formalist paradigm an 'artwork was self-constitutive and self-enclosed'. Its core doctrine is best expressed in Archibald Macleish's well-known aphorism from 'Ars Poetica': 'A poem should not mean / But be'. The watchwords here, words that in today's critical climate have all too glibly been dismissed, are autonomy and self-enclosure. Ostensibly inherited from a Euro-American context, the liberal/formalist movement is said to advocate that 'works emerged not from individuals or a class or a place or a time but from a hypothesised universal, transcendental, mind' (Cultural Imagination p. 135). It has been claimed – by Morphet among others – that once this hypothesis was uncovered, its hidden transcendent point of closure routed out, that the provenance of this movement 'began to break-up' (ibid.). According to Morphet, this break-up went hand in hand with the emergence of the 'revisionist' movement which, in turn, sought precisely to relocate the 'text' in the contexts of individual/class/spatial/ temporal productivities and agencies. Movements are commonly defined in, and through, a series of critical negations and advances. It is in and through these systemic negations that we have come to understand the meaning of history. For the purposes of critical productivity it is useful to advance these systemic negations to make sense of change. Nonetheless, given the contradictory conflation of these movements in the writing of Sachs and Ndebele, we should surely be alerted to the fact that these movements cannot be as easily parsed and spliced as Morphet would have us believe. In other words, are these movements not also coexistent, doppelgangers in an ongoing debate regarding the nature of the production and reception of a given text? And is this not precisely Sachs's point?

Reconsider Macleish's aphorism: 'A poem should not mean / But be.' Is this not the core doctrine of Pablo Neruda and Lionel Abrahams? Indeed, is this not also the core doctrine of *Life & Times of Michael K*? My assumption, then, is that any attempt, no matter how compelling, which forcefully distinguishes the so-called liberal/formalist and the revisionist periods in critical inquiry does a profound injustice to the nature of cultural production. The damage, of course, has already been done. It is as a consequence of this damage – this parsing and splicing of critical and creative productivity – that we have inherited a mutant critical discourse and industry which, in giving up the ghost of being so vital to Macleish, Neruda, Abrahams, Havel, Coetzee and Sachs, have devolved into a refracted and contentious sphere. This contemporary sphere of critical practice can no longer name itself other than as an after-effect, as the mutant fall-out of a lost tradition. This is evidenced in the *portmanteaux* of postmodernism or post-colonialism which, more problematically than ever, have come to accept adjectival insistence not as the constitutive dimension of great art or thought, but as the degraded and frustrated limit of contemporary critical inquiry.

Given the bleakness of the present critical moment – a moment not unlike that which Morphet defines under the heading 'incorporative irony', in which disparate elements are incorporated within a synthesis of 'civilised life' (Cultural Imagination p. 136) – the challenge remains one in which the freedom of expression is central to cultural inquiry and expression. That Sachs contradicts himself is not at all surprising. Indeed, it would be more surprising if Sachs were not to contradict himself, given the fraught and conflicting histories that impact upon his vision. What matters is not the contradiction but the aporia Sachs attempts to sustain in and through the relay of contradictions that bend and twist his paper. This aporia I have called the *epistemological leap* or the *post-dialectical moment*, or, returning to Macleish, *the being and not the meaning of cultural expression*. My argument is that critical inquiry need not assume itself to be a limit text that exists on the ironical margins of cultural expression, all the more so today when the very distinction between critical and artistic expression has, in the Derridean sense, been erased: at once cancelled and rendered visible. It is this realisation that critical inquiry and artistic expression coexist and infuse one another that gives Sachs's paper its continued currency.

Sachs, like Ndebele, knows – in the words of Morphet – that 'the revisionist period [is] simply a continuation and a reification of the previous formalist settlement. In [Ndebele's] argument liberalism turns, inevitably, into neo-Marxism or historical materialism, without effectively altering the "epistemological structures of South African oppression"' (Cultural Imagination p. 139). The key here is not only the compelling view that the two movements form a continuum, but that both, according to Morphet's reading, fail to answer the matter of oppression and, by extension, the matter of freedom. Both movements, in other words, remain reflexively closed.

I will not dwell here on the fact that Ndebele fails to unlock this paradigmatic closure; this is the subject of a later chapter. What interests me is how Sachs attempts to unlock this perceived closure in the name of artistic freedom. Morphet provides an interesting response, which is that 'Sachs's understanding of the revisionist settlement is both wider and narrower than that shown by Ndebele. Beneath his arguments and observations is a celebratory (rather than redemptive) narrative' (Cultural Imagination p. 140).

Morphet goes on to show how Sachs effectively contaminates his cultural vision by affirming the ANC 'as the fulfilment of the historical process foreshadowed in the revisionist settlement' (ibid.). Similarly, I have pointed out this crucial flaw; a flaw which, given Sachs's political affiliation and location in history, was unavoidable. However, irrespective of this flaw, what matters and will continue to thrive is the celebratory ethos that Sachs affixes to cultural expression. It is this celebratory ethos, which Sachs also describes as 'love' and 'joy', that I have interpreted as an aporia akin to Roland Barthes's post-dialectical notion of bliss or *jouissance*, an affect of being that bypasses the utility and closure of hermeneutic expression. It is this sense of celebration that I take to be the root of Sachs's notion of the 'cultural imagination'. Furthermore, to contradict Morphet, it is also this sense of celebration that is at the root of Macleish's aphorism. If this is the case, then to what extent is the aesthetic allegiance to, and value of, self-enclosure truly the core of the liberal/formalist movement? Surely the matter was never as simple as it seemed? Indeed, how can one reconcile transcendence and closure in artistic expression? To what extent is form not the inverse but the handmaiden of formlessness? To what extent is meaning not the adjunct or rider of being, but its first port of call? Finally, are these questions at their root not surpassed in Neruda's words: 'Life transcends all structures, and there are new / rules of conduct for the soul'?

The epistemic and aesthetic debate regarding closure versus openness, form versus formlessness, is a recurrent one. The very desire to contrast these fudged conditionalities in the sphere of cultural production has tended to restrict its complexity. My view is that these conditionalities are profoundly interdependent; that the one cannot, satisfactorily, be favoured against and above the other. In the context of Sachs's essay, it is utterly clear that, even though, in Morphet's words, Sachs presents 'the ascendancy of the ANC as something akin to the fulfilment of history' (Cultural Imagination p. 141), there remains in a paradoxically deeper and more evident sense a belief in artistic expression that precedes and exceeds this teleological claim. How, Morphet compellingly asks, can one resolve 'the indeterminate contradictions of human experience . . . to demonstrate the victory of a determinate ideological position'? (ibid.). 'Like Ndebele, Sachs's account of the cultural imagination remains incoherent,' says Morphet: 'Both founder on the issue of closure. Both appeal to the notion of incorporative irony for the sake of greater range, flexibility, complexity and openness, but neither is able to relinquish the fixed point of closure in the framework of social action to which they have committed themselves' (Cultural Imagination p. 142).

Clearly Morphet is begging for an alternative vision, one that need not contradict itself and that essentially frees itself from the pathological grip of the apartheid imagination that compelled its perpetrators as well as its detractors. In the concluding movement of his paper, which he calls a 'third settlement', Morphet notes: 'The unpicking of the lock (i.e. the opening up of the point of closure in which a correct historical position authorizes cultural practice) is likely to come through the continuing commerce between local and foreign notions of cultural practice (Cultural Imagination p. 143).

Unlike Neruda's position, which affirms the *élan* of art-making as that which 'transcends all structures' in the very instant that it defers to its constructive and material dimension, Morphet's is distinctly secular – cognitively bound by the materiality and textuality of an artwork, and, therefore, to my mind, problematic. By conceiving future transformation as a matter of reframing our aesthetic and geo-political inheritance and influence, Morphet sustains rather than confounds the very revisionist authority he contests. Deferring to poststructuralist and postmodern theorisations, that of Frederic Jameson in particular, Morphet notes: 'Whether history is, or is not, also only a text, is still under dispute; but what is no longer tenable is the view that it is accessible to us in some way beyond or behind texts' (ibid.).

This highly secular assumption, masqueraded here as authoritative, is, as I have suggested, in turn disputable: hence my deferral to being and not meaning. Cultural production is not the sum of its forms and meanings. Just as I have claimed that the new critical position is not reducible to the reification of forms, that, like Neruda, it hankers after a Bergsonian *élan vital*, a life that 'transcends all structures', I would argue that Morphet's third settlement is not only epistemologically limiting but, given this chapter's searching inquiry into cultural freedom, complacent and false. While I wholly concur with Morphet's desire to shift cultural and intellectual productivity from the closures of revisionism, this shift cannot be achieved by postulating textual inscription – whether perceived as bounded or open – as the frontier of meaning. There is, I would argue, an accessible world 'beyond [and behind] texts'. It is precisely this world that Sachs intuits and registers in, and through, the signs of 'freedom' and the 'imagination'.

Here, however, we must never cease to remember that Sachs conceived his cultural vision in the mid to late 1980s, that is, at roughly the same time that Coetzee, in his 'Jerusalem Prize Acceptance Speech', spoke of the ethical impossibility of freedom, of the fact that the 'gulag' of the apartheid imagination imprisoned each and every protest; that, in short, any critical or imaginative move beyond closure was nothing short of hopeless. It is therefore within, and against, this pathological inheritance that one must measure the pathos and wish fulfilment of Sachs's celebratory will. Given the bleak context of its inception it is a will that is all the more remarkable. That this will is hampered by the political vision that in part constrained it, by no means suggests that it is a will that has wholly failed. If Sachs fails, in Morphet's words, 'to unpick the crucial lock' of psychic entrapment, this does not mean that he has failed to sustain a way forward. The challenge is to develop the ethos of celebration that Sachs cherishes. The crucial challenge today is to rethink or re-imagine the negative closures that continue to dog cultural expression.

In his response to the controversy that raged over his paper, Sachs, in 'Afterword: The Taste of an Avocado Pear', noted: 'The culture of debate is perhaps more important than the debate of culture . . . Art and artistic endeavour need no justification. Perhaps we should not even try to define art, just do it and respond to it and argue about it. What I cannot regret is that there has been such a fierce discussion. *A conversa continua* – may the debate continue' (p. 148).

It is precisely here that Sachs challenges the critique of the new critical or liberal/ formalist position, for in stating that art and artistic endeavour need no justification he reinforces the ineluctable provenance of cultural production founded on Macliesh's aphorism. Freedom within the domain of art can never be a doctrine. No retrogressive or teleological system can ever contain it. My argument, moreover, contends that within the domain of critical praxis an equivalent value potentially pertains. It is the being of a thought and not only its meaning that will most surely break the deadlock and breach the divide between critical and artistic processes of expression, the boundaries of which have increasingly begun to blur.

Contrary to Sachs's last point, however, I believe that the agency of critical thinking does not only pertain to debate. While debate is an attendant necessity, it does not necessarily result in what Sachs most dearly values, which is a 'freedom of conscience', a freedom that Neruda eloquently describes as 'new rules of conduct for the soul'. Much remains to be said and done if South Africa as a society of thinkers and artists is to attain this vaunted freedom. Here perhaps Coetzee is absolutely right when he suggests that freedom, if it truly exists, is only possible in, and *through*, closure and entrapment. The ghetto and the gulag do not disappear when one announces an age of freedom. Freedom is conditional and, contrary to those who preach a newfangled positivism and relativism, freedom, today, is all the more difficult to achieve given a national and global inclination towards fear and compromise. If, then, I charge Coetzee of being a fatalist, it is because more than any other South African cultural analyst he well knows that fatality and freedom are not mutually exclusive and Janus-faced but interpenetrative, that they lie on the *same side* of a single coin. It is this acute and seemingly baffling insight that has set *Life & Times of Michael K* apart and has distinguished it as the greatest work of the imagination ever to have emerged from this psychically disfigured country. One cannot advance without first understanding this paradoxical intersection of fatalism and freedom. This, too, is an epistemological leap; a strange leap indeed, for today freedom is a pathological choice one assumes at one's own peril.

If we as a South African society are, increasingly, bypassing the doctrinaire legitimacy of the ANC, if we have embarked upon a fatalistic dance with globalisation, this does not mean that we have wholly lost our capacity as thinkers and artists to rethink the aporia in Sachs's paper. We remain children on the margins of hope. Though still trapped, we are beginning to articulate the dream of freedom. We may continue to live with the terrible unease of never having begun. We may feel to the depths of our being the terrible irony of Sachs's position, a position which in the 15 years since its utterance has been reduced to mere rhetorical wish fulfilment, precisely because the weak-willed and the ironical among us have deemed the vision impossible. Still, the struggle towards a transcendent and celebratory cultural imagination continues. Despite the fact that we are caught today in a global gulag that preys upon fear and hopelessness, we continue to 'live through the mutation of human order avidly'. Preparation is a permanent condition.

TWO

Embracing the Others of Our Selves

To come to the pleasure you have not,
 you must go by a way in which you enjoy not,
To come to the knowledge you have not,
 you must go by a way in which you know not.

— St John of the Cross

If from South Africa's jaundiced present moment Sachs's vision of a culture that 'overwhelms', 'ignores' and 'bypasses' oppression and 'establishes its own space' seems overly emphatic – a case of protesting too much – and if the desire to *establish* an alternative cultural topography implies yet another settlement or basis for permanence, this does not diminish its allure and veracity (Preparing Ourselves p. 21). For what Sachs invokes is the possibility of a society that could imagine itself otherwise, that could, through the creative act, restore the ability to dream, think, and taste the deferred promise of freedom. This promise is not easily achieved, let alone sustained. One should, therefore, be well aware of the arduousness and seeming impossibility of its fulfilment. A promise of this nature demands acts that cannot know themselves to be the freedom that is sought. If Sachs's paper stands at the threshold of this inquiry, it is because it stages a drama with no definable script and no perceivable end, in which thought, in the instant that it slips its casing, becomes exotic: other to itself. To arrive at this otherness one must – like Heraclitus, like St John of the Cross – go by a trackless and unexplored route and know that that which is sought is as much a source of terror as it is a promise of happiness. A journey of this nature is not for the faint-hearted, and it is certainly not one for those who make a virtue of reason and belief.

If a certainty exists in Sachs's appeal, then it lies in the words *bypass*, *overwhelm*, *ignore*, and in the imagined other space that these words gesture towards. Therein one will find the germ or seed for what Sachs vaguely terms a 'new consciousness' (Preparing Ourselves p. 21). Fifteen years later this consciousness remains disturbingly new. The South African imaginary has by no means overwhelmed, bypassed, or ignored the conditions for its continued oppression. Imagination remains in abeyance; freedom is but a word; the vision of a 'united South Africa with a free and equal citizenry' (Preparing Ourselves p. 19) a matter for the record books and the advertising industry.

Given the gnawing discrepancy between thought and its actualisation – and the simulacral displacement of this discrepancy – the burden of this inquiry will be to record why Sachs's vision has failed, and how and why it must be nurtured. In the broadest sense, the sphere for this inquiry is critical and cultural production. It is the latter that Sachs perceives as the source of liberation and the means whereby 'we constantly re-make ourselves' (Preparing Ourselves p. 22). The former – critical production – is the rider I attach to Sachs's quest. As I have stated in the preceding chapter, I do not perceive theory and practice as mutually exclusive disciplines, but, like Jane Taylor, I understand this inquiry to be 'a meditation on the translation between the realms of theory and practice' (Taking Stock: The Making of a Bourgeois Life). My own position, that of 'artist' and 'critic', should, perforce, draw me naturally to this conclusion; that is, if the matter of conclusion can be said to be a matter of nature.

If I attach this proviso then, it is because all too often, and all too insidiously, opinion manifests itself as belief, belief as nature. In 'The Novel in Africa' J. M. Coetzee affirms the need for this proviso when, through the character of Elizabeth Costello, he weighs the matter of belief: 'Things can be true . . . even if one does not believe in them, and conversely. Belief may be no more, after all, than a source of energy, like a battery into which one plugs the idea to make it run. Like what happens when one writes: believing whatever has to be believed in order to get the job done' (p. 4).

That Coetzee positions doubt as 'the other hand' of an unresolved debate should alert the reader to the openness of the matter of belief. Given the ineffability and elusiveness of my own inquiry, this openness becomes all the more critical. The imagination, and the writing of that, abhors certainty which is why, after George Steiner, I conceive my position – henceforth understood as a non-position – as that of 'an interpreter . . . a decipherer and communicator of meanings. [. . .] a translator between languages, between cultures and between performative conventions' (Real Presences p. 7).

Behind Sachs's paper stands J. M. Coetzee's Life & Times of Michael K, a work of fiction that brilliantly sustains the enigmatic agency of Sachs's vision. Its central figure, Michael K, is a squatter in systems who escapes detection, a condemned man who remains strangely free, uttering little, understanding even less, disclosing nothing, his passage through life inscrutable. He is a creature who is neither friend nor foe, who neither flees nor engages the world, a creature emptied of all need to be understood, loved, to understand and to love: the embodiment of that most austere of conditions – distance; not the calibrated distance between things but distance itself. It is this distance that enables Coetzee to bypass, though not ignore, the grim historical moment of the novel's inscription, a moment wracked by a state of emergency, in which oppressor and oppressed are both disfigured by the contestation of absolutes. Against and outside this reductive and prescriptive sphere of contestation, the novel invokes the other space, the other thought, which is the theme of this inquiry. Darkly impenetrable though it may appear, Life & Times of Michael K is not a prophecy of the 'apocalypse' as André Brink suggests (Reimagining the Real p. 152), but an exemplary fictional instance of what

George Steiner, speaking of Theodor Adorno, calls the 'questioning negativity [that] is also an allegory of hope' (A Little Night Music p. 3). This hope is not declared but enacted, arriving at its austere climax at the close of the novel, where we find Michael K before a bomb-blasted site. The final question that is posed is how to live in the midst of ruin. The answer: 'He [K] would clear the rubble from the mouth of the shaft, he would bend the handle of the teaspoon in a loop and tie the string to it, he would lower it down the shaft deep into the earth, and when he brought it up there would be water in the bowl of the spoon; and in that way, he would say, one can live' (p. 184).

The austerity and sublimity of this moment has, to my knowledge, not been matched in South African fiction. It stands as the defining moment of a psychically destroyed country struggling to re-imagine itself. Sachs's paper is the attempt, outside of fiction, to reaffirm this moment. That it is a moment destined to prove unsustainable, a moment few would imagine possible, does not in any way diminish its force. That Sachs and Coetzee have failed to sustain the hope that each has released should, all the more, reveal its tenuousness. The question, then, is how to nurture that which seems unsustainable. My belief – in the knowledge that belief can mean little – is that it is vital to develop a critical and cultural practice that would bypass and surmount a continued entrapment within the 'ghetto' (Sachs) or 'gulag' (Coetzee) of the South African imaginary. As meditations on psychic entrapment and freedom, Sachs's paper (1989) and Coetzee's fiction (1983) stand as critical entry points for *thinking the transition* within South Africa's jaundiced present moment.

If a shift occurs in the 1990s, then, as Loren Kruger observes, it is one in which 'the moral conviction and commitment of anti-apartheid [has] waned' and 'radical social transformation' is displaced by a 'postcolonial uneven development'. Kruger defines this uneven development as the 'post-*anti*-apartheid period' (Black Atlantics, White Indians and Jews p. 35). The formulation is suggestively stilted. While it locates an epistemic and psychic turning point, it does not memorialise that turning point. What matters is Kruger's pointedly disturbing insight: that the very radicality of transformation has been *diverted*. This diversion is summed up in the late-modern paradox: post-*anti*. How, one wonders, will the means be found to sustain Sachs's and Coetzee's vision in a period in history in which the capacity for a radical negativity is compromised at every turn by the ennui and insouciance of a culture of the posthumous? Precisely, I would suggest, in the hyphenated instant *between*. For that which must be overwhelmed, bypassed and ignored today is not only the oppressive past but also the oppressive present, which equally conspires against freedom and the imagination.

What is it within the South African cultural imaginary that compromises the imagination and displaces the fructification of a new consciousness? In the most general and inclusive sense, the root of the problem lies in colonialism and its surrogate, apartheid. The South African imaginary has by no means weaned itself from the oppressive legacy of the former or the shallow grave of the latter. The pathological inheritances of colonialism and apartheid have been further compounded by what Kruger tellingly describes as a 'postcolonial *uneven* development' (my emphasis). Within the present cultural imaginary, then, colonialism and apartheid remain obsessive fixations and fixities that at every turn threaten to utterly subsume radical transformation. Against this corrosive and over-determining influence, this inquiry poses a series of challenges:

How to rethink the human in South Africa and how, as a constitutive part of the process, restore the capacity for love?

How to divert the psychic and epistemic constraints that repress the unthinkable and unspeakable and how to make this – emergent – otherness the harbinger of an ethically revisionary project?

How to sustain this ethic in a society caught between national and global imaginaries: between persistent – pathological – dualities and their simulacral cessation?

How to affirm the project of thinking the transition in a country that, like Václav Havel's Czechoslovakia, 'history has condemned . . . to the unenviable role of mere unthinking experts in suffering' (p. 126).

How, in spite of the disfigurement of the human, to inculcate a spirit of play? How to redefine the ordinary on behalf of the numinous (sublime) or the awkward and experimental (queer)?

How, in a culture caught between secular rationalism and a casual fatalism, to nurture the radical alterity that is folly?

How to challenge an emergent cult of individualism and sustain a seemingly reactionary faith in the collective?

How to develop a syncretic logic that will not be subsumed by the metatropes of unity and sameness?

How, given that South Africa has been as emphatically named as it is unnameable, to *write* the country?

In his 'Jerusalem Prize Acceptance Speech' Coetzee memorably affirms the impossibility of the imagination given 'the *crudity* of life in South Africa, the naked force of its appeals' (p. 99). Coetzee prefaces his damning conclusion with the alluring yet thoroughly untenable possibility that, after Nietzsche, reads: 'We have art . . . so that we shall not die of the truth' (ibid.). For Coetzee, however, it is 'truth' which negates imagination. My contrary view is that art and truth are not exclusive but interdependent *urgencies* caught in the interstices of their expression and interpretation and ceaselessly subject to revision. Coetzee's view, therefore, cannot be the last word on the fate of South Africa and that of its culture. There is, however, no disputing the intractability of his critical vision. Indeed, his 'Jerusalem Prize Acceptance Speech' – the psychic inverse of Sachs's 'Preparing Ourselves for Freedom' – will continue to toll its truth in this inquiry. Neither vision, however, is adequate in itself. In distinct and opposed ways, both point to a revisionary ethic defined by the desire to affirm creativity as that which absorbs, displaces, and surpasses the numbing contestation of opposed conditions.

In 'The Postcolonial and the Postmodern: The Question of Agency' Homi Bhabha conceives this revisionary ethic as that which is 'part dream, part analysis' (*The Location of Culture* p. 181). This fusion of seemingly incommensurable states points to the bypass Sachs would effect. Located 'outside . . . the hierarchy and the subordinations of the sentence', this ethic affirms the '*definitive discontinuity*' (p. 180, my emphasis) of epistemic engagement and textual inscription. Non-positional, this ethic exists *between* the contrapuntal, and there sustains thinking as a hesitance or stammering, as that which is 'not quite experience, not yet concept' (p. 181). Situated between an *a priori* certainty (definitive discontinuity) and an epistemic and psychic immanence (not quite, not yet), Bhabha names this hesitance, this stammer, the 'hybrid moment' (ibid.). It is this – imprecise – moment that cannily echoes Sachs's epistemological leap and which negatively affirms the veracity of Michael K's agency. For it is in this ever-shifting moment that thinking eludes both subjectivity and objectivity and becomes that which is 'neither signifier nor signified' (ibid.). It is this beguiling and stupefying proposition that I have taken to heart and chosen to affirm as a vital way out of the impasse that defines South Africa's present cultural predicament. For what Bhabha's logic suggests is that it is only by passing through the ambivalence of the post-*anti* – the after-shock of a prior and delimited contestation of absolutes – that we will be able to reinvigorate the displaced and radically transforming agency which Sachs regards as vital to the sustenance of culture.

In 'Taking Stock' Jane Taylor reflects upon the ambivalence of the present cultural moment. The object of her reflection is *Confessions of Zeno*, a theatre production inspired by Italo Svevo's post-World War I novel, for which Taylor wrote the libretto, with music by Kevin Volans, shadow play by The Handspring Puppet Company and direction by William Kentridge. A late-modern variant of what Muthobi Mutloatse defined as 'proemdra' (p. 5) – the fusion of prose, poetry, and drama, to which, here, we can include song, puppetry and music – *Zeno* signals a further – aggravated – interpenetration of aesthetic modes in the service of a syncretic exploration of culture which, increasingly, has come to express an 'ambiguous relationship to absolutist authority and power'. For Taylor it is this ambiguity that allows for the 'deeply unpredictable processes of making'. What interests Taylor, moreover, is 'indirection': '[W]e are no longer so sure of the merits of the penetrating gaze of truth, and oftentimes we prefer to look a little askance, holding stubbornly but affectionately on to an impression we think we have seen, as if this little glimpse is more significant than a more obvious point of view' (p. 7).

If Taylor favours the incidental or glancing look it is because she is well aware that South African theatre – and here I would say critical and cultural production in general – is caught in the 'unenviable space of performing into a kind of vacuum' (ibid.). What this 'vacuum' suggests is that the absolute contests that persist must at some critical level be simulacral projections that, despite their continued impact, can be thought *against*. This process of thinking against and outside absolute contestation distinguishes the *raison d'être* of the play's central character who 'stays outside his own borders, always watching himself, holding back from expressive range, in some way anatomising his own malaise' (ibid.). Here Taylor conveys the non-positional and hybrid moment that defines my own inquiry. Nonetheless, my venture does not restrict itself to the pathological and solipsistic constraints that shape *Zeno*. While this inquiry undoubtedly shares an affinity with Taylor's reflection, it works through the pathology that *Zeno* thematises in order to forge an alternative consciousness that has not been scripted in advance by that which would constrain and over-determine it. Hence the immense allure of Bhabha's formulation: *not quite experience, not yet concept*.

Compelled beyond – yet caught within – the discontinuities of its enunciatory process, this inquiry not only resists the absolute, conceived here as simulacral; it also challenges the latent threat that would render this inquiry complacently and speculatively gestural. What drives this inquiry is the bid to affirm *the ethical veracity of its constitutive ambivalence* rooted in the shiftiness of what we have come to name the postmodern and postcolonial condition. When read in the affirmative, Kruger's logic of the post-*anti* aptly defines the psychic and epistemic indeterminacy that characterises Taylor's reflections, as it does my own endeavour. Weaned from the grand narratives of resistance and freedom, South African cultural practitioners are increasingly faced with an ambivalence that is as enabling as it is dangerous. The challenge, as I understand it, is to convert the liminality and partiality of a given insight into a saving revisionary ethic.

This is the burden of Bhabha's thinking. Characterised by a charged ambivalence, or hesitance, it is a method of thinking caught *between* and compelled *beyond* the polarisation of the unknowable and the knowable. Advancing by way of a detour – a trajectory akin to Taylor's glancing impression – a thinking of this kind understands that its putative 'object' of study is as imperilled and uncertain as the method used to understand it. Conceived under erasure, both the 'subject' and 'object' of thought convey the interstitiality of the intentional and the interpretive. Bhabha has never ceased to reiterate this point, which, all too often, has been blithely and reductively deployed. Emptied of its ethical moment, this differential and ambivalent logic has come to mark yet another aspect of the ennui and insouciance of the late modern mind. It is not surprising, therefore, that in a country defined by the notoriety of its historical burden and increasingly and corrosively influenced by the aforementioned ennui and insouciance, Bhabha's position has largely been regarded with suspicion. Against this suspicion I would suggest that it is precisely the critical praxis that Bhabha has developed which will yield a more incisive and enabling vision of the country.

Indefinitely pronominal, South Africa resists intention and interpretation to the precise degree that it begs it. The question is: How does South Africa *want* to be read? And what is occluded in the instant of reading? What is the *vacuum* that faces the interpreter? For if Taylor is correct, if indecision is increasingly operative, if substance is ineffable, then how is one to *ground* meaning? These are giddy times indeed. The challenge and the pleasure lie in an affirmative relation to reflexive inquiry. Against the penetrating and moral gaze of truth, and, as compellingly, the gaze fixated upon an untruth, this inquiry assumes a non-position that, after Bhabha, I would define as 'the 'midst ness' of the intermediary in its relation to the other' (Aura and Agora p. 13). To not assume this 'midst ness' would be to fall prey to one of three tendencies that characterise critical appraisal and cultural production in South Africa. I have already noted two: fatalism (nihilism) and positivism (voluntarism). The third, which closely shadows and endangers my own thought, is relativism (opportunism). Since these contesting terms recur, it is vital to foreground them. Each seeks to define what South Africa is and the role of its culture. By aligning myself with none of the three, but by emphasising their contiguity, I hope, in the mix as it were, to develop the alternative perspective and sensibility invoked by Sachs, which, since it is the performative sum of this thesis, I will not summarise here.

I will, however, turn to one particular vision of South Africa, Coetzee's, which appears in his 'Jerusalem Prize Acceptance Speech'. The vision is that South Africa is as 'irresistible as it is unlovable' (p. 99). I duly note this vision because it stands as a remarkably durable and deeply troubling summation of the country. That this vision recurs 13 years later in Coetzee's essay on William Kentridge's animated film *History of the Main Complaint* affirms its durability. In brief, Coetzee posits that Kentridge's film reintegrates the past within the present in a manner that mixes 'loathing . . . with . . . attachment'. This observation leads Coetzee to the following rhetorical question: 'is not precisely the mix of loathing and attachment what defines obsession?' (History of the Main Complaint p. 87). What I regard as fixation within the economy of cultural production and reception in South Africa, Coetzee reads as obsession. I would suggest, furthermore, that Coetzee's reading points to a founding pathology. Indeed, in his 'Jerusalem Prize Acceptance Speech' he speaks of 'pathological attachments' (p. 98).

Loathing and attachment, then, like their echo, the unlovable and irresistible, define the pathological matrix whereby South Africa is perceived and experienced. That Coetzee embraces the very pathology he assesses reveals the extent to which he finds himself incapable of attaining the psychic and epistemic turn that, he knows, is critical to the re-envisioning of South Africa's predicament. I address this conscious failure later. For now I wish to affirm a deeply ingrained pathological economy of cultural production and reception which is not only Coetzee's, but which forms the constitutive seam of the South African imaginary, a seam which I have pitted myself against. Its psychic and epistemic impact has been so consuming and overwhelming that it has left virtually no room for an alternative vision. All the more, then, the necessity – and not the need – to develop an other logic.

My counter proposition, then, is that South Africa is as *resistible as it is lovable*. This conceptual shift is no mere inversion. Rather, it allows me to unmask a dominant – fatal – perception of South Africa that, if we are to advance, must be resisted. That this fatality can be found even within highly reflexive and immanent cultural offerings such as *Zeno* should alert us not only to its durability, but also to its guile. Fatality absorbs and deactivates contradiction. Its object: to hold all in bondage. Coetzee hauntingly sums up this entrapment in his 'Jerusalem Prize Acceptance Speech'. He conveys bondage so insidious, so inclusive, that even exultation falls victim to its rule. One even finds an 'entrapment in infinitudes' (p. 98). To develop a notion that South Africa is as resistible as it is lovable, therefore, demands a differential and inconclusive logic that negates the instrumental (polarisation) and the pathological (obsession). A logic of this nature will allow one to slip the ties that bind, namely the Manichean logic of the master and slave – inverted, mirrored – which lies at the root of South Africa's continued psychic disfigurement.

To conceive South Africa as resistible and lovable, one will need to defound South Africa's bonded economy and effect a psychic and epistemic embrace that works against fear and denial and gestures towards love. I cannot satisfactorily stress the immense importance of the shift that I propose. Love, we will discover, has formed no place within the oppressive system(s) that have marked and marred South Africa. Indeed, one could say that the history of South Africa has been shaped by the very lack of love, a lack so profound, so damaging that no retrospective project of healing can easily – if ever – remedy it. This tenebrous position is certainly deeply ingrained in South Africa's imaginary. My position, however, is not as hopeless. After Sachs, it would regenerate a blighted capacity for love, a love 'immune to fate and criticism'. After Kentridge, it would achieve this regeneration in a manner as unenamoured by fatality as it is by hope, a manner that, in 'a state of siege', would keep nihilism at bay and optimism in check (Art in a State of Grace p. 103). It is this position – or rather non-position – that will allow for both resistance *and* love. Nevertheless both gestures must be conceived under erasure, for what I understand to be resistance and love – that which is resistant and lovable – must defy closure and summation (fixity and obsession). Consequently my wager is that for the imagination to liberate itself, for freedom to become realisable, thought must resist closure *in the name of love*. I am of course well aware that love, like its cognates freedom and imagination, has been traduced and commodified. The television show *All You Need is Love* (SABC 1) is a typical instance. Having unmasked the absurdity of the programme, Darrel Bristow-Bovey notes:

> Love is a beautiful thing, but it is tricky, because many other things can be mistaken for love. Fear, for instance, and tiredness and loneliness and – on more than one occasion – hunger. Sometimes love is just another way of saying you have nothing left to say (p. 10).

Here, though, it is as the liminal moment between longing and its betrayal that love assumes its enabling agency. Notwithstanding the fraught ambivalence that stalks love, it can, contrary to Bristow-Bovey's just though ironical view, also serve as a resistant act, an act that furthers the attempt to rethink – dream and experience – the inherent heterogeneity of the South African cultural imaginary which, until now, has been intuited as symptomatic of a pathology rather than as that which, all the while, was resistant to pathology.

The pathological is not the heterogeneous or hybrid. The pathological is the obsessive fixation upon a single thing at the expense of all others. South Africa's failure to imagine or dream what Bhabha describes as the 'hybrid moment' marks the precise extent to which it has negated itself: exchanged radical difference for sameness, blurred gradation for fixed and separable terms. This gesture – loveless, or defined by self-love or the love of one's caste – has by no means come to an end in the new South Africa. It continues to thrive at the expense of an incommensurably heterogeneous reality. The slogan '*Simunye* we are one', flashed obsessively on SABC 1, is the axiomatic new South African metatrope of unity in difference and sameness, though, as Kentridge notes, the new South Africa cannot be so easily glossed: 'the very term "new South Africa" has within it the idea of a painting over the old' (Felix in Exile p. 127).

In his 'Introduction: South Africa in the Global Imaginary', Leon de Kock similarly conveys the layering and the stresses and strains inherent in a bonded and repressive conception of the country:

[A] crisis of representation has been endemic to the geographical and cultural conjunction that has become South Africa and that 'it,' the country conceived as a third-person singular entity, is a seam that can be undone only at the cost of its existence. Its very nature, its *secret life*, inheres in the paradoxes of the seam (Introduction: South Africa in the Global Imaginary p. 284, my emphasis).

The question is: how to affirmatively refigure South Africa as an indefinite category and as an experiential paradox? If the method that Bhabha invokes is of value in this regard it is because it allows for a cognitive slippage that enables the sustenance and the interrogation of a fraught 'seam' that would, at every turn, undo the seeming integrity of South Africa. The 'hybrid moment' or the 'seam', then, are conceptual attempts to convey that which is irreducible to thought, yet nevertheless the product of thought. Kentridge's *pentimenti* – a new painting over the old – similarly conveys the differential and resistant nature of a given construct. However, it is when Kentridge turns to sonar that he most compellingly and persuasively conveys what Leon de Kock calls the 'crisis of representation'.

Explaining why he favours charcoal drawing Kentridge states that the medium, better than any other, traces the ineffable. 'Oil paint, or pen and ink, would be a dissimulation', whereas charcoal captures 'the smoky transitions in X-rays, the discrete marks of a sonar scan, the diagrammatic clarity of an MRI' (The Body Drawn and Quartered p. 140).

Dissect as deep as you like and you will never find the mimetic reference of the sonar. They are *already a metaphor*. They are messages from an inside we may apprehend but can never grasp. In their separation from the apparent they come as reports from a distant and unknown place (ibid., my emphasis).

Kentridge's appraisal of his art echoes Bhabha's hybrid moment and affirms my own fascination with the ineffable and resistant trace. After Kentridge, I would suggest that the descriptor – South Africa – is at best improper, subject to erasure, and irreducible to mimetic reference. This decision to conceive of South Africa as the figuration of sonar is undoubtedly a peculiar one given the country's weightedness in the global imaginary. As the title of Kentridge's film *Weighing . . . and Wanting* suggests, South Africa's very weightedness also implies a blotting out: a fixed presence which erases as much as it reveals. If I defer to this weightedness, then, it is as a decoy. For what matters here is the desire to explore and reflect upon cultural expression in South Africa that does not echo the familiar and the apparent and is not subject to the reactive and nostalgic, but which emerges from *a distant and unknown place*. To access this other place – which, after Sachs, I take to be culture's quest – one will need to till that which Coetzee calls an 'unacknowledgeable desire' (Jerusalem Prize Acceptance Speech p. 97).

André Brink's recent novel, *The Other Side of Silence*, gestures towards this quest. In an interview with Maureen Isaacson in the *Sunday Independent*, Brink noted: 'Everything is written for the sake of what cannot be said' (p. 17). If writing speaks the unspoken, it also *speaks the unspeakable*: that which forms the allegorical cornerstone of the South African cultural imaginary. I would suggest, however, that the intensification of an exploration of this nature – be it in writing, or visual and dramatic expression – is increasingly emergent, indeed ascendant. Contrary to popular opinion, this ascendance of the unspeakable is not indicative of a putative freedom, but the marker for a heightened awareness of the unspeakable within the South African cultural imaginary which freedom cannot or must not – yet – name. The repressed does not go away with putative freedom. Certainly, by virtue of its sun-struck and freshly minted newness and self-presence, freedom in South Africa cannot countenance, let alone sustain, the knowledge of the unspeakable and unnameable. With each proclaimed step towards clarity and resolution a slippage occurs. If this is so, it is because in South Africa it is not a newfound settlement that prevails but a further, aggravated, unsettlement. Within this inquiry it is this unsettlement that assumes centre stage, in the full knowledge that unsettlement cannot be centred or staged. To do so would, in Kentridge's words, be an act of dissimulation. Better, then, to conceive of this inquiry as a metaphoric impress, which, on the hither side of its enunciation, emits 'the codes, dots and dashes of a sonar' (The Body Drawn and Quartered p. 140).

These substantive yet ineffable markers echo what Bhabha – after Roland Barthes – describes as 'writing aloud' (*The Location of Culture* p. 181). This echo occurs all the more forcefully in Maria Anna Tappeiner and Reinhard Wulf's documentary film *Drawing the Passing*, in which Kentridge describes his art as a 'handwriting' and a form of 'thinking aloud'. As metaphor, 'writing' for Bhabha and Kentridge harbours no referent. This does not mean that it is intrinsically irreferential. Rather, the notion of writing aloud, like the figurations of sonar, affirms the paradox of metaphor as that which is ineffable *and* ontological. For Bhabha and Kentridge metaphor is not the estranged echo of that which exists outside; it is not, after Nietzsche, the equation of the unequal. Metaphor is the partial figuration of meaning within and despite an existent vacuum. For Bhabha and Kentridge there is nothing outside of metaphor.

Given this controversial conclusion, the resistance that Bhabha, in particular, has faced within the South African socio-political and cultural sphere is not surprising. For Bhabha it is precisely the metaphoricity of the lived world that makes it all the more profoundly ambivalent. Because he rejects every polarisation, preferring the incommensurability of the liminal instant in which one is neither one nor the other, he has roundly been charged with sophistry. Here, though, one should note the source of this charge: Platonism, a source that founds the varied ideological positions that comprise secular rationalism. Lest we forget, it was Plato who condemned the sophist to the dungeon. That this condemnation should fix itself upon Bhabha's thought is as inevitable as it is predictable. Nevertheless, my purpose is not to defend Bhabha against his detractors. Withdrawing from the reactive frisson, I have chosen to reflect on the importance of Bhabha's 'hybrid moment' to the revivification of Sachs's thwarted quest for an other space.

In 'Aura and Agora' Bhabha defines his thought as 'an interpretational ethics and an interventionist aesthetics that is at once liminal and luminous' (p. 15). Here, in the name of rapture – which I read as love and, in due course, as magic – Bhabha addresses a mode of expression – through art and writing – which 'hover[s] on the edges of inscription and spectation' (p. 11). By sticking to the edges and keeping the seeming fullness of understanding at bay, Bhabha ushers forth the 'spectres of memory, phantoms of the future, proxies for the present' (p. 15). These spectres, phantoms, and proxies are akin to Kentridge's codes, dots and dashes. What Kentridge understands as sonar, Bhabha reads as the 'interstices of intention and interpretation' (ibid.). Neither objective nor subjective, sonar evokes the 'liminal and luminous'. If, for Kentridge, the messages from the 'inside' may be apprehended but never grasped, then for Bhabha, who defers to an unbounded 'outside', there is no finitude to the processes of understanding. I would suggest, here, that the outside and the inside are one and the same. Both spaces traverse the subordinations and sententiousness of meaning. By fracturing and rendering fluid meaning's components – experience, concept, dream, analysis – Bhabha qualifies their relative autonomy and reveals their interpenetration in the instant in which meaning comes into being. Thought does not occur at a remove and neither is thought self-present. That which occurs outside also occurs within; hence Bhabha's insistence upon what he calls the definitive discontinuity of textual inscription.

If Bhabha is the critical lynchpin that drives this inquiry it is because no thinker has further impelled my own aggravated and agonistic desire to fuse the somatic, the oneiric, and the analytic. That Bhabha locates his inquiry at the edge that links and separates the (post)modern and the (post)colonial all the more reinforces his critical provenance and value. In an interview with Gary A. Olson and Lynn Worsham, 'Staging the Politics of Difference', Bhabha reminds us that 'what was some people's modernity was somebody else's colonialism' (p. 17). If earlier he points to the definitive discontinuity of textual inscription, here he points to a related discontinuity in which 'modernity [. . .] emerg[es] in and through a very complex negotiation with its own colonial *double life*' (ibid., my emphasis). For those engaged in the question of South Africa this complex negotiation is unavoidable.

Caught *between* modernity and colonialism/postmodernity and postcolonialism, South Africa exemplifies what Bhabha describes as a double life and Kruger the post-*anti*. Like other emergent nations, South Africa has repressed its colonial anteriority in favour of modernity. This denial – factored into the workings of colonialism itself – has assumed full-blown proportions today. In the name of democracy, modernity lays claim not to its colonial past but to a 'Greek ideal'. Here Bhabha adds 'it should also, at that point, make a claim to the colonial reality in relation to which it has elaborated its own modernity, whether that modernity be the notion of nationhood or civility or civil society or civic society or civic virtue' (Staging the Politics pp. 17–18). Bhabha does not construct an opposed set of choices but asks that the Greek ideal be examined *in relation* with colonial reality, that the ideal and the real, in turn, inform modernity. This logic has not come to pass in South Africa. Rather, it remains the very culture of division and rule – a culture masked today by indifference – that has further estranged the emergent nation from itself. Bhabha's multi-tiered notion of modernity, in which nationhood segues into civility, civil society into civic society and civic virtue, is anything but apparent. Rather, if modernity can be said to define present-day South Africa, then it is as the simulacral double of a repressed or displaced past.

The challenge, then, is to understand how this rift has come about and how it can be bridged. The solution I offer is not one in which the split between the ideal and the real in South Africa is synthesised. Rather, the solution invoked here is one which bypasses the sententious and exegetical claims of South Africa's emergent modernity and constructs, instead, a critical and cultural vision which thrives between and within the inconclusiveness that is experience/concept/dream/analysis. By occupying an inter-mediate and reflexive non-position such as this, one is better able to qualify *both* the ideal and the real. Thereby modernity and coloniality, which problematically and unevenly segue into the postmodern and the postcolonial, are perceived as constructs which afford an ongoing inquiry in which the subject and the object of analysis are both understood as shifting – *not quite, not yet* – and, therefore, at no point reducible to the order of signification. What matters here are not the putative mimetic fixities – such as modernity or colonialism or apartheid – but, given the nature of their cultural inscription, what these fixities cannot and must not say. Kentridge's sonar and Brink's silence are figures for this elided and 'fissure[d] [. . .] form of knowledge' (Staging the Politics p. 11). That Kentridge, in an interview with Carolyn Christov-Bakargiev, describes drawing under erasure as 'a model for knowledge' (In Conversation p. 8) should, all the more, affirm the link I have drawn between the theoretician and the artist.

John Noyes's 'The Place of the Human' and André Brink's 'Interrogating Silence: New Possibilities Faced by South African Literature' similarly map the interpretational ethics and interventionist aesthetics which distinguish this inquiry. The first paper, after Theodor Adorno, postulates a 'negative dialectic of the human' (The Place of the Human p. 60). The second, while it sustains the efficacy of a negative dialectic, also leans enigmatically towards what Bhabha terms the 'hybrid moment' that is 'neither signifier nor signified'. What both papers have in common is the desire to think reflexively within and against the Manichean system. At once over-determining and symptomatic of the oppressive conditions of colonialism and apartheid, this Manichean system provides 'the synthetic resolution of a contradiction' and 'historicize[s] difference as a step on the way to unity' (The Place of the Human p. 59). Within and against this defining epistemological system, Noyes and Brink – along with Kruger, Taylor, Kentridge and Bhabha – seek, instead, to reflect on yet another dimension to critical and cultural expression which could be said to form a supplement – Sachs's other space – to this omnipresent system of understanding South Africa's past, its present, and its future.

For Noyes this supplementary critical and cultural expression demands the *'reluctant articulation* of utopia, and the form in which it announces itself in everyday life, the idea of the human' (p. 53, my emphasis). If Noyes qualifies, indeed resists, the very impulse that impels him, it is because he is well aware of the profligate and simulacral currency of the utopian vision in South Africa. His very insistence upon the agency of the term alerts one to a dimension of thought that fuses the everyday with the transfigural, or, after Bhabha, 'the liminal and the luminous'. Brink, similarly, explores the efficacy of the *imagined real* which he also terms the magical. Well aware of the abuse of the term, he nevertheless insists upon its value as a trope through which to grasp the somatic, oneiric, and cognitive processes at work in the project of decolonisation. Both thinkers, then, deploy terms – utopia/magic – which have been abused and/or suppressed. It should be noted, however, that the utopian and the magical are not conceived as means through which to access a cognitive or experiential absolute. On the contrary, after Bhabha, they make possible an apprehension within the liminal moment of that which is *not quite experience, not yet concept*. What matters to both Noyes and Brink is an epistemic and psychic agency that, in *passing through* and *sustaining* contradiction, opens up what has largely been a closed and prescriptive depiction of South Africa's past and an enervated depiction of its present.

If – unlike Brink, for whom there are 'more things in heaven and earth than have been dreamt of in philosophy' (Interrogating Silence p. 25) – Noyes chooses to work within the constraints of a negative dialectic, this does not diminish the salience of his insight. To be sure, the very contradiction which each in their own way dramatises should alert one to a lack, attendant upon a desire for closure, that is resident in the Manichean system of cultural critique and expression. Within South African cultural studies Noyes and Brink are not unique examples of an emergent and ascendant resistance to this system. Kruger, Taylor, and Kentridge are other cases in point. If I have elected to locate their respective positions in relation to the nodal position which Bhabha occupies in my schema, it is because their positions, as well as those of Noyes and Brink, not only echo Bhabha's critical insight but, in their inflected distinctiveness, help me to account for the tension that marks my own non-position which, by turns, is shaped by the reflexive rigour of a negative dialectic and by the *élan* or quest for the post-dialectical and post-philosophical thought – experience/concept/dream/analysis – which traverses and confounds the dialectical.

The defining means through which to access this unthinkable – the utopian and the magical – as I have already suggested, is through bypassing a received position, perceiving at a glance, and at every turn allowing for the reflexive moment when one catches oneself in the instant of thinking: in the instant, that is, when thought slips its casing and becomes other to itself. In this manner one opens up and enriches the question of what it means to be, to create and to think, in South Africa at this present moment. The defining term for this process, foregrounded in Noyes's paper and active in Brink's writing and Kentridge's art, is *reflexivity*. It is a term to which I will insistently return. As Noyes suggests:

> To write in a particular place about the location of theory and the concept of the human is to enter a reflexive mode where the writer is at the same time writing culture and, in this process, *testing the conceptual limits of key ideas on culture* . . . [T]he key to understanding how conceptualization relates to the moment of its performance, that is how in the act of theorization, a specific constellation of ideas comes together to define and delimit the individual's position in a particular social and historical order (p. 49, my emphasis).

Reflexivity emphasises and loosens a given position. In so doing it defines a given position as a performative act that *in part* is constrained by, and inscribed within, the particularities of place and history. If I stress the partiality of a given position it is because, unlike Noyes, I am not wholly convinced that an 'individual's position' is defined and delimited by a '*specific* constellation of ideas . . . a *particular* social and historical order' (my emphasis). In accordance with Bhabha and Brink, I believe that there are factors at work in the constitution of a given position other than the ideational and the received particularities of the social and historical. It is precisely my divergence, here, from Noyes, which leads me towards what I define as a non-position. This non-position not only deconstructs itself in the instant that it deconstructs its prey – be it the Manichean system which divides the better to synthesise and reify a given social and historical position or the new South African ennui and insouciance distinguished by indifference – but also loosens and aggravates the constraints which Noyes affixes to reflexivity. Its objective – at best a problematic assignation, since the non-positional challenges the teleological agency which resides even in reflexive engagements – is to disinter that which critical and cultural engagement has heretofore failed satisfactorily to access and foreground: that is, the hybrid moment.

In 'Interrogating Silence' André Brink describes this *other* dimension of human experience as that which '*eludes* or *defies* understanding' (p. 20). For Brink it is precisely this cognitive impasse or failure to '*imagine the real*' (p. 24) which thwarts social and cultural transformation in South Africa. 'I certainly am convinced,' says Brink,

> that without the attempt to grasp, *with the creative imagination*, the past and its silences, South African society as a whole may get bogged down in mere materialities, sterile rationalizations, and the narrow mechanics of retribution or amnesty (p. 25, my emphasis).

Brink's fears have already been realised. Against the realisation of these fears, however, I have elected to 'attempt to grasp' that which Brink describes as the *real* and Noyes the *human*. In a sense akin to sonar, these terms *defy* understanding. This does not mean, though, that the *real* and the *human* exist wholly beyond the increasingly blurred limits of intellection. Certainly, the perceived inaccessibility of the *real* or the *human* is as much a product of their inherently confounding nature as it is a product of systems of interpretation which, when confronted by the resistance of these terms to cognition, have suppressed their enigmatic agency and constructed them as the markers for an unbreachable limit or silence. In the final movement of his paper Brink suggests why that which he defines as the *real* has not, epistemically, come to pass:

> Many times in the past Africa has been conquered; its true discovery – certainly in white literature – is still awaiting its moment (ibid.).

The implication, here, is that the act of conquering presupposes a suppression and a silencing. The reticulated question which follows is: what has been suppressed, and why? What is it that 'white literature' lacks? What is the discovery that must be made? And what is the moment that awaits those engaged in the production of culture? By way of an answer one could say that that which awaits, that which is missing, is precisely the *real*, the *human*. The inverse of this assumption is that it is precisely that which is *unreal* and *inhuman* that has assumed a hegemonic control over the South African imaginary. By working against this imaginary, Brink hopes to issue forth a supplementary logic under the sign of magic. Well aware of the difficulty implicit in an attempt of this nature, Brink nevertheless can find no other alternative. His problematic discriminatory position that ascribes this lack to 'white' literature alone is symptomatic of the strain that inhibits that which Brink would realise. In targeting the problem in such a discriminatory manner, Brink reinforces the privative binary that marks and mars the very conditions for the production and reception of literature, and culture in general, in South Africa. This limit aside, there remains definite merit to Brink's attempt to grasp 'the other side of silence'.

If Brink awaits this redemptive moment in white literature then Lewis Nkosi, in a paper entitled 'Postmodernism and Black Writing in South Africa', explores the foil in this privative binary. While the counterpointing of white and black writing may prove instructive, it remains a restrictive and distinctively historical debate that does not satisfactorily further my own inquiry, which, more generally, and more inclusively, explores a lack within both so-called white and black literature. For Brink that lack is 'magic'. Located at the limits of intellection and split like the literature of this country into 'white' and 'black', magic, for Brink, forms the missing link between the past and the future. If Brink valorises the term it is because, in the literary guise of 'magic realism', it fosters a mode of writing which links the probable and the improbable, the inhuman and the human, the unreal and the real. Nevertheless, the marked rarity of this mode of writing in South Africa suggests, all the more, the deferred and persistent inscription of a lack that, for Brink, is tantamount to the continued failure to *imagine the real*. The reason for Brink's cautious restitution of magic is that it fosters a counter-logic – Bhabha's hybrid moment, Kentridge's sonar, Sachs's other space – that could reinvigorate cultural practice and render fluid the fixity of cultural difference.

Brink's compelling intuition that the South African cultural imaginary will be able to source the magical only 'once the mind has become, in Ngugi's sense of the word, decolonized' (ibid.), reaffirms the cogency and urgency of my own project of recovery which, in returning to a repressed silence and definitive discontinuity, would refigure and re-think South Africa's past, its present, and its future. That this epistemic (oneiric and somatic) turn has not, to date, been sustained reaffirms the extent to which critical and cultural practice has remained defined by the pathological. It is precisely because we remain unfree that we have failed to imagine the real. To be sure, it is our continued *resistance to freedom* that has sustained the stuntedness and deformity that remains the defining characteristic of critical and cultural engagement in South Africa. For Brink, then, it is the resuscitation of magic – 'a free interaction between the worlds of the living and the dead, a rich oneiric stratum' (ibid.) – that will all the more make possible the sustenance of a transforming critical and cultural vision.

Epistemically and psychically, then, this inquiry engages with an ongoing, ceaselessly thwarted, and seemingly unending process of decolonisation. At best, after Brink, it is a blasphemous and redemptive attempt 'to speak the unspeakable, to eat of the forbidden fruit' (Interrogating Silence pp. 20–21), 'to play with the future on that needlepoint where it meets past and present; and to be willing to risk everything in the leaping flame of the word as it turns into world' (p. 27). A position of this nature, marked by an attenuated hope, a charged ambivalence, and a heightened reflexivity, must, necessarily, eschew any aggrandising and exegetical desire for closure or settlement. All the more critically, it must not allow itself to fall prey to an ironical and enervated late-modern stance that stages ambivalence as an empowering limit. By challenging closure – whether self-inflicted or defined by others – it must further aggravate the received conditions that, until now, have sought to prescribe and over-determine the nature of a given place, a given history.

George Steiner echoes this position when, in his autobiographical work *Errata*, he finds himself incapable of renouncing the validating wonders of love and the future tense. Critchley points out that Charles Baudelaire, in 'Chacun sa Chimère', similarly conveys this complex of renunciation and desire when he speaks of being 'condemned to hope' (Very Little p. 1). Renunciation and condemnation are not perceived here as impediments, but as the reflexive and conditional prerequisites for inquiry into a terrain which, historically, has been distorted and stultified by the Manichean dualities of despair and longing, oppression and freedom; dualities which have at no point permitted the erasure and contiguity of opposed terms which the phrase *condemned to hope* suggests. By fusing these privative dualities, yet falling prey to neither, Noyes, similarly, invokes the ethical possibility of hope in a place and time which threatens to reduce such hope to mockery:

> I permit myself this leap from the idea of utopia to that of the human via practices of everyday life, because one of the first moves in reconstituting our damaged civil society will have to be countering the way a particular idea of the human – the one that held sway over the ideology of apartheid – relates to the material basis it arose from and which persists in many ways in South Africa after apartheid. For a utopian discourse, social damage is measured as a discrepancy between what might be called the non-racial imaginary and the practice of everyday life. But the idea of utopia, or any utopian bent in theory requires the recognition of the theoretical impossibility of a coherent identity in any one location (as is indeed inscribed in the etymology of the word *utopia* itself) while at the same time acknowledging the political urgency of located identities (The Place of the Human p. 53).

Here Noyes maps what he later describes as the essential function of the negative dialectic, which is '*to keep alive the difference at the heart of the human*' (p. 59, my emphasis). For Noyes it is this negative dialectic which, by foregrounding 'the impossibility of the human as a moment of theoretical closure . . . enables the enactment of human rights in practice' (p. 60). In this striking conclusion to his paper Noyes weans himself from a prior reflexive rigidity in which the 'act of theorisation' defines and delimits a given position. Here, in this seemingly improbable yet strangely consoling wager – that liberates the rights and the *rites* of the human – Noyes allows for the ethical position that defines this inquiry. This position, which I have described as a non-position the better to affirm what Noyes postulates as *the theoretical impossibility of a coherent identity in any one location*, reaffirms my aversion to the synthetic stratagems of dualism, the rigidification of reflexivity, and, latterly, the metatropes of indifference and sameness. While I concur with Noyes when he states that 'the dialectic is not to be wished away by a simple critique of dualism', I do not believe that a negative dialectic remains the final arbiter of intellectual inquiry. More enigmatically, and certainly more vulnerably, I have called upon a dimension to critical and cultural expression that precedes and exceeds the constraints of dialectics. This dimension, which cannot *quite* be named for it defers to the a-significatory and the a-categorical, is not merely the inverse of a system founded on closure. It defers to a cognitive (somatic, oneiric) process that forms the *other* constitutive seam of this inquiry. This *other* finds its tropological echo in the auratic (Benjamin), the epiphanic (Joyce), the *ek-static* (Coetzee), the hybrid moment (Bhabha), the magical (Brink), sonar (Kentridge) and the imagination (Sachs). This other dimension, which I claim to be a property of thought, is at no point deployed in this inquiry at the expense of the negative dialectic, but, rather, as its critical supplement.

Bhabha succinctly defines this supplement as the logic of 'cultural difference'; a logic which 'add[s] to' that 'doesn't add up' (Staging the Politics p. 15). It is important to note that this supplementary logic is never a *fait accompli*, but that it marks an incommensurable bid on behalf of the ongoing project of decolonisation. Brink's leaping flame that *turns* word into world is an instance of this project of decolonisation, understood, at this point, as the decolonisation of the hierarchy and subordination of the sentence. Brink knows that writing is *not quite* convertible, *not quite* subject to its object. A radical alterity – love, rapture, or magic – exists, which is irreducible to the economy of its inscription. The *turning* of word into world is not a seamless operation, but one that acknowledges the constitutive role of alterity in the instant of signification. This instant – *a turning away and a turning towards* – is one which, in its agonistic rotation, releases the flame of magic from the furnace of signification which produces it. It is this agonistic process, Brink suggests, that releases the agency of magic realism: 'the leap of the imagination towards grasping the larger implications of our silences' (Interrogating Silence p. 24). Importantly, for Brink, the magical does not constitute the surreal but the *real*. It is the latter that has been suppressed. By working to decolonise closed epistemic systems, and by opening up the processes of inscription to the unthinkable and magical, Brink seeks to *rehumanise* the processes of thought and creation, the troubling implication being that it is precisely a system founded on the unity and closure of ineluctable differences, or a system which promotes indifference and sameness, that is inhuman and unreal.

To support his argument Brink turns to Steiner who, in *Language and Silence*, states: 'The world of Auschwitz lies outside speech as it lies outside reason' (in Interrogating Silence p. 19). South Africa, I would suggest, lies similarly on the outside of accepted systems of signification. Staying with Steiner, but turning to *Real Presences*, Brink argues for the regenerative power of critical and cultural inscription. For Brink, after Steiner, it is literature which gives to reality 'the greater permanence of the imagined', because 'without the arts, form would remain unmet and strangeness without speech in the silence of the stone' (in Interrogating Silence p. 19). These are undoubtedly far-reaching gestures of the mind and the spirit, gestures which heighten the grotesquery of the

Manichean construction of South Africa's past, its present and its future, which has persisted in perceiving a country – as nameless as it is emphatically named – through a reductive and foreshortened lens. The very clarity that founds a privative dualistic vision is symptomatic of blindness. If secular rationality has failed to register the complexity of lived experience in South Africa, then, all the more, one is compelled to interpret otherwise. This is why, along with Brink, I have highlighted an awareness that there are 'more things in heaven and earth than have been dreamt of in our philosophy' and forged a line of thought which I have called the post-dialectical. From a secularly rational point of view this position is undoubtedly problematic. To date, however, I have found no other way of accounting for the riddle of the South African condition other than by asserting the efficacy of an epistemology that fuses the immanent and the improbable.

Like Leon de Kock, who wrestles with an equivalent dilemma in his introduction to *South Africa in the Global Imaginary*, I am well aware that the name – South Africa – is ubiquitous, that it means different things to different people and that it refuses to contain the meanings ascribed to it. A designation as improper and as evasive as the *real* and the *human*, *South Africa* emerges in the pages of this inquiry as the figuration of a 'crisis' that, for de Kock, 'belongs as much in the country's history of suffering as it does in university seminar rooms' (p. 273). This conclusion leads de Kock to propose that 'an exploration of South African signifying economies *appears essential* to an understanding of its literary and cultural production' (ibid., my emphasis). In the equivocal fusion of the apparent and the essential, de Kock alerts us to a fraught commitment to inquiry in and through the analysis of 'signifying economies'. Moreover, he heightens the realisation that an inquiry of this nature pertains not only to intellectual and cultural practice but also to 'the country's history of suffering'. Any undertaking of an intellectual or cultural nature will not advance without the acute knowledge that its condition for engagement is coterminous with a history born of pain. The questions that I persistently pose are: What to make of this pain? How to think and create through, and in spite of, this pain? How, given the pathological dominance of pain in South Africa's imaginary, to sustain Steiner's validating wonders of love and the future tense? My view is that it would be ethically catastrophic if one were not to do so. The question, however, remains: What awaits those who would pass beyond fatality and beyond the strictures of sterile rationalisations and the lure of simulacral hope?

As Njabulo Ndebele, in 'Redefining Relevance', has stated:

> The greatest challenge of the South African revolution is the search for ways of thinking, ways of perception, that will help to break down the closed epistemological structures of South African oppression, structures which can severely compromise resistance by dominating thinking itself. The challenge is to free the entire social imagination of the oppressed from the laws of perception that have characterized apartheid society. For writers this means freeing the creative process itself from those very laws. It means extending the writer's perceptions of what

can be written about, and the means and methods of writing (*South African Literature and Culture* p. 67).

That the challenge Ndebele first posed in 1986 remains an urgent one all the more reinforces its intractability and complexity. My allegiance lies with those who would 'break down the closed epistemological structures of South African oppression' in the full knowledge that if they do not do so, the very processes and agency of resistance and decolonisation will be compromised. By foregrounding the epistemic root of oppression Ndebele points to the sphere in which the hindrance persists and where the reckoning must be focused: the sphere of representation, of signs. Nonetheless, this sphere is not reducible to the sum of its parts. Epistemology is not a closed theory of knowledge. Rather, as J. M. Coetzee in his 'Jerusalem Prize Acceptance Speech' suggests, epistemology supposes an engagement with the 'psychic representation' of oppression (p. 98). This evocative fusion of the occult with the representational allows precisely for a reading of cultural production that could confound and bypass an epistemic closure that, as Ndebele reminds us, 'can severely compromise resistance by dominating thinking itself'.

To engage with the persistence of oppression and to uncover the 'means and methods' whereby this oppression can be undermined and a culture of transformation and decolonisation sustained, it is critical that one understand not only the veracity of signs, but also their *inadequacy*. If words are cognates for lived experience, they are also phantoms. Hence Bhabha's 'hybrid moment' which is 'neither signifier nor signified'. Sachs and Ndebele intuit this lack. So does Coetzee. His haunting phrase *psychic representation* allows for a reading of South Africa's cultural predicament that incorporates the agency of the magical, the unthinkable, the repressed, the irrational, a-significatory, and a-categorical. That Sachs, Ndebele and Coetzee finally shut down this intuition marks the self-inflicted limit of their critical engagement rather than the veracity of their respective insights.

Regarding Coetzee, it should be noted that I am responding specifically to the 'Jerusalem Prize Acceptance Speech', which exemplifies an acute response to the monstrous logic of colonialism and apartheid. However, this speech cannot be said to serve as a blueprint for Coetzee's critical and cultural vision. I have already pointed to *Life & Times of Michael K* as a negatively conceived allegory of hope. Later, under the sign of Folly, I will explore Coetzee's resistance to secular rationality and his attempt to access what he has called the *ek-static*. For the purposes of this chapter, though, I have restricted myself to the fatal wager that Coetzee makes in his 'Jerusalem Prize Acceptance Speech': a wager that poses no escape from entrapment. Like Sachs's 'ghetto', the 'gulag' is Coetzee's figure for this entrapment. The psychic and epistemic descriptor for fatality and closure, the gulag characterises a country benighted and isolated, caught in the rictus of a state of emergency, a country that damns the very redemptive processes of the imagination that Coetzee elsewhere invokes. That I am able to read *against* the paralysing enclosure in which Coetzee finds himself, and thereby discover a way forward *through* the very psychic deformation which Coetzee acutely describes, surely means that a redemptive seed, no matter how thwarted, remains operative within what, undoubtedly, is an utterly inconsolable vision.

The case of Ndebele is a markedly different one. Unlike Coetzee but like Sachs, Ndebele *does* make a claim for a transformative cultural vision. As I have already noted and will develop later, the epistemology that founds Ndebele's claim is beset with problems. Bhabha provides a key to unlocking the problem inherent in Ndebele's critical epistemology when he states that what is needed is not an apodictic and subjunctive logic of transformation but 'a way . . . of *thinking the transition* that is involved in making the transformation' (Staging the Politics p. 14, my emphasis). If Ndebele resists closure, he does so *reactively*. What Ndebele does not reveal is that any closed epistemological system – whether founded on division or indifference – must presuppose *a constitutive and prior openness*. While I wholeheartedly support Ndebele's call for the development of new ways of thinking and perception, my point is that these new ways do not only form a reaction to closure, but precede, exceed, and immanently defound the oppressive laws of closure. Coetzee alerts us to this immanent discordance when he states that

> the deformed and stunted relations between human beings that were created under colonialism and exacerbated under what is loosely called apartheid have their *psychic representation* in a deformed and stunted *inner life* (Jerusalem Prize Acceptance Speech p. 98, my emphasis).

His fusion of the psychic and the representational reinforces the rupture that results from a system founded on division and rule. That Coetzee and Ndebele fail to develop the transformative power that their respective insights beg does not – to repeat – diminish the suggestiveness of those insights. One could reasonably argue that as victims of history they, like Sachs, are at best bound by paradox. That both reify oppression and render their thought subject to that oppression, so that even in those moments when an emergent freedom beckons it is swiftly thwarted, suggests a pathos of the time, a blindness willed or otherwise, that is defined by the preternatural and hegemonic dominance of colonialism and its surrogate, apartheid.

Coetzee and Ndebele are not the only ones who represent this marked failure. Indeed, this failure – a failure that knows itself as such – has proved to be the distinctive trait of cultural inquiry and expression in South Africa. By thinking against the grain of this reflexive and highly conscious failure, this inquiry seeks in turn to speak that which is intuited and felt but has not succinctly been expressed, the better to access the *psychic representation* of a lived experience, past and present, that is not wholly defined by oppression. In order to do so I must venture in and through, then beyond, the prison-house of dualism that has characterised cultural inquiry and expression, a dualism exemplified in Coetzee's all-too conscious fatalism and Ndebele's apodictic hope. My residual point, of course, is that it is precisely this legacy of oppression and freedom – evinced in Coetzee's fatalism and Ndebele's protracted longing – which, *together*, has resulted in a third more enervated strain: the malaise of the present moment which sustains and cancels the binary which defines it, and, in so doing, produces yet another prison-house: indifference.

Confronted thus, I propose that cultural inquiry and expression take up the challenge exemplified in the thinking of Bhabha, a mode of thinking that others – Kruger, Taylor, Kentridge, Noyes, Brink, Ndebele, Coetzee and Sachs – have, in distinctive ways, also provoked. I do not ask that we forget the stifling and pathological hold which the 'gulag' or the 'ghetto' has had – and continues to have – over our social and cultural imaginary; rather, I suggest that by thinking in and through its logic of entrapment we may begin to resuscitate the distorted and heterogeneous life which, despite the efforts of colonialism and the subsequent systems of oppression that are their mutations, has never successfully been pronounced null and void. In repressing the heterogeneous complexity of life, colonialism instituted a culture of guilt and shame, fear and denial, anger and suspicion. Today these pathological traits continue to mark and mar all attempts to create a celebratory cultural and social imaginary. The mockery that is the substance of transformation in South Africa is the direct result of an inability and a perverse refusal to forego a burden of pain that, for most, remains the defining crux of human existence.

There are those who will baulk in the face of what appears to be a gratuitous and falsely dismissive response to changes in the country; these include Nadine Gordimer, for whom the historical passage between 1991 and 1994 marked 'the grand finale when South Africa emerged amazingly, a great spectacle of human liberation, from double colonization' (Writing and Being p. 114). My point, however, is that these changes have remained largely cosmetic, that the psychic disfigurement which Coetzee so chillingly describes has by no means been vaulted. If, therefore, I insist upon defining change at this present moment as a mockery, it is because that which has been deemed to be change has been achieved *in spite* of a constitutive psychic perversion that continues to hold the country in its thrall. This, surely, is why Coetzee's inconsolable vision remains so attractive and loathsome today.

Coetzee's telling phrase – that South Africa is *as irresistible as it is unlovable* – sums up the complex of compulsion and disgust that defines the burden of our response to the nation's past, its present and, all the more alarmingly, its future. Here, again, Coetzee alerts us to a constitutive paradox that defines the seductive and perverse logic that moves cultural inquiry and expression. To desire in the name of South Africa, it seems, is to be party to this perverse embrace, an embrace that one does not will, but which wills one. If I have challenged this perverse embrace it is because I believe in the psychic and epistemic *possibility* of thinking (dreaming, feeling) South Africa as *resistible and lovable*. This possibility marks a process of thinking that works against the pathological dualism of despair and hope that defines a country still caught in absolute contests. No matter how intensely one engages with, or is subjected to, this contest, it is fast becoming apparent that this contest is simulacral: the domain of alienated and polarised fixities and fixations. In probing deeper, though, one discovers an incommensurable psychic burden, at the gnawing root of which lies 'fear and denial: denial of an *unacknowledgeable desire* to embrace Africa, embrace the body of Africa; and the fear of being embraced in return by Africa' (Jerusalem Prize Acceptance Speech p. 97, my emphasis). This fear and denial prevails. Today it afflicts not only the 'closed hereditary caste' (p. 96) that, under apartheid, rendered it totemic. Indeed, today, this fear and denial afflicts South Africans irrespective of 'caste'. That this fear and denial persists in this putatively new age of freedom is all the more remarkable and alarming. If we do not and cannot speak each to each it is because no call to national unity has been able to shift the balance of power from a psychic dependency on fear and denial. As Coetzee has insisted, our inner and outer lives remain deformed and stunted. Hence our continued uneasiness, our continued shame and despair, as a culture.

The root of this pathological mixture of loathing and attachment is by no means solely domestic. It is a pathology that afflicts Africa as a whole. In 'Ali Mazrui, *The Africans*' (Stranger Shores pp. 240–49) Coetzee notes:

> Africa remains a place that one studies, to which one sends teachers and aid: Africans are not people from whom one learns. The richness of Africa's resources is acknowledged, but the resources referred to are natural, not human. What Africa has to offer is always raw: raw produce, raw ores, *raw people, raw experience*. What Africa gets in exchange is finished: systems of government, health clinics, computers (p. 240 my emphasis).

For Coetzee, Africa's stuntedness, its deformity and rawness, are directly linked to the ongoing iniquities of empire that, today, manifest itself in global corporate 'investment' in the so-called underdeveloped and developing world. Closed or 'finished' epistemological systems are *imports* that sit uneasily in the context of Africa. Coetzee polemically and predictably adds:

> [P]erhaps it is time for the West to accept that almost any African intellectual, asked to speak about Africa, will speak about a continent abused, exploited and patronised by foreigners, an Africa still living in the aftershock of colonialism, bitter, angry and suspicious (p. 241).

This bitterness, anger and suspicion form a morbid counterpoint to fear and denial. Both sets of responses are inherently compromised and conditional. Any representation thereof is necessarily invested in the psychic link between anger and denial, suspicion and fear. As responses they are riven, fraught, and unresolved. If closure has a psychological role in this regard, it is because it allows for a didactic *reduction and fetishisation* of mental and emotional torture. Here closure – inflicted upon, imported from without, absorbed within – turns from stranger to intimate and nightmarish familiar. Coetzee is the exemplary victim – the one who knows himself as such, the one who assumes the authority of the pathologist – through whom those engaged in cultural inquiry pertaining to colonialism and racial strife have come to understand their own entrapment and disfigurement. The 'embrace' Coetzee offers, however, is as challenging as it is confounding. For Coetzee the body of Africa is the body of psychic strife. By fusing the psychic with representation Coetzee not only locates the psychological and epistemic root of a pathology born of oppression but, unwittingly, also points to the area or interzone – Bhabha's 'hybrid moment' – which I have made the elusive object and subject of this inquiry. For, as I have stated, if one takes Coetzee's perception as given, then reads against the grain of his conclusion, a more enabling perception emerges. To read South African culture in the light of this perception it is necessary that one effect an epistemic shift away from Coetzee's fatalism, unlock the hidden and secret life, albeit deformed and stunted, and, having done so, shift the psychic matrix from oppression to freedom.

However, if we follow Coetzee's view in his 'Jerusalem Prize Acceptance Speech' we would be compelled to conclude that the venture I propose is impossible. For Coetzee we remain psychically in chains. South African literature – Coetzee's reference point through which he accounts for this psychic entrapment, his own included – is 'unnaturally preoccupied with power and the torsions of power, unable to move from elementary relations of contestation, domination, and subjugation to the vast and complex human world that lies beyond them' (p. 98). In his insistence on the unnatural, Coetzee once again points to a constitutive perversion. Caught in this perversion, he finds it impossible to imagine a world that he knows exists beyond the gulag in which he finds himself. Be that as it may, I have suggested that resident within the logic of psychic entrapment lies a counter-logic which, having passed through the fraught contingencies that mark and mar critical thought and cultural expression in South Africa, could make possible entry to the *complex world that lies beyond*. I wholly concur with de Kock when he states that this world cannot be invoked, embraced, or entered by deferring to the metatropes of unity in difference or sameness. These metatropes, omnipresent today, are not only illusory, but also as ethically perverse as the pathology they react to. This other 'complex' human world will be achieved only by tilling the very ills that inhibit, and unwittingly intuit, the development of this alternative strain of thinking and being.

This is the wager that governs my inquiry into cultural production in South Africa. Caught in the fold of fatalism and hope, it is a wager that, while it listens to the toll of the former and the clarion call of the latter, yields to neither. Bhabha succinctly defines the psychic and epistemic agency of this inquiry when he states:

> It is the trope of our times to locate the question of culture in the realm of the *beyond*. At the century's edge, we are less exercised by annihilation . . . or epiphany . . . Our existence today is marked by a tenebrous sense of survival, living on the borderlines of the 'present', for which there seems to be no proper name (*The Location of Culture* p. 1).

If Bhabha rejects the epiphanic, and by implication the *ek-static* and the magical, he cannot, however, wholly wean his thought from these states. This is evident in his conceptualisation of the 'hybrid moment' that is 'part dream, part analysis', in his valorisation of an interpretational ethics and interventionist aesthetics that is 'at once liminal and luminous', as well as in the question he poses: 'Within the unease of negotiation is there a kind of sublimity?' (Aura and Agora p. 13). At this juncture, Bhabha's invocation of the constitutive yet partial, evasive and ineffable is evident in his deferral to that which possesses no *proper* name. This compelling statement – which extends the epistemological reach to be found in the writing of Kruger, Taylor, Noyes, Brink, Kentridge and Sachs – cannily characterises the dramatic counterpoint in South Africa between psychic annihilation and simulacral hope. By electing neither condition, Bhabha paves the way for a third space that he locates *between* and *beyond* this polarisation of states that, I would suggest, also form a continuum. By stating that this third space has no proper name, Bhabha also points to an alternative strain of thinking and being that is informed by an eschewal of the pronominal and by the reflexive and intuitive embrace of the agency of the irrational, a-significatory, a-categorical, or magical. This third space, Bhabha argues, allows one to 'elude the politics of polarity and *emerge as the others of ourselves*' (*The Location of Culture* p. 39, my emphasis).

For Bhabha our very survival is thoroughly dependent upon this psychic transubstantiation from self to other. This process does not imply a causal shift from one fixed position to another; rather, by pluralising both positions, and by conceiving their engagement as perpetually active and undecidable, Bhabha, like Noyes, affirms *the life of difference at the heart of the human*. For both Bhabha and Noyes, it is precisely this definitive differential that allows for *the enactment of human rights in practice*. It is this translocative and non-positional shift which affords an *other* embrace – the embrace not only of otherness, but the embrace of others – which I posit as the surest means, within the ever-shifting present, through which to recover a past and promote a future freed from the spectre of colonialism.

Many will conceive this project of recovery – none other than the *acknowledged desire* to embrace the body of South Africa – as utopian. That few have elected to sustain this desire reveals the persistence of fear and denial that grips the mind and heart. By reifying the problem of colonialism and apartheid, and turning the problem into the object of critique, critical and cultural inquiry has, in the process, displaced this desire. As Coetzee reminds us, neither colonialism, nor what is *loosely called* apartheid, are objects. These systems of oppression are embattled processes, ceaseless actions, which are sustainable to the precise degree to which they continue to interpellate, psychically subject, and reduce to victimhood, all those within its orbit of influence. Any critique defined by and founded within the system of colonialism and its surrogate, apartheid, is, by this means, over-determined by allegiance and/or refutation. What Taylor, Kentridge, Noyes, Brink, Sachs and Bhabha invoke are ways of interrogating, resisting, by-passing, and surpassing these systems of oppression which, irrespective of a putative democracy, persist today. If each, in their own way, must engage in the pathology that is colonialism and apartheid, then it is because each knows that this pathology cannot be countered other than by advancing through it. To bypass, overwhelm, or ignore, therefore, supposes a radical negation from *within* an oppressive economy. The change for which each calls cannot be achieved by solely focusing on the problem, but by focusing on what the problem *occludes*. Colonialism, and its subsequent manifestations, is the chimera – the monstrous and intimate familiar – which each of us carries on our backs. Thereby we are condemned; thereby we are compelled to hope. The inextricability of this bondage to a law we cannot shake is not the root of our travails. Rather, the root of the problem, whether understood consciously or not, lies in our willingness to be the subjects of this law, be it as a victim or as a resistor. Neither response, because of its reactive nature, is adequate.

What urgently needs to be sourced, then, is what Coetzee calls the *unacknowledgeable desire*, a desire which I, in turn, would foreground and transmute. Without this desire there can be no change, be it cognitive, emotive, psychic, or aesthetic. For Brink it is the recovery of this suppressed and destroyed desire that matters, a recovery captured in the figure of the 'leaping flame' which turns word into world. It is this selfsame turning away and turning towards which allows for the enigmatic moment in which we become 'the others of our selves'. Without the achievement of this turn we will remain the victims of a relentlessly invasive, conscriptive and parasitic law that feeds upon, exists alongside, and consumes its victim.

If colonialism is the parasite that still thrives today, then what is the host? In the context of this inquiry, the host is the body of South Africa, a body irreducible to division or simulacral unity. *Resistant and lovable*, it is a body we have failed to love, which we have yet to embrace (Jerusalem Prize Acceptance Speech p. 97). It is the body of freedom that remains unfree. Indefinitely pronominal, hidden and suppressed, this body is 'struggling to give birth to itself' (Preparing Ourselves p. 19). This birth – the birth of the imagination – occurs in those hybrid moments when the increasingly blurred edicts of oppression *and* freedom that distort inquiry and expression are bypassed and overwhelmed. It is in those moments that this inquiry will seek its sustenance.

THREE

Restlessness and Redemption

There was no gate to rattle, no doorbell to ring. After a while something came to him, a phrase he had heard in a film about the Wild West, and he tried it out: 'Hail the camp!'

– Ivan Vladislavić

George Steiner's statement that 'art develops via reflection of and on preceding art', where 'reflection' signifies both a 'mirroring', however drastic the perceptual dislocation, and a 're-thinking' (*Real Presences* p. 17) applies to the development of cultural practice in general. Here it affirms the connection I establish between the thought of Theodor Adorno and Homi Bhabha. Writing at different points in history – the first after Auschwitz, the second at the 'edge' of the twentieth century – both address the tenebrous question of survival, the limit of imagination, and the desire, in the face of this question and limit, to develop a 'restless and revisionary' ethic (*The Location of Culture* p. 4). Key to the development of this ethic is an innovative engagement with the categorical imperatives of the self, the house, and the nation-state. That these imperatives have thrived despite the psychic and epistemic upheavals of modernity reveals the extent to which the critique of them has largely, and unnervingly, proved to be simulacral.

My allegiance lies with those who, like Adorno and Bhabha, have examined the impertinent and posthumous life of these imperatives. That these imperatives persist – in Nietzsche's cursed sense of the eternal return – does not mean that their validity is given and beyond reproach. A degree of derangement clings to the need for self-possession and permanence. I am reminded of Ivan Vladislavić's *The Folly*, to which I will shortly turn, and a scene in Wim Wender's film *Wings of Desire* in which, through a bomb-blasted wall of a tenement building, we see a woman making her bed. All about her is rubble. She airs the sheets before laying them down and delicately pleating them. Given the gutted setting, the procedure is as eerie as it is movingly familiar. If history hurts, if history is that which refuses desire, as Frederic Jameson has memorably stated, then to endure one must put history aside. How else make the bed in which one must lie?

It is this putting *aside* of history, this psychic negation, which, explored further, defines the thought of Adorno and Bhabha. Neither is concerned simply with the re-enactment of a gesture – the making of a bed – which functions against an existent truth.

Neither is solely – morbidly and obsessively – concerned with the negation of a history that has made the imperatives of the self, the home, or the nation-state, impossible. What each attempts to do is invigorate an other thought that exists because of, in spite of, and outside these imperatives. Against history, then, that which Adorno and Bhabha hold on to is *desire*: the desire to pass through the pathological re-enactment of a scene which can never be repeated in the same way, the desire to shift the emphasis away from the aftershock that is pain or pain's forgetting, and forge, out of and in spite of pain, the promise of a saving ethic.

At every turn, it is history that cauterises desire. History's implacable logic supposes that destruction feeds regeneration: destroy one house and build another; destroy one self and another will grow. It is not life that inhabits the house of history, but death. The scene of a bomb-blasted tenement building, a woman within its gutted nest making a bed, is not an affirmation of the regenerative power of the living, but of a death in life. The bed is made: desire sustained. But, reversing Jameson's formulation, it is not desire that refuses history so much as it is desire which enacts the toll of history – protracted desire, then, desire repeated in the name of history. This, though, is not Adorno and Bhabha's conception of desire. Each believes that there exists an other – unconscripted – desire that could drive thought onward, a desire that would not turn the making of a bed into a pathological reiteration, but make possible desire's unconscionable and unrepeatable furtherance of itself. This desire – echoed in Sachs's conception of an imagined other space, and in Brink's notion of silence and magic – does not dispel the fact that history knocks even on the doors of those who will not heed its call. On the contrary, Adorno and Bhabha both know that history is the wake-up call that they cannot, yet must, refute.

In 'Cultural Criticism and Society' Adorno announces the brutal and summary arrival of history as 'the *final* stage of the dialectic of culture and barbarism' (*Prisms* p. 34, my emphasis). This finality, which presages the end of the dialectic, also marks the full-blown and virulent re-emergence of barbarism: the hegemonic process whereby thought becomes reified, a process which, in its grim wake, suppresses uncertainty and wonder and cancels every transforming and radically negating desire. The sentence that follows, by now thoroughly ingrained in a fatal global imaginary, reads: 'To write after Auschwitz is barbaric'. For Adorno it is history under the sign of barbarism that becomes *de rigeur*. The dialectic that sought to stave off horror, ground to a standstill, results in an increasingly agonistic relationship to the very procedure that makes thinking possible. This agonistic relationship is all the more intensified and aggravated in Bhabha's writing.

Given the full-blown extremity of the barbarous condition that inhibits and provokes Adorno and Bhabha's insights, what interests me – indeed compels me – is the pertinence of their respective visions to a re-thinking of the present condition in South Africa. My wager is that South Africa after apartheid, like Germany after Auschwitz, is a society and culture still caught in a stranglehold from which, against all hope, it finds itself unable to liberate itself. Caught between the notoriety of its brutal history and a longing to surpass this history, South Africa finds itself enmeshed in a legacy of absolute contests. By reactively sustaining its predicament, South Africa reinforces the endgame in which, as an outpost of empire, it was always already caught. That South Africa, in the guise of change, elects to choose prescriptive solutions to problems it cannot countenance, all the more reinforces its incapacity to think and interpret itself otherwise. The root of the problem, I venture, lies in a psychic and epistemic inability to reconcile its inherent and restless heterogeneity with a redemptive and revisionary ethic.

By turning to Adorno and Bhabha – thinkers who foreground heterogeneity and thwart reification – I argue that a more invigorated reading of South Africa's present predicament becomes possible. If Bhabha, in particular, has received a bad rap in the arena of South African cultural studies, this in itself reaffirms a resistance that I regard as detrimental to the furtherance of critical and cultural inquiry. A notable example of this bad press is Zoe Wicomb's essay 'Shame and Identity: The Case of the Coloured in South Africa'. The root of Wicomb's misreading of Bhabha lies in her failure to give credence to the agonistic source of his thought. By claiming that Bhabha 'echoes . . . the tragic mode where lived experience is displaced by an aesthetics of theory' (p. 101), Wicomb forges precisely the polarised logic which Bhabha rejects. This tendency to dismiss the theoretical on the assumption that it exists at an apparent remove from lived experience marks a threat to the generative and humane power of thought, a threat which represents yet another face of the new barbarism.

My view is that Bhabha, like Adorno, fuses the ontological and ethical, aesthetic and theoretical. By fusing these dimensions – which Wicomb mistakenly claims that Bhabha divides – Bhabha, like Adorno, reaffirms the immanent agency of thought in the world. The redemptive ethical solutions each offers are by no means transcendent or otherworldly. Rather, as Simon Critchley suggests, Adorno's thought (and Bhabha's, to whom Critchley does not refer) makes possible a 'preparation for action in the world, however minimal' (Very Little p. 20). By invoking a blighted stage that affords 'very little . . . almost nothing' – the very stage which Adorno conceives as 'final' – Critchley, at the last, calls upon the infinitesimal grain of a saving insight. It is here, at this blasted point, that Adorno and Bhabha achieve their ethical turn.

The task of this chapter will be to unravel what exactly this saving insight and ethical turn is, and why, in spite of what Lucy Graham terms 'the limits of imaginative empathy' (Yes, I am Giving Him Up p. 10), this insight must be sustained. Linking the atrocities of Auschwitz to those effected under apartheid, Graham searches for a saving ethic that could help us endure both in spite of, and because of, the impossibility of imaginative empathy. Given this impossibility – typically rejected on the grounds that it gratuitously negates practical and pragmatic human engagement – this chapter works to develop a way forward which – while caught in the fraught circuitry of restlessness and redemption, and defined at the outset by the erasure of a saving telos – nevertheless sustains a negative capability or a non-positive affirmation.

In South Africa a perceptual dislocation of this nature will prove to be critical. South Africa has also been influenced by what I have described as a psychic and epistemic faithlessness – the culture of late modernity – and the resurgence and ascendance of faithfulness – the culture of barbarism. In saying this, I do not of course mean that South Africa's citizenry can *in toto* be defined by these contiguous sensibilities, or that the instrumentality of the so-called 'miracle' of democracy is, as a consequence, no longer operative. I am gesturing towards the gnawing realisation that a discrepancy persists between desire and its fulfilment, that in South Africa a lag, or lack, continues to mark and mar the process of change. Instead of conceiving this lack in the negative I will, after Johnny Mercer, whose refrain forms the epigraph to Bhabha's *The Location of Culture*,

> Ac-cent-tchu-ate the pos-i-tive
> E-li-mi-nate the neg-a-tive
> Latch on to the af-firm-a-tive

The very fragmentation of the wording, together with the closing sentence to the refrain – 'Don't mess with Mister In-be-tween' – points to the interstitial agency of Bhabha's critical vision. Echoing Steiner, Mercer's refrain marks a perceptual dislocation of the refrain's given components. Each word teeters before an abyss. For Bhabha, writing at the edge of the twentieth century, in an era marked by epistemic violence, it is fitting that the subjunctive nature of the refrain be cathected and cut up. Each word must be reinvigorated. Each invigoration must undo the fatality that stalks the subjunctive.

As Bhabha well understands, perceptual dislocation occasions the betrayal of the very hopes that one cherishes. What is needed is a mode of thought that is transgressive and dislocative in the instant a given insight is re-fashioned. This, as I understand it, is what the theoretical projects of Adorno and Bhabha offer South Africa, a country whose dislocation has not been matched by a revisionary insight but marked by a resistance to, and suppression of, the root of its dislocation in the mistaken belief that change is possible only through reaction and subsumption. The past, however, is not another country. The perceptual dislocation effected in the Constitution, for example, is not an answer unto itself. There can be no wholesale removal from a prior history, no easy reification and displacement of it. A removal of this nature constitutes a dislocation of the most degraded order, which is why, against remembrance, we find forgetting, against the regenerative spirit that consecrates the rites of the past, the quick-fix smash-and-grab culture which believes not in the future and its link to the present and the past, but in *futures*. What is needed is the sustenance of the means to re-think and reinvigorate the dialectic – when and where the dialectic is sustainable – and to discover, through this process, a revisionary ethic that could save South Africa from itself. If there has proved to be no continuum between South Africa's past and its present, if we are caught in a perceptual dislocation that signals a psychic, epistemic, aesthetic and ethical vacuum, then how, as a society, will South Africa advance?

The second epigraph to *The Location of Culture* provides the clue. From Frantz Fanon, the epigraph reads: 'every human problem must be considered from the standpoint of time'. This insight has rarely been factored into the conceptualisation of change in South Africa. Consider the conceit of a television commercial designed to sell a detergent: we see a beaming black woman miraculously transform a filthy garment into one 'whiter than white'. What is operative is a narrative divested of a temporal point of conversion. The movement from filth to cleanliness is intransitive. Only two temporal figures matter: the past and the future, before and after, figures which, when not conceived immanently, exist outside time. Extrapolating from this telling elision, I would suggest that the popular imaginary in South Africa is done with transition. The very phrase 'whiter than white' suggests a glare so blindingly apparent – a glare which affirms Jean Baudrillard's formulation of the simulacral nature of the postmodern as that which is more visible than the visible – that it leaves no room to reflect upon the shift that has made this glare possible. Extrapolating further one could say that the blinding intensity of the glare suggests a radical forgetting motivated by the desire, tellingly dramatised within the domestic sphere, to erase the stain not only of the past, but also the stain that distinguishes the present.

An assessment of the news reportage on political and cultural engagement with regional, national, and international concerns reveals a similarly overwhelming desire to pass beyond the particularities of the present moment. This desire defines government policy as much as it does the popular imaginary. Concerns for the particularity of the local are characterised either by a mock piety, a barely suppressed impatience, or a bloated rhetorical intensity that lacks all connectedness to its object. What is invariably absent is a purposive engagement with the human problem considered from the standpoint of time. Instead, the evidence suggests an overriding, desperate and dangerous bid to advance beyond the past at the expense of the present. A leap of this kind, the product of denial and wish-fulfilment, is nothing short of catastrophic. Hence my insistence that we rethink the perceptual dislocation in South Africa within an ever-shifting, restless and heterogeneous present. Here Loren Kruger's formulation of South Africa's present moment as post-*anti* becomes all the more resonant. Caught between a waning resistance and an ennui and insouciance, what is needed is to rethink and reinvigorate the hyphen between, which, like a flatline, has come to signal a dead time in the South African imaginary. It is this time – the time *between* – which Adorno and Bhabha accentuate and locate as the core of a revisionary ethic.

Scripted in the aftermath of Auschwitz, the resonance of Adorno's 'Reflections From Damaged Life' in *Minima Moralia* possesses an intractable relevance to the predicament experienced after apartheid. 'Dwelling, in the proper sense, is now impossible,' writes Adorno.

> The traditional residences we grew up in have grown intolerable: each trait of comfort in them is paid for with a betrayal of knowledge, each vestige of shelter with the musty pact of family interests (*Minima Moralia* p. 38).

That this horror of home predates the catastrophe unleashed by the Second World War does not diminish the force of Adorno's insight. One discovers this great malady of home in the writings of Baudelaire, Pascal, and others. Nietzsche, prescient always, anticipates the corrosive rise of German nationalism and the wreckage that is the bitter fruit of global migration when, at the close of the nineteenth century, he calls for no more fatherlands, no more forefatherlands.

The residence that Adorno finds uninhabitable is not only the physical home, but also the home that is language and ideology. Distrust becomes the abiding register of his thought. An 'intellectual émigré' (*Prisms* p. 97), he is necessarily and historically denied any filial ties – be it to physical location or received ideas. After 'the European catastrophe' (ibid.) the thinker is impelled to think in flight, to forge his thought in a manner contingent and provisional. Ours is the age of the 'sleepless . . . alert and unconscious at once,' says Adorno (*Minima Moralia* p. 38). We can no longer embalm ourselves in houses, be they of words or mortar. No domus is purely functional. Structures disintegrate before our eyes. Having broken free of their purpose, structures must, henceforth, be ceaselessly negotiated, for as Adorno blisteringly announces: 'The house is past . . . Today . . . it is part of morality not to be at home in one's home' (*Minima Moralia* p. 39).

In Ivan Vladislavić's *The Folly* one finds a canny echo of Adorno's disavowal. Like Adorno, Vladislavić constructs a liminal point between dream and wakefulness. There, the very desire for a home recoils in the face of its lack of substance. That *The Folly* emerges on the South African literary scene in 1993, when South Africa stands on the verge of its first democratic election, is telling. For Vladislavić that transitional point becomes the marker for a fraught ambivalence. As the novel *de*volves, the dream of impending change is defounded. In the place of certainty we find a gnawingly intrusive sense of a lack: the house will not be realised. The very phantasmal venture – the creation of a house that does and does not exist – defines an imaginary in the infant stage of its conception. In the place of the empirical and instrumental we find doubt: 'That wall of yours, with the suns – are they rising or setting?' (*The Folly* p. 24). Hallucinatory projection rather than mimetic representation, the house in Vladislavić's *The Folly* marks a key psychic shift from the real to the hyper-real. At the very point of its putative consolidation we find the increased estrangement (and derangement) of the South African imaginary.

Vladislavić does not make the large claims that I infer. However, within the intensively reflexive literariness of its inscription – the very world exists as a constellation of ceaselessly dissolving signs, a deconstructed house of fiction – Vladislavić reinforces the impertinence of the imperative. The simulacral nature of the fictive construct is affirmed in the following:

> It was a magnificent place, every bit as grand as Malgas had thought it would be, but it had its shortcomings, which he was quick to perceive too. It had no depth. It had the deceptive solidity of a stage-set. The colours were unnaturally intense, yet at the slightest *lapse of concentration* on his part the whole edifice would blanch as if it was about to fall to pieces (*The Folly* p. 116, my emphasis).

Hyper-real rather than, in Brink's sense, magically real, *The Folly* imputes nothing beyond its metaphoricity. Like Kentridge, Vladislavić affirms metaphor as that which, in itself, is ineffable *and* ontological. Like Mercer, and by extension Bhabha, Vladislavić understands the ineffable and ontological as a fraught emanation and not as a nomination. Meaning is imperilled in the moment of its enactment: '"*House*," he mumbled, as if he were praying, and the verb itself shattered into spillikins against his palate' (*The Folly* p. 103).

Like Adorno, Vladislavić invokes the impossibility of a settled sense of place. Rather, it is restlessness – the restlessness of an imagination confronted and thwarted by the abyssal nature of signs – which comes to mark a work distinguished by regression and erasure, rather than by causation and fulfilment. Contrary to an observation made within *The Folly* – 'We are condemned to renounce and repeat, the head and the tail, the one barking and the other wagging, with the body of the same old dog between them' (p. 143) – the book performs a psychic and epistemic deconstruction of difference as the repetition of the same. A shift has occurred. The question is, what might this shift mean? How, in other words, to measure the impact of the past upon the present? How to negate that which refuses desire? And what are we to make of this emergent desire?

If *The Folly* is a castle made of air, it is not, however, satisfied with its own delusional architectonics. Lodged within an enterprise as absurd as it is wondrous is the negative turn that, aesthetically and ethically, understands that what matters is the moment in which one *thinks* the transition. *The Folly*, then, is an exemplary instance of this fraught and restless project. The epistemic and psychic upheaval that Vladislavić experiences in South Africa finds its pre-echo in 'the European catastrophe' (*Prisms* p. 97) against which Adorno pits his thinking.

What matters here is the pertinence of Adorno's thought for those who, like Vladislavić, grapple with the catastrophe of place, the malady of placelessness. For what makes the 'negative moment' (*Prisms* p. 22) of Adorno's thinking decisively relevant is the hope that resides within it. Confronted with the final stage of the dialectic, at which point culture turns into barbarism, Adorno discovers an austere consolation within a state of arrest and restlessness. This curious sense of hope in the face of disintegration and fatality is echoed in *The Folly*:

> . . . hurrah. Threads unravelled noisily. Whirlwinds swirled out of teacups and ripped through paper bags. Hooray! Portraits of Nieuwenhuizen's ancestors fell from the walls. Hip, hip, joints disjointed and screws unscrewed . . . and so on and so forth, hubba hubba . . . (p. 141).

This collapse, as I have already suggested, does not merely mark a renunciation. Rather, what Vladislavić foregrounds is definitive discontinuity. Things are insubstantial and atomic. History – the pageantry of portraiture – tumbles. Hysterical glee is all Vladislavić can muster in the face of catastrophe, a glee that brings with it an unconscionable reason for happiness, which, we will discover, marks the austere and illuminating ventures of Adorno and Bhabha and, before them, Benjamin.

Like Vladislavić, Adorno finds himself in a disjointed world in which there is no capacity for illusion other than illusion in-and-for-itself. His is a world gutted, destroyed, 'uncommitted, suspended' (*Minima Moralia* p. 39). What is left? In which direction can he turn when tragedy mocks victory? Recklessly – what other stance is left? – Adorno, like Vladislavić, 'sets up house' in the book he writes – *Minima Moralia* – a book whose vaunted aim is to render darkness visible. We read:

> Just as he trundles papers, books, pencils, documents untidily from room to room, [the writer] creates the same disorder in his thoughts. They become pieces of furniture that he sinks into, content or irritable. He strokes them affectionately, wears them out, mixes them up, re-arranges, ruins them. For a man who no longer has a homeland, writing becomes a place to live (p. 87).

What is this house in which the writer lives? Is it not, as Adorno elsewhere concedes, a 'refuge for the homeless'? (p. 38). What, then, is this refuge? And what sanctuary does it provide? For Adorno the answer to this question seems clear. The refuge is the 'text', a house of words in which he 'sinks', shiftless, caught between contentment and its mockery, in which the 'disordered' room upon room of words mirrors his own disorder. There cherished beliefs wither; acts of affection turn into acts of ruination. No thought, no feeling, escapes the thinker's estranging and withering glance. That which must be abolished is kinship, be it to a 'homeland' or a received and worn-out idea. Uprooted and displaced, Adorno finds refuge in the aphorism, the charged detail of the fragment. The seeming structural formlessness of *Minima Moralia* – 'the disconnected and non-binding character of the form, the renunciation of explicit theoretical cohesion' (p. 18) – refracts the writer's displacement. Itinerant passions consume the spine of narrative. The process, uncompromising, is also utterly corrosive. In the end there is no refuge for the would-be occupant, for 'the writer is not even allowed to live in his writing' (p. 87).

Here Adorno arrives at the critical and vulnerable turning point that founds his restless vision. In principle, for Adorno, there is no home, be it in the realm of things or words. Rather, 'he who contemplates does not absorb the object into himself' (p. 90). This estranging moment of apperception Adorno terms 'a distanced nearness' (ibid.). This seeming contradiction allows Adorno access to the piecemeal freedom he seeks and would nurture. It is a freedom, structured negatively, which recognises that indictment, in itself, is insufficient. If the writer is not allowed to live in his writing then this is so not only because the assumption of this possibility is flawed, but because writing precedes and exceeds such a claim. What matters is why the writer has no place in his words. Only when we ask this question will we begin to arrive at a truth, scarcely even thinkable, which bypasses any claim to belonging. Moreover, it is this *not* belonging which, for Adorno, explains why, at best, the only recourse is 'a distanced nearness'. It is not a melodramatic sense of fatality and insignificance that draws Adorno to this conclusion but, rather, an intuitive sense that 'hope' and 'freedom' are possible only once we have moved beyond the perception of an existent error or illusion and, significantly, beyond the mere unmasking of the error or illusion. This is why, in the concluding fragment to *Minima Moralia*, Adorno famously states:

> The only philosophy which can be responsibly practised in the face of despair is the attempt to contemplate all things as they would present themselves from the standpoint of redemption. Knowledge has no light but that shed in the world by redemption: all else is reconstruction, mere technique. Perspectives must be fashioned that displace and estrange the world, reveal it

to be, with its rifts and crevices, as indigent and distorted as it will appear one day in the messianic light (p. 247).

Adorno's understanding of 'redemption' is a curiously eviscerated one. At best it is the after-life of an *a priori* disarticulation. The perspective he offers must further displace and estrange an already displaced and estranged world. Only then will we move beyond knowledge and despair and rediscover a founding and enabling restlessness. Therein lies the thinker's grasp of 'morality' and its uses. To be ill at ease, to record the history of unease, is to surpass 'mere' reconstruction and technique. In one fell swoop the object of contemplation is 'negated, fulfilled and surmounted' (*Prisms* p. 29). The understanding of this threefold movement is critical if we are to advance an affirmative reading of the bankruptcy of the integrated self, home, or nation-state, as well as the source of this bankruptcy and its fallout: restlessness.

Having fallen apart, the world cannot be put back together without embracing the latent threat that defounds the world at every turn. We cannot go forward without going back. Moreover, this traffic backward and forward will not save us unless we absorb that which constitutes this traffic – a corrosive *untimely* present. For Adorno there is no safe vantage point from which to mediate our fate, not even the 'hair's breadth' or 'distanced nearness' which he associates with redemptive thought. Suspicious and exacting, his is indeed a despairing vision. Nevertheless – and here lies the marvellous paradox – Adorno's position, which he also attributes to Walter Benjamin, is one that is 'no less a source of terror than a promise of happiness' (p. 235). The paradox serves as a striking index of the affirming nature of Adorno's exacting vision.

'Thought is not content with intentions', says Adorno in his essay on Benjamin. Rather, 'the thoughts press close to its object, seek to touch it, smell it, taste it and so thereby transform it'. The tactility and 'secondary sensuousness' of Adorno's approach to thinking works against the process of reification which he abhors. It is a process that penetrates to undefined spheres, a process that eschews the contingencies of both classification and 'blind intuition' (p. 240). This process emerges as the surest way in which to grasp the complex nature of restlessness and its provenance as both the condition of our present moment and the elusive object of our thought. Classifications that juxtapose place against placelessness, the campfire against the pyramid, nomadic versus sedentary culture, invariably fail to grasp the paradox that infuses and ceaselessly disturbs our being and its attendant consciousness, which is why the thought of Adorno, because of its critical re-enactment of the constitutive force of restlessness, remains a vital point from which to contemplate the unease of late-modern life.

In his introduction to *The Location of Culture* Homi Bhabha cites an excerpt from Martin Heidegger's essay 'Building, Dwelling, Thinking': 'A boundary is not that at which something stops but, as the Greeks recognized, the boundary is that from which *something begins its presencing*' (p. 1). From the outset, then, we are alerted to a movement of mind that would negate, fulfil and surmount any reified notion of the border as a constitutive and founding limit. In the instant of its rigorous assertion a boundary opens the world to that which exists outside, for contained within the logic of a limit is the realisation that there is no limit. The boundary is always already corrupted, frayed and porous, the charged locus of an other *presencing*.

If Bhabha embarks with Heidegger, the sentence that follows possesses a restless residue, the source of which can be found in Adorno:

> It is the trope of our times to locate the question of culture in the realm of the *beyond*. At the century's edge, we are less exercised by annihilation – the death of the author – or epiphany – the birth of the 'subject'. Our existence today is marked by a tenebrous sense of survival, living on the borderlines of the 'present', for which there seems to be no proper name other than the current and controversial shiftiness of the prefix 'post': postmodernism, postcolonialism, postfeminism (ibid.).

Here the plight of restlessness that, for Adorno, lies in 'the far-reaching effects of the European catastrophe' (*Prisms* p. 97) is not so much revisited as it is further aggravated at the *edge* of the twentieth century. As I have already noted, Adorno trumped the mistaken opposition of 'annihilation' and 'epiphany' by recognising that any critical thought worthy of the name must synthesise, undo, and reach beyond both categories. Adorno's 'promise of happiness', his call for an embattled yet redemptive logic, finds its late or *post*modern echo in Bhabha's 'realm of the beyond'. This realm, it is vital to note, 'is neither a new horizon, nor a leaving behind of the past' (*The Location of Culture* p. 1). Here Bhabha precisely challenges the prevailing orientation in South Africa that cancels the present in the instant that it rejects the past in the name of the future.

For Bhabha that which is elided in this cancellation is the critical 'moment of transit where space and time cross to produce complex figures of difference and identity, past and present, inside and outside, inclusion and exclusion' (ibid.). The pertinence of this insight has enormous resonance in South Africa today. As I have noted, South Africa is precisely caught in the intersection that cancels, or renders vulnerable, all received dualities, what Bhabha describes as 'a sense of disorientation, a disturbance of direction' (ibid.). *The Folly* re-emerges here as an exemplary instance of this vertiginous disturbance of direction.

Instead of purging this disorientation and repressing an existent loss of direction, Bhabha suggests that we sustain and rethink this disorientation in the affirmative. Furthermore, Bhabha echoes Adorno's belief in 'withstanding' all disturbance and disorientation and, in the 'unalleviated consciousness of negativity holding fast to the possibility of what is better' (*Minima Moralia* p. 25). Like Bhabha, Adorno advocates a 'suspension of objectification' and the sustenance of the moment of transit. 'No authentic work of art and no true philosophy . . . has ever exhausted itself in itself alone, in its being-in-itself', Adorno declares. That which matters necessarily stands 'in relation to the actual life-process of society' (*Prisms* p. 23), a process which, in South Africa, is in danger of being abandoned in favour of a simulacral and reified idea.

As Bhabha repeatedly reminds us, for theory to be 'innovative' and politics to be 'crucial' it is vital that we begin to think beyond originary and prescriptive narratives and 'focus on those moments or processes that are produced in the articulation of cultural differences'. Clearly Bhabha's favoured focus is on the interstitial and the micrological.

Like Critchley, Bhabha well understands that no claim upon the past or the future can be sustained without an attenuated understanding of the ramifications of heterogeneity lodged in the shifting instant. Bhabha can, and has, been accused of navel gazing, though, in the face of another facet of barbarism – generalisation – Bhabha's fractal consciousness gives substance to what J. M. Coetzee in the *Narrative of Jacobus Coetzee* calls the annulus between wilderness and number, an annulus which is repeatedly crisscrossed in *The Folly*, to the point that it becomes impossible to distinguish the head from the tail, let alone the body of 'the same old dog' between. Substance, then, is by no means given. It is that which is discovered, that which is *performed*. Its shifting location is in 'in-between spaces' that 'initiate new signs of identity, and innovative sites of collaboration, and contestation, *in the act of defining the idea of society itself* (*The Location of Culture* pp. 1–2, my emphasis).

The relevance of Bhabha's thought to this inquiry is all the more reinforced by his reappraisal and proactive refiguration of the destiny and fate of the colonial subject. Bhabha knows that this is not possible by simply returning to 'indigenous cultural traditions and retrieving their repressed histories' (p. 9). The innovation for which he seeks is not defined by an archaeology of the pre-colonial. A return to a mystical past will not save us. Rather, turning to Frantz Fanon, and again cannily echoing Adorno, Bhabha calls for a 'negating activity' that

> captures something of the estranging sense of the relocation of the home and the world – the unhomeliness – that is the condition of extra-territorial and cross-cultural initiations' (ibid.).

In his concluding fragment to *Minima Moralia* Adorno anticipates Bhabha's strategic displacement of what it means to be at home:

> Perspectives must be fashioned that displace and estrange the world, reveal it to be, with its rifts and crevices, as indigent and distorted as it will appear day one in the messianic light (p. 247).

In the thought of Bhabha and Adorno we find a perceptual dislocation of a self-aggrandizing sense of place – of homeliness – that is psychically and epistemically enabling. By estranging received imperatives, by highlighting the indigence and distortion that reside within these imperatives, Bhabha and Adorno do not, as a consequence, opt for a nihilistic conclusion. What is most striking in the moment of estrangement is that it turns the possibility of something new – 'an extra-territorial and cross-cultural initiation' – into a gift. That few have grasped this initiation, that even fewer have understood this initiation as a harbinger of light, reveals, all the more, the benighted nature of the mind and the spirit. In a barbarous age it is easier to believe in the impossible – another certainty – than to conceive the *presencing* of the possible.

It is crucial to remember that this presencing, this messianic light, does not suppose an informing ur-historical and transcendent elsewhere. Bhabha and Adorno's conception of time remains immanent and contiguous: time shot through by the untimely present. Only by admitting this other presencing will thought escape 'the trance-like captivity of bourgeois immanence' (*Prisms* p. 236), which, for Adorno, remains a fatal and hopeless conception of human agency. Adorno's notion of a captive 'bourgeois immanence' here finds its echo in Bhabha's idea of a 'culturally collusive present' (*The Location of Culture* p. 9). Importantly, for Bhabha, the present 'can no longer be simply envisaged as a break or bonding with the past and the future, no longer a synchronic presence' (p. 4). Rather – revealing the critical influence of the Frankfurt School – Bhabha states:

> Unlike the dead hand of history that tells the beads of sequential time like a rosary, seeking to establish serial, causal connections, we are now confronted with what Walter Benjamin describes as the blasting of a monadic moment from the homogenous course of history, establishing a conception of the present as the 'time of the now' (ibid.).

If Bhabha would move us beyond a sequential and synoptic conception of history, he, as urgently, wishes to move us beyond what Adorno has called 'the trance-like captivity of bourgeois immanence', which is why he is so damning of so much that falls under the name of postmodernism, postcolonialism, postfeminism. Notwithstanding the 'shifti-ness' of the prefix 'post', Bhabha notes:

> If the interest in postmodernism is limited to a celebration of the fragmentation of the 'grand narratives' of postenlightenment rationalism then, for all its intellectual excitement, it remains a profoundly parochial enterprise (ibid.).

It is at this point, this moment of renunciation, that Bhabha – through Benjamin and Fanon – arrives at what Adorno calls a 'messianic light'. In Bhabha's words, what is needed is a 'restless and revisionary energy' (ibid.) that at no point allows 'a smooth passage of transition and transcendence' (p. 5). Rather,

> being in the 'beyond', then, is to inhabit an intervening space . . . But to dwell 'in the beyond' is also . . . to be part of a revisionary time, a return to the present to redescribe our cultural contemporaneity; to reinscribe our human, historic communality; *to touch the future on its hither side* (p. 7).

One does not have to be a philosopher in order to perceive the constitutive restlessness that founds being. Restlessness and despair is certainly a condition that predates the catastrophic impact of the Second World War on a figure such as Adorno as it does the edge of the twentieth century, which continues to define us. One need only turn to the 'Notebooks' in Bruce Chatwin's *The Songlines* to discover the prevalence of restlessness through the ages. What matters here is the proposition that restlessness founds being – and the consciousness of it – and, more important, that it is in and through restlessness that human redemption is possible.

As Chatwin throughout his life and work insisted: human nature is nomadic. Chatwin conceived of his own life as a journey in pursuit of the miraculous. His tragically thwarted aim was to write 'a kind of "Anatomy of Restlessness" that would enlarge on Pascal's dictum about the man sitting quietly in a room' (*Anatomy of Restlessness* p. ix). The allusion here is to Pascal's belief that incarceration breeds illness.

Chatwin echoes Pascal's supposition that 'our nature lies in movement, complete calm is death' (*The Songlines* p. 183): 'Monotonous surroundings and tedious regular activities [weave] patterns which produce fatigue, nervous disorders, apathy, self-disgust and violent reactions' (*Anatomy of Restlessness* p. 100). Needless to say, Chatwin's detractors have a vested interest in sustaining a shuttered sedentary culture of the house, the state, the diocese, the church. Conversely, Adorno and Bhabha have posited that those who have willed the provenance of a monadic or arborescent culture are today forced to revisit and re-evaluate their idols and the horror that founds them.

This revisitation and re-evaluation reveals itself in Baudelaire as 'a study of the Great Malady; horror of home' (*The Songlines* p. 183). In *Routes: Travel and Translation in the Late Twentieth Century*, James Clifford reprises the study in a laconic though equally corrosive manner:

> Dwelling was understood to be the local ground of collective life, travel a supplement; roots always precede routes. But what would happen, I began to ask, if travel were untethered, seen as a complex and pervasive spectrum of human experiences? Practices of displacement might emerge as constitutive of cultural meanings rather than as their simple transfer or extension. The cultural effects of European expansionism, for example, could no longer be celebrated, or deplored, as a simple diffusion outward – of civilization, industry, science, or capital. For the region called 'Europe' has been constantly remade, and traversed, by influences beyond its borders . . . And is not this interactive process relevant, in varying degrees, to any local, national, or regional domain? Virtually everywhere one looks, the processes of human movement and encounter are long-established and complex. Cultural centers, discrete regions and territories, do not exist prior to contacts, but are sustained through them, appropriating and disciplining the restless movements of people and things (p. 3).

Clifford's proposition is the mainstay of Chatwin's critique. Whereas Chatwin would will us to a pure embrace of our originary disarticulation and restlessness, Clifford conceives his vision 'under the sign of ambivalence, a permanently fraught hope' (p. 10). For Clifford the world is perceived in terms of 'diasporic conjunctures'. 'Location . . . is an itinerary rather than a bounded site – a series of encounters and translations' (p. 11). Clifford echoes Bhabha, and like Bhabha, Benjamin: 'I see no future resolution to the tension', says Clifford. Rather, 'in the tradition of Walter Benjamin' he would 'track emergence, new orders of difference' (p. 10). As before, location is equivocal. The unease and 'ambivalence' which founds Clifford's 'fraught' vision is that which, at best, touches what Adorno has called a messianic light and Bhabha the hither side of the future. The thought of each is determined by an originary disarticulation. After Walter Benjamin, each intuits that 'origin is an eddy in the stream of becoming' (p. 281). Bereft of a way out of immanence, each forges a snarled and restless tale. While Clifford, Adorno, and Bhabha may concur with Chatwin that 'we are travelers at birth' (*Anatomy of Restlessness* p. 102), none of them can find an easy recourse to an untainted primordial restlessness. For each, we are 'indigent and distorted' creatures. Our thought, therefore, must necessarily mirror and further dislocate this inherent indigence and distortion.

If, as Chatwin states, 'our mad obsession with technological progress is a response to barriers in the way of our geographical progress' (ibid.), then for Clifford, Adorno and Bhabha, what matters is how this obsession impacts upon the way we live, the way we negotiate barriers. Why is it, they ask, that settlement has gained ascendancy over the cultural imagination? And why is it that, at every turn, this ascendancy is undone by the restlessness that founds it? Perhaps, in his haste to overleap the barrier and reclaim the past, Chatwin fails to grasp the founding undertow of restlessness that remains with us today? Perhaps, unlike Adorno or Bhabha, Chatwin cannot conceive of a radical politics implicit in restlessness. Indeed, it would seem that Chatwin's strident call for change is ensnared in the very processes of commodification that revolted him. We need 'Diversion. Distraction. Fantasy', says Chatwin. 'We need them as the air we breathe. Without change our bodies and brains rot' (p. 100). The declamatory ease with which Chatwin wills change unwittingly enfolds itself in the ample arms of the very consumerist and corporate culture he deplores. This begs the question: What if the very air we breathe is policed? What if 'freedom of movement' is nothing more than a corporate logo? This seems to be what Adorno is suggesting when he speaks of 'the open-air prison which the world is becoming'; a world in which

> all phenomena rigidify, become insignias of the absolute rule of that which is. There are no more ideologies in the authentic sense of false consciousness, only advertisements for the world through its duplication and the provocative lie which does not seek belief but commands silence (*Prisms* p. 34).

This prescient indictment exposes the deadly capacity to discipline and punish the earth and its people – in the name of freedom no less. With its instinct to absorb any insurgent unrest, the so-called free market has, in turn, commodified restlessness.

Now it is precisely this will to contain and moderate the restless movement of people and things – and here I include words – that Adorno and Bhabha have challenged. The 'open-air prison' which the world is fast becoming cannot, however, eliminate the outside. No *cordon sanitaire* will stopper restlessness, no border delimit the world. 'Risk is full: every living thing in siege' writes the poet A. R. Ammons (Corson's Inlet p. 1257). Integrity is parasited at every turn. Any affirmation today must admit that which it would disavow, which is why the logic of Adorno and Bhabha – and here we should include Clifford and Vladislavić – is not a logic founded on affinity or contradiction but on a radically negative and affirming immanence.

If every living thing is in siege, as Ammons notes, the demand remains 'life, to keep life' (ibid.), which is why the exacting 'negative moment' of the thought of Adorno or Benjamin continues to haunt us, and why it is reprised in the thought of Fanon and Bhabha. These thinkers serve as our ethical arbiters; they guard us against both pessimism and optimism. As Adorno says of Benjamin: 'From the very start his thought protested against the false claim that man and the human mind are self-constitutive and that an absolute originates in them' (*Prisms* p. 235). Today this protest has become all too familiar, its intelligence enervated, its truth reduced to a parochial adage. Such is the fate of any profound thought when it is subsumed by what Adorno has called a 'bourgeois immanence'.

To truly 'live', then, to 'revision' and redeem the world, our selves and others within the world, demands a method of thinking that is conditional *and* transfigural. One must inhabit the very doctrine one would disavow, for there is no vantage point outside that is not also inside. As Adorno reminds us: the more passionately thought denies its conditionality for the sake of the unconditional, the more unconsciously, and so calamitously, it is delivered up to the world. 'One must have tradition in oneself, to hate properly' (*Minima Moralia* p. 52). Contrary to Baudelaire or Chatwin, there is no pristine elsewhere. Snagged in the anomy of the present moment, we remain faithless in faith.

The despair that attends a belated realisation of the 'horror of the home' is all the more felt in a country such as South Africa in which, in the midst of attempting to sustain a belief in nationhood, a sense of place, a new beginning, there is, at the same time, an escalation in faithlessness, a sense that the home – domestic, regional, national – is under siege, traversed and cut apart by an unnameable and terrifying outside. I am not strictly referring to the invasive and devouring free market that, hand in hand with the 'new South Africa', has split and fragmented the axis of location and identity. Together the so-called free market and the belated enlightenment project that is nationhood have undoubtedly triggered and reinforced the unrest and faithlessness that characterises South African culture today.

Turning to the imploded confines of the home we find that the faith in a sense of place has not only been radically compromised but also catastrophically abused. The membrane that divides the inner and outer worlds is broken. The house is a stain. There is no recourse to permanence, no basis for sustenance, let alone the largesse of hope. Fear is omnipresent, vengeance and terror commonplace, the belief in safety mere wickerwork. Any system of protection is both a defence and a lure. Therein and thereby we embalm ourselves alive (p. 38). Open a South African newspaper on any given day and the 'horror of home' will be omnipresent. Amongst the bourgeoisie – as well as those who refute or do not understand the label – dinner table talk is driven by the need for intensified security and/or the longing to emigrate. Baudelaire's call – anywhere but here – is the plea not only of those who have the capacity to flee, but also of those, devoid of the means, who instinctively will a world that exists beyond this fraught and besieged place that, today, cannot be controlled or mediated. This frustration and fear, the paradox of entrapment and the desire to flee, is omnipresent, worse, commonplace: in Bhabha's scorching sense, 'parochial'.

What interests me, though, is not the searing presence of this paradox but the promise latent in the restlessness – indeed the terror – that founds it. In other words it is not the either/or of the off-shore or the trellidor, the capacity to flee or to reinforce the prison-house but, rather, the *aporia* that subsists in grasping what it ethically may mean to be neither here nor there, the interstitial and enabling unrest that comes from confronting the seemingly impossible position of being stuck between a rock and a hard place. For it is in grasping this liminal position of belonging-yet-not-belonging that we will begin, in turn, to grasp the exacting and redemptive position that is Adorno's and Bhabha's.

Today we live in a world that seemingly affords a surplus of alternatives and no alternative. The door is open, yet there is no exit. We stand on a threshold of an unfree world. Deprived of sleep we are 'alert and unconscious' (p. 38). This paradoxical state of surveillance and blindness is a state which conspires against a sovereign capacity to mediate the world and is undoubtedly debilitating, which, of course, is why a sense of hopelessness and fatality has, with a stealthy rapidity, consumed the imaginations of many South Africans. There is no refuge. As Adorno never ceases to remind us, 'the hardest hit . . . are those who have no choice' (p. 39). The pathos and the irony is all the more difficult to bear in a country freshly weaned from the shallow grave of apartheid, hurled into a world of seeming possibility, which, with a treacherous ease, has within the very depths of its psyche accepted the bankruptcy of any saving future.

I am well aware of the controversy that dogs this statement. In making such a claim I do not wish to reinforce the currency of this culture of entrapment and fatality, but in acknowledging its preternatural presence, to discover, with Adorno and Bhabha, a way to access a saving vision of the present moment. This way 'beyond' cannot be sourced through a blind intuition and neither can this way be served by permitting thought to be the handmaiden of secular rationality. Either route would be calamitous. If, then, it can be said that the home – and its correlatives, the self and the nation-state – are ethically bankrupt, then where would that leave us? Restless yes, but restless how, and to what end? What possible redemption can be salvaged through ruin, be it the ruination of received beliefs, notions of place, or the integrity of things?

For Adorno and Bhabha ruin is, at best, a rune in and through which history returns us to the present moment. Ruin politicises and thereby enables change. Through sleeplessness and terror all illusion – potentially – falls away and we are returned to a heightened awareness of our indigent and distorted natures. Hardly a conclusion to write home about; but then, lest we forget, there is no home to write to, let alone one out of which we could spin a redemptive narrative. Which of course is not to say that the home as a shelter, as an intricately pervasive and invasive system of identification and belonging, does not remain operative. It is not the existence of the home that I question; rather, it is what the home is speedily becoming. Increasingly, I have argued, we have witnessed what Bhabha has called 'the estranging sense of the relocation of the home and the world – the unhomeliness – that is the condition of extra-territorial and cross-cultural initiations' (*The Location of Culture* p. 9). This is also Clifford's and Vladislavić's point. 'To be unhomed', however, 'is not to be homeless, nor can the "unhomely" be easily accommodated in that familiar division of the social life into private and public spheres'. Rather, 'the unhomely moment relates the traumatic ambivalences of a personal, psychic history to the wider disjunctions of political existence' (p. 11). It is precisely here that we see why, for Bhabha, 'unhomeliness' is enabling: it galvanises awareness, transmutes solipsism and pain, sensitises one to the wreckage of global displacement, forges a 'restless and revisionary energy' that turns an 'incredulous terror' in the face of a nameless present into 'an expanded and ex-centric site of experience and empowerment' (p. 4).

Take it or leave it; this, according to Bhabha, is the debilitated and incisive ethics of a "new' internationalism' (p. 5), an emergent twilight ethics bereft of certainty, infused with hope, which Bhabha conceives as a 'Third Space'. Only therein and thereby can one

> open the way to conceptualizing an international culture, based not on the exoticism of multiculturalism or the diversity of cultures, but on the inscription and articulation of culture's hybridity. To that end we should remember that it is the 'inter' – the cutting edge of translation and negotiation, the in-between space – that carries the burden of the meaning of culture. It makes it possible to begin envisaging *national, anti-nationalist histories of the 'people'*. And by exploring this Third Space, we may elude the politics of polarity and emerge as the others of our selves (pp. 38–39, my emphasis).

Here it is critical to emphasise that the concept of totality – be it the totality of the self, the nation or the people – is not abandoned but infused with the wakeful negative moment that, as we have seen, is equally critical to Adorno. This notion of a re-envisaged and enabling totality, 'disconnected and non-binding' in character, allows Bhabha and Adorno to salvage hope in and through the wreckage of exhausted and/or defunct ideas and beliefs. If Bhabha eschews polarity – offshore or trellidor, flight or fear – it is because he believes that such logic is intrinsically false and, moreover, that it will not save us. What matters all the more is the manner in which we construct a saving ethos – be it of the home, the nation, and the self – which, as we move forward, will come to determine the outcome of our fate. For Bhabha this outcome is best served by an ethos of 'translation' and critical 'negotiation', an ethos which at its shifting core embraces 'hybridity' as the decisive figuration of our present and our future, a figuration which at every turn seems under threat.

Confronted with 'the hideous extremity of Serbian nationalism' – and here we can include the scourge of all exclusionary and fundamentalist political movements, all rigidifications, whether local, national, or international – Bhabha notes: 'This side of the psychosis of patriotic fervor, I like to think, there is the overwhelming evidence of a more transnational and translational sense of the hybridity of imagined communities' (p. 5). Resident in Bhabha's phrasing is Clifford's fraught and anxious hope. The question which dogs Bhabha, as it does all those who would re-imagine the world, is whether or not the world can truly be redeemed? Has fatality or simulacral hope – opposed views that, increasingly, appear to be in collusion – become *de rigeur*? The jury is certainly out. What must we make of the fervour, indeed the hysteria, which seems the defining characteristic of ascendant fundamentalisms worldwide? Here one could include nationalism, irrespective of the so-called democratic tenets that found it, as a variant of fundamentalism. How does one negotiate the staggering irony of the desire for settlement when settlement is disrupted at every turn? What of the unhoused millions throughout the world who, each day, negotiate the treacherous boundary between belonging and not belonging? What sustenance could an enabling restlessness possibly offer? After Critchley one could say: precious little . . . almost nothing. Still, it is the precious within the little that matters. What Adorno and Bhabha offer is a mode of thinking the present that frees us from captivity, a thinking which George Steiner defines as a 'questioning negativity [that] is also an allegory of hope' (A Little Night Music p. 3). The 'beyond' is within and all about us. We can and must 'emerge as the others of ourselves'. Only therein and thereby will we touch the hither side of the future in which to not belong, is to be at home in the world. For Adorno and Bhabha it is this very 'unhomeliness' which will redeem us.

Hail the camp!

FOUR

The Navigating Harlequin: Speculations on the Syncretic

Dervishes in ecstasy believed that they flew. Their dancing costumes were adorned with symbolic wings. Sometimes their clothes were deliberately shredded and patched. This denoted that the wearer had ripped them to bits in the fury of the dance. A fashion for patchwork has a habit of returning with ecstatic dance movements. To dance is to go on pilgrimage, and people dance more in periods of distress.

– *Bruce Chatwin*

Derived from philosophy and theology, syncretism denotes 'the merging of different inflectional varieties of a word during the development of a language' (*Concise Oxford Dictionary* p. 145). From the Greek *sunkrētismos*, of two parties, syncretism combines elements or parties 'against a third'. Of particular note is syncretism's deliberately *inconsistent* refusal to unify differing schools of thought, styles, or languages, and its foregrounding of the reflexive merger of discrete elements. In so doing, syncretism exposes the sleight of hand at work within aesthetic and epistemological practices founded on a dialectical synthesis of inherent differences. Strategically, syncretism is anti- and post-dialectical. As an aesthetic and epistemological strategy syncretism informs surrealism and Dadaism, movements that have had a major impact on late modernity. The following formulation by surrealist Max Ernst, reported by Sarane Alexandrian, provides the key to the agency of syncretism: 'The exploitation of the chance meeting of two remote realities on a plane unsuitable to them' (*Surrealist Art* p. 61).

Here Ernst compellingly points to a strategy of inscription and representation that is founded on disarticulation and reflexive exploitation of the liminal threshold which links, separates, and challenges the parity of discrete elements that make up a given artwork. Ernst's formulation, furthermore, de-territorialises the very ground, or 'plane', upon which a convergence of elements takes place. Disarticulation is not only a process that is imposed but also one that is integral to the *resistant ground* that fosters the syncretic. Hence the premise that syncretism is strategically anti- and post-dialectical.

In the context of cultural production in South Africa we will see that the radical agency associated with syncretism has not held sway. Rather, syncretism has been largely divested of its reflexive power and reduced to an arbitrary and facile fusion of differences. 'If plumes make plumage, it is not glue (*colle*) that makes collage' (p. 64). Ernst's scabrous retort serves as a reminder of the limit and threat implicit in what I will term *reactive syncretism*.

As an article of faith or a fashion, syncretism is a double agent, for it can as easily reinforce a received order of faith and fashion or forge an interstitial and radical unmasking of a given faith and fashion. Because of its very duplicity and inconsistency – its inherent corruptibility – syncretism can reinforce cultural stasis or promote change. Since it refutes any transcendent point of reflection and chooses to exist *in media res*, syncretism offers no teleological or deterministic value. And it is for this reason – given one's point of view – that syncretism is both the ally and the enemy of systems of cultural production. An immanent factor in the development of the languages, faiths, and styles of late-modernity – a period distinctly characterised by the conflation and erosion of cultural differences – syncretism has become the most strident characteristic of contemporary culture, a culture in which traditions have been supplanted by makeshift influences and each and every sacred order desacralised – converted and perverted – so that what today has come to be accepted as truth is nothing more than the bastardised remnant of a long-forgotten and – putatively – once-integrated and essential system of values.

By posting a doubt regarding the veracity of an integrated originary system of values I do not wish merely to dismiss any investment in such a claim. I wish to awaken the reader to an epistemic and psychic unease – generally perceived as the aftermath of World War I – which accelerated and ramified the ascendant hold of the syncretic on Europe's cultural imaginary. Rushing cites Barnett Newman, writing after World War II, who reasserts this perception in the following words:

> You must realize that . . . we felt the moral crisis of a world in shambles, a world devastated by a great depression and a fierce world war, and it was impossible at that time to paint the kind of paintings that we were doing – flowers, reclining nudes and people playing the cello (The Sublime is Now).

What Newman, like Ernst, brings to our attention is the growing – modernist – realisation of the impossibility of painting in a tradition that had been reduced to rubble. For Newman and Ernst, certainty is replaced by uncertainty and chance. The very ground, or plane, has become untethered and unsteady. Every reified and representative ideal – flowers, reclining nudes – has fractured. By locating the root of this disorder in the First World War I do not wish to reify that historical moment as the source of a disorder that prevails today, but rather to point to its impact upon systems of thought and cultural production, in relation to which South Africa was by no means exempt.

Crisis, generally perceived as the source of cultural innovation, occurs in many different geographic locations and at many different moments in history. What interests me, though, is the moment when a crisis becomes a given and innovation turns to enervation: a mere affect of that given. This shift is said to characterise the cultural logic of late or post-modernity. The relevance of this moment to South Africa's present condition – when the resistant dimension within innovation freezes and novelty becomes a disposable affect – will duly become apparent. But first, I wish to extend upon a doubt regarding the existence of an integrated originary system of values, and its rider, an originary disarticulation of systems of values that, until now, I have not contested. Both points of view, *when conceived antithetically*, are inadequate to the understanding of the past, present, or future. What the binary of integration versus disintegration represses is an active and reflexive engagement with the question of value and the processes of cultural signification. Therefore, when I insist upon a prior disarticulation it must at no point be understood as a mirror of an articulated order. Disarticulation as it is understood here exists in a radical sense that eschews all mirrors or stabilising counterpoints. In South Africa – as I have intimated throughout this inquiry – it is precisely this radically differential moment in signification that has been repressed. Any reading of cultural production in South Africa today must, as a result, bear witness to this repression and the pervasive emptiness of signs: the shift from innovation to enervation. In this regard, Jane Taylor's reflections on *Confessions of Zeno* as an 'unenviable' theatre performed 'into a kind of vacuum' become all the more telling.

My non-position, which seeks to restore the radically differential agency of syncretism, pits itself against this ascendant emptiness and enervation. If Ernst's formulation is critical to this chapter, it is because it reflexively *performs* the syncretic instead of posting it as a given within a received polarisation. In the clutches of those less dexterous than Ernst, this radically differential and reflexive vitality becomes rigidified in the instant of its ephemeral construction as a new disposable order. There lies the threat of the reactively syncretic. If I regard this ascendant reactive syncretism as symptomatic of what Newman would call a moral crisis, it should be noted at the outset that this crisis is not generally perceived as such. If innovation is still cherished today, then it is cherished as something consumable and disposable. To understand the agency of the syncretic within the present moment, one must acknowledge its reactive and absorptive force. Its marked tendency to displace radical difference in the name of a simulacral unity should alert us to a critical loss that such a process incurs. That loss is the loss of the reflexive, resistant, and radically other.

As this chapter unfolds we will find that the syncretic is not only the result of an after-shock of the Great and Second World War, as Newman would have us believe, but, in the context of South Africa, it serves as the marker for a *prior,* persistent, and unacknowledgeable crisis. By asserting that crisis is persistent I wish to draw the reader's attention away from the tendency to root and to frame a given crisis – be it the Great War or South Africa under apartheid – and, in so doing, read innovation and change as an aftershock thereof. While there is justice in this slant, it is, I believe, inadequate to an understanding of how change comes about and the role of the radically resistant. I wish, therefore, to engender an awareness relevant to a rethinking of South Africa's cultural predicament, which will allow us to conceive of the syncretic not only as a foreign importation – the aftershock of a European crisis – but as a constitutive seam of lived experience in South Africa which, despite the Manichean system which would shape its fate, was always already a primary influence in shaping what South African society was and what it would become. Between the suppression of the syncretic under colonialism and apartheid and its full-blown emergence today lies a story that has yet to be satisfactorily addressed. What it means to be a South African is not reducible to the crucible of colonialism and apartheid. The task of this chapter will be to unlock this other story.

What is striking in the particular context of South Africa is how swiftly and how easily the radical agency of the syncretic has been disposed of. That others, such as Loren Kruger, have also noted the swift cessation of a culture of resistance does not mean that the root of this cessation has been grasped. More often than not those engaged in the problem remain in a quandary. How, it is asked, does one rethink and reinvigorate a culture of resistance, given that that which has consumed South Africa's cultural imaginary has so thoroughly emptied resistance of both its purpose and its content? How, in other words, to shift the syncretic from its predominantly enervated and reactive mode to one that is more critically and reflexively engaged with the processes of change? This question is more easily posed than answered. There is no doubt that every aspect of cultural production – the clothes we wear, the food we eat, the music we listen to, the languages we speak, the values we propound – has been bastardised/hybridised/modernised through the mill of syncretism. What are the implications behind this systemic – indeed endemic – de-territorialisation of traditional values, integrated cultures, classical aesthetics? What does this overriding syncretism tell us about late-modern life? What, more particularly, does syncretism tell us about the agency and vision of culture in South Africa?

Turning to the epigraph, which is taken from Bruce Chatwin's 'It's a Nomad *Nomad* world' (*Anatomy of Restlessness* p. 105), we find a distinct fusion of the ecstatic and self-conscious, the metaphysical and the physical. The clothes of the dervish, 'adorned with symbolic wings . . . deliberately shredded and patched', is perceived by Chatwin as a two-fold denotation: a sign for a psychically transfigural condition and a deliberately conscious posting of the syncretic within the secular realm. By emphasising this seemingly contradictory fusion, Chatwin points to the key value of the syncretic as the means through which to announce and incarnate a divestiture from, and impossibility of, faith and fashion as properties that are uniform or seamlessly integrated – the figure of the dervish, then, as the figure of the late-modern syncretist. What makes Chatwin's observation all the more compelling is that it presents this tactically strange fusion of disparate and contradictory elements as symptomatic of 'periods of distress'.

Returning to Taylor's reflections on the *Confessions of Zeno* – an exemplary instance of the syncretic – one finds a canny resonance between *Zeno*'s heightened reflexivity – its 'anatomizing [of a] malaise' – and Chatwin's observation. Here reflexivity heightens but does not alter distress. Reflexivity remains subject to enervation and reaction. Given this limit, one could say that *Zeno* is a syncretic work that is symptomatic of its time, that it represents a contemporary attempt to navigate an increasingly confusing and desperate shift from oppression to freedom, a shift defined by what Taylor terms an 'ambiguous relationship to absolutist authority and power' which necessitates a makeshift utilisation of varied forms of expression, that, in sum, *Zeno* occupies a middle ground between innovation and enervation: it is reflexive about enervation, enervated in the act of reflexivity.

Zeno exemplifies a contemporary South African culture that is forced to inhabit a contradiction in which resistance remains a claimant at the very instant in which its claims have been divested. The art produced out of this contradiction has, as a consequence, been forced to evoke this distress. Consequently, if syncretism today is the hallmark of an emergent culture in South Africa, it is also the charged marker for a further stage of emergency. That this state of emergency has not been projected or perceived as such in no way diminishes the fact that the emergency – or crisis – persists. The subject and the object of the crisis may have shifted – 'matters of historical and psychological weight . . . treated . . . as meringue; and the trivial minutia of the bourgeois condition become matters of monumental psychic drama and ethical quests' – yet the emergency persists.

As Taylor notes: *Zeno* is an 'extravagant and playful farce teetering on the brink of tragedy'. That *Zeno* is an adaptation of a modernist work written after the First World War, yet distinctively rooted within the South African imaginary, ramifies the doubled link I have thus far drawn. That *Zeno* is structurally fractured, and utilises this formal breakdown to convey aphasia – the disintegration of speech and the continuance of an unspeakable mental activity – defines, furthermore, the psychic rupture which distinguishes the present historical moment. That that which is unspeakable is projected onto a screen, the audience made privy to the unspeakable, should draw our attention to the syncretic and tactical exploitation of chance elements. South Africa's present moment is anything but transparent or fluent. Rather, for Taylor, the art produced out of an existent 'trauma' must, necessarily, function as 'psychological allegory'. There the anatomy of a malaise emerges in shreds that at no point add up, but add to an unabated dilemma. For Taylor, it is the 'wilfully anti-naturalistic' nature of *Zeno* that proves the source of its immense liberation. Taylor concludes her reflection with another 'chance meaning'. This last pertains to Volans's discordant music and the visual metaphor produced by the presence of a string quartet on stage. The musicians, she says, were '"bowing" the world into existence'. This is no mere theatrical conceit. By contrast Taylor compellingly draws us to the sacred within the syncretic. No matter how conventionally flawed, how uneven and incomplete, *Zeno* gifts to South African culture an act of love as desperate as it is mystifying. In addition, as 'a meditation on the translation between the realms of theory and practice', *Zeno* conveys the unspeakable and unforeseeable, which is critical to thinking the transition in the process of transformation.

Turning now to what I call reactive syncretism – a syncretism co-opted by nationalism and the market forces of late-modernity – we find that it has largely been divested of its integral and challenging force. While reactive syncretism may foreground the merger of conflicting interests and elements, it has reduced this merger to a matter of fashion and style. This reduction – traducement and commodification – converts resistance into a disposable affect; the property and sign of a life-style rather than an integral and gnawing agency that could challenge or engage with a dominant or ascendant order. This reduction of the agency of resistance is by no means peculiar to South Africa. It is within the particular context of South Africa – in the full knowledge that the country cannot be perceived as a bounded and distinct site – that this chapter assigns its focus.

How, then, in the loosely defined context of South Africa, does reactive syncretism work? Broadly, it is apparent in the opportunistic alliances of political parties, the disingenuous deployment of affirmative action and the quota system, the simulacral multiculturalism of media representation. These initiatives, seen in an 'affirmative' light, promote what until now has been accepted as an impermissible and incommensurable marriage of races in a shared society. The very term 'separate development' suggests a cellular rather than a syncretic society. Against this cellular conception, the syncretic promotes a more positive engagement with difference, although my argument is that the dominant deployment of syncretism in contemporary South Africa merely constructs the illusion of a positive engagement or merger of difference. If the economy of syncretism remains defective as a result, it is because in glossing difference it has failed to address a radicality or heterogeneity that subsists at the core of South Africa's differential condition. The problem lies first in the elision and suppression of the incommensurability of difference (foregrounded as aphasia in *Zeno*); second in the way the shift from lack to fulfilment – oppression to freedom – has been undertaken and recorded in South Africa. Perceived causally as a shift from one state to another the shift has been defined by a process at once fixated and reactive. In other words, the shift has recast the dualistic system it purportedly sought to negate (rather than the psychic, epistemic, and formal fragmentation evinced in *Zeno*). Freedom, as a consequence, has remained a reified and constrained ideal, the inverse of oppression and not its radical negation. Given this conceptual limit, the syncretic culture that has emerged has remained bounded, moderated, and circumscribed by a dualistic law. The problem does not stop there. I would suggest that a vested interest exists in circumscribing and containing change: in monitoring and moderating difference. The shift, then, is a shift from a separate to a contiguous and relatively autonomous development. In that lies the *unevenness* that Loren Kruger has noted (Black Atlantics, White Indians, and Jews p. 35).

At first glance this appears to be a favourable move. Nonetheless, irrespective of the shift, reification remains in place. What this continued investment in reification reveals is the desire to maintain a system defined by causation and fixation. The content may shift, appear more plural, but the epistemic system that defines the content remains more or less the same. What this realisation indicates is a process of rationalisation, which remains coercive and opportunistic. This opportunism I understand as the reactively syncretic in cultural production. If it is reactive it is because it fixates on causes that are no more than symptoms. In order to maintain its cultural dominance as a signifying system it must manufacture a motive: call it freedom, call it change. In the instant in which this call is made it must understand itself as ephemeral, for the simple and beguiling reason that the ephemeral invokes a doubled logic of disposability *and* perpetual newness. Freedom and change, consequently, are relativised, made incandescent. In the process we find that the continued desire for reification is not lost. Its emphasis is shifted from the instrumental to the ideational. That which is reified is not some *thing* but some *idea*: the idea of freedom, the idea of change. The very ephemerality of the syncretic – the belief in endless combinations – in no way negates the constitutive belief that is glanced in the present and projected into the future. The upshot of this psychic and epistemic approach is that it freezes the account and lightens the load. With the idea of freedom and change in mind, one withdraws from the past, advances towards the future, and moves – in passing – through the present. Urgency, if it has a place within this schema, is dissimulated, for at every turn this urgency is compromised by a contrary and ascendant belief that, as a society, South Africa has – putatively – advanced beyond its resident ills. There lies the critical and constitutive misprision, there Taylor's vacuum.

Split between local, regional, national, and international needs and concerns, it is not surprising that cultural expression and production in South Africa has found it impossible to reconcile these distinct and refracted needs. The politics and aesthetics forged through civil society are markedly different from that forged within and for an international economy. Because the fusion of these diverse concerns is deemed impossible, culture has tended to give up the ghost and fragment its focus. What has withered as a consequence is the very notion of, and desire for, a collective national identity at a level other than that of the ceaselessly broached and ceaselessly deferred idea. Today the very notion of such an identity exists as a floating signifier; a simulacral and reactively syncretic ploy that can be utilised or set aside at any given moment. Contrary to the hopes of an activist such as Albie Sachs, there has in fact been no sustained attempt to produce a cultural imaginary that could unify the citizenry of South Africa. Given South Africa's psychic and epistemic inheritance, my daunting and unsettling assumption is that this desire for unity will never be realised. The hegemonic dominance of reactive syncretism as a marker for the South African cultural imaginary serves as a testimony to this impossibility. What interests me is why a unified cultural imaginary is impossible, and how, in spite of this impossibility, one can sustain a regenerative cultural vision.

This impossibility is certainly not merely the glib result of logic of the post-nation or the transnational. My assumption, rather, is that the impossibility is rooted in an unthinkable and impossible prior disarticulation which Leon de Kock, in his 'Introduction: South Africa in the Global Imaginary', has termed a radical heterogeneity. This radical heterogeneity is not merely the foil for a colonial and apartheid culture founded on division and separate development, or an emergent democratic culture founded on contiguity and relative development. Radical heterogeneity is the key to defounding a psychic and epistemic system which, in spite of putative change, has maintained a culture of privation and enslavement in the very disingenuous instant in which it has invoked a culture of abundance and freedom. As a result, a radical epistemic shift remains profoundly lacking. Max Ernst's formulation (and its performative correlative *Zeno*) provides the key to unlocking the endgame which characterises South Africa's present moment. After Ernst what is needed is *the exploitation of the chance meeting of remote realities on a plane unsuitable to them*. This meeting must surely have occurred in the distant past as it occurs today. That little has been done to reshape and remake this encounter – an encounter which, within the divisive and repressive constraints of an inhuman Manichean system, has largely been erased – should remind us all the more of the catastrophe of the past, and the catastrophe that awaits us.

If apartheid's perverse virtue was to keep the country out of step with capital, its undoing – albeit partial – has resulted in the subreption and displacement of every ideal associated with resistance culture. How, then, can those engaged in cultural production effect a societal fusion when there is no faith in – and no possibility of – a collective core? How can syncretism work proactively when, increasingly, there is no sustained quest for an ethical means to negotiate the loss of once perceivable and sacralised origins? Seemingly plotless and incoherent – in the double sense of failing to cohere and confusing – syncretic culture in South Africa has largely devolved into indifference, an indifference marked – in part – by an investiture in a global economy and cultural imaginary at the expense of the needs of the nation's people. Simulacral, syncretism has largely chosen to mirror its corruption rather than convert that corruption, explain the constitutive lack therein, and, in so doing, transform this lack into a power. What is strikingly evident today is that the artist who works in the syncretic mode – unlike Chatwin's dervish, who navigates between the ecstatic and secular realms – largely has no access to the subversive and transfigural power of the mode that is used. If this is so it is not because the syncretic artist has no access to a primary faith, be it aesthetic, philosophical, political or theological, but because the artist has fallen victim to reactive ambivalence, unthinkingly accepted the fall from grace, and embraced the web of affects and fashions which over-determine a disposable economy. It is not surprising, then, that the distress – acknowledged or repressed – that accompanies this embrace is all the more acute.

With specific regard to South Africa, my assumption is that reactive syncretism is not merely the affect of late modernity. To understand from whence South African society has emerged and what it is fast becoming, it is critical that one rethink the hegemonic primacy of dualism, and, in its place, fashion an other more heterogeneous logic. By doing so one will all the more compellingly reveal that South Africans do not only live in the aftershock of empire and racial strife – and its rider, the aftershock that is modernity – but also within a *prior* epistemic and psychic irresolution which empire and racial strife sought to displace, yet could not. A reconceptualisation of this nature will all the better account for the lack which resides in any attempt at producing a national unity, a lack embodied in the cultural signification that is reactive syncretism. If syncretism *appears* to stem from beyond the nation's borders it is because there is a vested interest in perceiving it to be such. If this is so, it is because it has been impermissible to conceive of South Africa as a nation whose deeper psychic aspirations – indeed, its truth – had always run counter to both the projects of oppression *and* liberation. My point is that the liberation that South Africans sought is not reducible to a shift from white to black control, or, more loosely, from colonialism/apartheid to democracy. This transfer of power occludes as much as it yields. The syncretic, as I pointed out at the outset, foregrounds the corruption in the instant of a given displacement and merger. This corruption, which eschews any moral arbitration, is, I believe, the more persuasive root of the South African cultural condition. That this root has not been rigorously addressed merely reveals the symptomatic provenance of denial. I would suggest, therefore, that South Africa has a vested interest in *not* knowing itself.

Startlingly hypocritical in its understanding of itself, South Africa has not sought to ramify the psychic needs of its myriad constituencies but, rather, to blithely contradict and diminish those needs at every turn. If this is so it is not, as it is commonly assumed, because South Africa embraces plurality and diversity, but because it has been incapable of attaining, let alone sustaining, a coherent knowledge of itself as a country. Plurality and diversity serve as a transference or displacement of the will to cohere a society whose people do not – yet – speak each to each. Divested of a framing myth or master narrative at the very outset of its inscription, South African society was confronted with two choices: to accept its heterogeneous and syncretic state or choose balkanisation. The former was seen as horror, the latter as reason. This claim does not of course dispel the repeated attempts to cross the physical and psychic boundaries that continue to divide people; rather, the claim serves to draw the reader's attention to a founding and persistent abnormality that militates against and disfigures each and every attempt to do so. Within the sphere of cultural expression, what interests me is the resultant nature of the culture produced given the characteristic abnormality that over-determines its expression. My insistent point is that any attempt to vault the divide between people does not produce a synthesis, but a reactive syncretic convergence. What is needed is to track the impact of this reactive syncretic convergence, to ascertain the degree to which it is wholly symptomatic of a withering and schizophrenic globalisation of culture or whether it is also rooted in a domestic incapacity to conceive a realisable unity in difference. Could it be that South Africa, forged in and through empire and racial strife, was always already doomed to a simulacral and reactive syncretism?

To the extent to which South Africa's present remains psychically over-determined by the Manichean systems of colonialism and apartheid, the answer would be yes. My conclusion is that the South African cultural imaginary has not been wholly defined by these systems of oppression. There remains a constitutive and repressed heterogeneity that is irreducible to the systems that sought to deny its very existence. Projected as a horror, this radically syncretic and heterogeneous reality is not merely latent but emergent today, existing on the hither side of the dominant compromise. By projecting its release, I anticipate a cultural vision that, after Bhabha, would not only be a new, radically differential intertext, but a symptomatic projection of a past that has hitherto been disregarded or suppressed. In order to coax this radical syncretism conceptually – somatically, experientially – into being it has been necessary to emphasise what I consider a constitutive and critical elision and suppression of resistance in this newfangled age. After all, how is it possible to post the emergence of a radical syncretism when the very force of resistance that would make possible its release has been so thoroughly compromised?

We live in the shadow of two insidious logics: that of the post-nation and the post-resistant: hence the cultural dominance of the twinned states of fatal ennui and hysterical glee. That South Africa has absorbed these twinned states with consummate ease is not merely the result of its investment in a global culture, but also the result of a divestment of the radically syncretic. If the reactive and simulacral have proved preferable it is because the burden of change – a burden marked by a return to the past as well as an advance into the future – would otherwise be too great. By disinvesting itself of this burden – defined by and preceding colonialism – the South African cultural imaginary has chosen to forego and bypass a black hole that exists at its core. By returning to this black hole – a descriptor for a radically syncretic and heterogeneous reality that has been repressed – I wish to reveal that which links South Africa's past to its present moment, rather than that which separates it. The causal and the consecutive, I have suggested, is a disruptive logic. If this is so it is because it favours the novel (development) over an indifferently heterogeneous continuum. It is this conceptual misprision that is the root of South Africa's estrangement from itself.

This estrangement, or lag, recurs in recent history at the point when South Africa shifts from immoral pariah to moral exemplar of a democratic, trans-cultural and trans-national imaginary. This so-called transitional point – which I read as an intransitive falsification – is not one in which South Africa addresses the notoriety of its past or the lost encounter which precedes this notoriety, but, rather, it is the point at which the past – good and bad – is effectively erased. This erasure cannot of course be achieved in its entirety. Furthermore, the erasure must not be seen to be such. Rather, that which must appear to be ongoing is the embattled engagement with a reified past in the name of a changed present. Therein lies the illusion. This illusion – call it the transition or interregnum – presupposes a reckoning and a reparation. Nothing of the sort occurs. Or, more precisely, nothing of the sort is sustained. In its haste to wean itself from the notoriety of its past, South Africa replaces the need for reparation with a consuming, deeply ingrained and wanton need, namely the need to be inducted as swiftly as possible into a global economic and cultural imaginary. It is this overwhelming need that makes a mockery of every act of resistance during the apartheid era and the era that preceded it. How did this overwhelming need come about? How long had this need lain dormant? Was this need already deeply rooted in South Africa's isolated and benighted years? Surely it must have been? How else explain its overwhelming and consuming presence? And where, in the midst of South Africa's history of resistance, was this desire lodged? Everywhere, it seems now: even at the heart of resistance itself.

To say that South Africa is merely a latter-day collaborator in the global pandemic that is late capital is to belie the fact that it is the economy of this consuming desire, more than any other, which had defined its cultural imaginary. Consider the dictum TOO MUCH IS NOT ENOUGH, which succinctly defines the cultural logic of late capital. Therein we find that desire is all consuming, yet ceaselessly regenerate. Lack challenges and spurs excess. My hunch is that something akin to this process lies at the root of South Africa's libidinal economy. Historically caught between lack and excess, the received assumption was that what South Africa needed was moral arbitration. This burden of arbitration would fall on the ANC. In retrospect we can see that this burden proved not to be sustainable, indeed, more troublingly, that the burden has proved superfluous: hence the ascendance of a marked absence of morality, an ascendance evident in the opportunistic rise of reactive syncretism.

Surely the fact that syncretism has subsequently assumed the form it has is connected to the fact that there never was a point at which the country could truly conceive of itself as a unity, a core, or an integral store-house of durable values? This wager deserves further consideration. The assumption that fuels it is that a constitutive disingenuousness characterises South Africa's putative shift from oppression to freedom. This disingenuousness, I have suggested, lies in the dislocation and suppression of an originary heterogeneity. In that moment when South Africa psychically estranges itself from itself, it erases every regenerative possibility and rigidifies difference. It is at that moment – a moment that will recur – that South Africa forges an impossibility that will prove to haunt and disfigure every bid for change. Henceforth no bid for unification, no eventual nation-hood, will absolve South Africa from a constitutive fracture. Dis-articulated at the point of its inscription, South Africa would come to know itself as intrinsically estranged from itself. This haunting estrangement from an originary heterogeneity would never cease. Even today, in the midst of seeming freedom, this haunting persists. It emerges all the more when South Africa dresses itself up as a picture-perfect Benetton moment in which difference is glossed, oneness endorsed. For in eliding radical difference, reactive syncretism has failed to smother a deeply lodged psychic discordance and failure that – after J. M. Coetzee – I have called the failure of love (Jerusalem Prize Acceptance Speech p. 97). This failure – the failure of self-love and the love of others – suggests a society that could never conceive of itself as either whole or as other to itself. Fragmented at the core, it would attempt to give up the ghost in favour of an international cultural imaginary that, all the more, would fracture its already fragmented self. The cost of this loss remains to be counted. What is certain, though, is that a black hole exists which widens and deepens by the day. A consummate fraud – decreed by national and global accord to be a miracle – has been perpetrated at the expense of the nation's people. A late inductee into a defunct Enlightenment ideal, South Africa, along with its more illustrious cohorts, is learning today to run on empty. Reactive syncretism is the marker for this emptiness.

This is the fatal condition of South Africa's past and its present. This fatality I have termed reactive syncretism. The challenge, now, is to ascertain how this fatality can be overcome, not by replacing difference with unity, but by returning to the radical agency that is resident within syncretism. I have already pointed to *Zeno* as an attempt, through performance, to address the incommensurable ambivalence of South Africa's present moment, a moment that, paradoxically, I claim to be perpetual.

Flora Veit-Wild, in her paper '*Festivals of Laughter*: Syncretism in Southern Africa', provides a further opening to a rethinking of syncretism. In accordance with the opening observations of this chapter, Veit-Wild begins by reading syncretic culture pro-actively. Syncretism, she says, 'has to be revalued and freed from its pejorative connotations'. She defers to the original meaning of syncretism in art and religious history: 'the impure, the deviation from the canon, the anti-hierarchical', then adds, 'syncretism is close to bastardisation, hence implies being outcast, marginalized' (p. 27). My argument is that it is not syncretism's bastardised, outcast, or marginalised history and agency that has assumed dominance in South Africa's cultural imaginary, but rather its centralisation as the key trope and index of a market-driven ethos defined by nationalism and by multi-nationalism and globalism. What's more, I have suggested that it is the very forgetting of the eccentric and outcast nature and power of syncretism that has resulted in the withering of its radical and transformative impact. Co-opted by capital and by nationalist rhetoric, evident in glib phrases such as '*Simunye* we are one' and the 'rainbow nation', syncretism has not in fact produced the level of critical inquiry and cultural signification which it is capable of.

In failing to perceive the opportunism at the root of reactive syncretism, Veit-Wild is in danger of falling victim to the very treacherous flowering of optimism spawned by the heady days of the 1994 'democratic' election. She problematically links the National Arts Coalition's *Festivals of Laughter* – a haplessly reactive attempt at triumphalism – to Bakhtin's conception of carnival in literature

> which mobilizes all 'abnormal' and fantastic human instincts and desires in order to ridicule and subvert dominant cultures and discourses. Carnivalesque laughter . . . is festive laughter. 'The entire world is seen in its droll aspect, in its gay relativity . . . [T]his laughter is ambivalent: it is gay, triumphant, and at the same time mocking, deriding. It asserts and it denies, it buries and it revives. Such is the laughter of the carnival' (*Festivals of Laughter* p. 27).

While I may concur with Veit-Wild's reading of syncretism and acknowledge its link to Bakhtin's notion of carnival, I am at the same time reminded that the very vivacity she affords the syncretic also conceals a deeper unease. This of course is Chatwin's compelling observation regarding dance as a synecdoche for a period of distress. Here one could exchange dance for other cultural phenomena and arrive at the same reading. What matters to me, in the broadest sense, is how and to what end syncretism converts the indissoluble link between festivity and despair. If syncretism can either nullify or transform a society, then how is the more positive dimension of syncretism to be achieved?

Before returning to this favoured vision of syncretism, I wish to reinforce the reader's vigilance regarding the persuasive and negative impact which syncretism has had when it has been associated with a culture of festivity. A striking and macabre example that reinforces Chatwin's point would be the dance marathons during the Depression in America in the 1930s. In South Africa it was precisely dance movements, notably Gibson Kente and Mbongeni Ngema's internationally renowned musicals, which have been perceived as instances of liberation and joy in township culture. But to what extent are Kente and Ngema's musicals – trumpeted as triumphal depictions of 'ordinary' township life – truly instances of release in an oppressive time? Are they not also the surest ciphers of an anxious and desperate attempt to vault the very oppression in which these musicals remained snagged?

The point Chatwin makes is that oppression is not only evident in moments of resistance but, more acutely, in those very moments commonly perceived as the ordinary-and-transcendent manifestations of pleasure. J. M. Coetzee echoes this view when, acknowledging the corrupted link between freedom and entrapment, he states: 'All expressions of [. . .] inner life, no matter how intense, no matter how pierced with exultation or despair, suffer from [. . .] stuntedness and deformity' (Jerusalem Prize Acceptance Speech p. 98).

It is precisely this stuntedness, this deformation then, that is the psychic root of reactive syncretism. Coetzee's point is that distress, when informed by the legacy of empire and apartheid, can in no way be easily vaulted. If syncretic musicals such as Kente and Ngema's *Sarafina* and David Kramer and Taliep Petersen's *Kat and the Kings* have been hailed both nationally and internationally as triumphal depictions of joy in a dark time, it is because at their root they have displaced the very threat at the core of their dramatisations of flight. Neither work is carnivalesque in the Bakhtinian sense. They may be droll, gay and celebratory; they may be mocking and derisive. Nonetheless, they lack a radically reflexive and transformative dimension. In both works the pain of history is mediated and moderated by a foreknowledge that the very context for expression – whether locally or on Broadway and the West End – cannot countenance the real threat of psychic and physical pain. Festivity becomes a diversion rather than an inversion and transformation of distress. Jeanne Colleran, in 'South African Theatre in the United States: The Allure of the Familiar and the Exotic', and Jerry Mofokeng, in 'Theatre for Export: the Commercialization of the Black People's Struggle in South African Export Musicals', address at greater length what I have noted here as the reactively syncretic manner in which South Africa performs itself for itself and for others.

Consider the comparatively less exotic, local, and global phenomenon of rave culture. Tellingly associated with a drug called Ecstasy, rave is a late-modern manifestation of a collective outer-body experience. It is a corrupted culture of the dervish that in its ecstatic and secularised manifestation imputes a horror of home, a desire to be anywhere but here. Driven by music that is ritualistic, anaphoric, and largely synthetic – music designed to transport the dancer into a wild and furious state of delirium – rave is a phenomenon that denies all consequence in the mortal and secular sphere. Its vaunted will is to forget all cares, all ills, and, without consequence, to fashion the dancer anew. Irrespective of rave culture's transcendent claims it is also, all the more troublingly, a culture governed by amnesia and denial. As a syncretic phenomenon, rave signals a contemporary miscarriage of a radicalised sense of self in the world. It is a form of carnival that offers the participants no capacity to either reintegrate themselves within or transform the society from which they have fled. While furiously energetic, rave is a phenomenon that is also curiously passive, since it foregoes the agency of the self and institutes the values of a marooned tribe.

As a reactive syncretic phenomenon, rave is very different from both the traditional conception of carnival and the more subversive conception of carnival described by Veit-Wild and Bakhtin. What traditionally distinguishes the carnivalesque is that it is a ritual of inversion that, while momentarily dispelling a prevailing order, in no way sustains the inversion of that order but, rather, presupposes the return of its authority. It is this re-integrative and Manichean conception of carnival that informs the musicals of Kente,

Ngema, Kramer and Petersen. Veit-Wild, however, does not share this traditional perception of the carnivalesque. For her the inversion is not momentary. It supposes a perpetual and active negation of the very authority that seeks to reassert itself. Notwithstanding my own belief that Veit-Wild has misread the seeming vitalism in South African resistance culture – in particular the National Arts Coalition's 1994 *Festivals of Laughter* – there remains a salience to the radical agency she has factored into the syncretic. For her the force of the radically syncretic in cultural production is sustainable.

Fusing the syncretic with the hybrid, Veit-Wild progresses by deferring to hybridity's principle avatar, Homi Bhabha. She distinguishes between syncretism as 'a fusion of elements of different yet still recognizable origins; and hybridity as a completely new subject position and consciousness arising out of a fusion' (*Festivals of Laughter* p. 28). For Veit-Wild – after Bhabha – syncretism makes possible the production of a third space

> where people, in times of transition, 'are now free to negotiate and translate their cultural identities in a discontinuous intertextual temporality of cultural difference . . . The process of cultural hybridity gives rise to something different, something new and unrecognisable, a new era of negotiation and representation' (ibid.).

Clearly Veit-Wild's conception of syncretism, like Bhabha's conception of hybridity, is conceived in the affirmative. What matters is not that the syncretic contains a refracted and definable set of origins, but that as a fusion of diverse elements it issues forth *a completely new subject position and consciousness.*

The question I ask is whether or not this new subject position and consciousness is indeed the distinguishing trait of contemporary cultural production in South Africa. My assumption is that it is not. If this is so, it is because there has been no transforming ecstasis, no subreption of received states of being, but instead a displaced, nullified and hapless fusion of influences. The economy of desire, and the representation of this desire through culture, has been defined not by a radical translation of the existing terms for change, but by a set of reactive tactical adjustments which, while appearing to address the needs and desires of society, have in fact eschewed any attempt to answer for those needs and desires. Reactive syncretism, then, is founded at a remove. Hence the prevailing confusion and desperation – Chatwin's 'period of distress' – which, today, is characteristically expressed as ennui and fatality and/or as hysterical glee. If this distress prevails – and I see no end to its pathological persistence – it is because syncretism in its ascendant reactive mode has not produced a psychically immanent reconfiguration and radicalisation of a differential cultural inheritance, but a heteroglossic, patched, and disposable fashioning of the so-called new. It is happenstance and opportunism – ruled by a local and international market economy – which characterises cultural production in South Africa today.

This is undoubtedly a distressing view. It must be remembered, however, that it is a general view which in no way dispels the fact that alternative subject positions and consciousness remain possible, indeed, realisable. While I am intimately concerned with the capacity of the syncretic to denude, unmask and uproot oppressive power structures, I am as intimately concerned with the canny capacity of existing power structures to absorb contradiction and, disingenuously, dissimulate the dance of its own demise and reinvigoration. While I may wholly endorse Veit-Wild and Bhabha's vision of the syncretic and the hybrid as the means through which to issue forth *something new and unrecognisable, a new era of negotiation of meaning and representation*, I wish, once more, to qualify the extent to which this era has come to pass in South African culture. My point is that no matter how judicious and critically necessary this vision may be to the development of culture in South Africa, it remains a vision that, at best, exists as a fission-flare.

Notwithstanding a cultural phenomenon such as the nationally televised Truth and Reconciliation Hearings — which in its flawed phrasing cancels the very truth it purportedly seeks to return to South Africa's citizenry, since reconciliation, an arduous if not impossible task, is perceived as a *fait accompli* — South Africa, on the contrary, is a society perversely and bizarrely distinguished by its staggering capacity to erode and distort its originary heterogeneity. Hell-bent on reinventing itself, South African society has sought to set aside the pathological root of its continued ills by choosing to manufacture and implicitly edit its history, its present, and, pre-emptively, its future. History, though, cannot be manufactured. Contrary to received opinion, history is not a system of signs alone. Rather, as Bhabha reminds us, history, when conceived as 'something new and unrecognisable, a new era' is the product of the 'negotiation of meaning and representation'. History is not a product, but a series of intersected and often fraught interpretations and actions.

It would seem, here, that Bhabha does not quite access the complexity of the engagement with systems of meanings and representation when he speaks of 'negotiation'. The word appears too tame, too Platonic and rational. Nonetheless in 'Aura and Agora' Bhabha notes that

> negotiation is the ability to articulate differences in space and time, to link words and images in new symbolic orders, to intervene in the forest of signs and mediate what may seem to be incommensurable values or contradictory realities. If rapture erupts as ineffable experience, negotiation insists on the *necessity of narrative* (p. 8).

In a more charged and radical sense then, syncretism can be said to uneasily negotiate meaning and representation, to narrate rupture and rapture, and foreground the *unsuitability* of the very plane that founds a given system of meaning and representation. The implication is that for a system such as colonialism or apartheid to have an impact it must presuppose that which necessarily resists it. It is this resistance, under the sign of the radically syncretic, which I have made the subject of this chapter. After Walter Benjamin, I would argue that radical syncretism thrives in the abyss of mediateness. This more vertiginous and immanent conceptualisation of a radical reflexivity, which defines the highest power of syncretism in cultural production, is the surest way to achieve what Bhabha calls 'something new and unrecognizable, a new era'. While I wholly concur with Bhabha's subjunctive formulation – a formulation which echoes the call to novelty expressed by the modernists – I am at the same time aware that the syncretic is not merely about newness, but also about an age-old and deeply residual seam of radical difference that runs non-parallel with the dominant systems of colonialism and apartheid. Therefore, one could say that the 'new and unrecognizable' which Bhabha invokes is also something *old and recognisable* that has historically been occluded. Contrary to so much talk, including my own, that syncretism is a thing of innovation that results from a crisis which produced modernism, it could also be argued that the syncretic is a thing of infinite durability that reaches further back in time. Therefore, whether conceived as a vestige of a lost past or as a figuration of the thrill of the new, the syncretic remains, in the most compelling and reflexive sense, the indissoluble manifestation of radical difference.

What matters to Veit-Wild and Bhabha is the capacity of syncretic culture to achieve an eccentric and transforming vision. For each the development of a new subject position and consciousness is a profoundly immanent and reflexive syncretic act. Like Chatwin's dervish, who consciously denotes the transfiguring affect of his conscious will through shredded and patched trappings, the contemporary pioneers of a radical and transforming syncretism must signpost their flight and figure a radical disfiguration of received perceptions and aesthetic modes. Veit-Wild points to Wopko Jensma as an example of the radical potential of syncretism. Referring to his 1977 collection *i must show you my clippings*, Veit-Wild notes Jensma's eclectic blending of poetry with photographs and wood cuts, his mixing and morphing of English, Afrikaans, and street slang, and the Dadaistic play with and on words, letters, and graphic patterns. Veit-Wild then quotes the following 'anaphoric incantation':

> yes, open the sluices, suck me into the crowd!
> it's long been time – time's long overdue
> i jensma, i have come to blow all that boodle
> i jensma, i the incarnate of vincent van gogh
> i jensma, i am also a socalled real artist.
> (*Festivals of Laughter* p. 71)

What is interesting here is Jensma's desire to be sucked into a human mass and, at the same time, his self-appointed messianism. The dialectic that could mediate these spheres is shattered. The shattering is telling not only because it signals the desire, in Veit-Wild's words, to 'explode the shell of white-dominated South Africa' (ibid.), but because it declares a self-willed agency at the same time as it challenges and expresses an anxiety regarding the reality of this agency. The pronominal and percussive 'i jensma, i' undermines the reified self and releases the self's openness and fluidity. Self-possession, for Jensma, becomes an action rather than a given, and biography a fraught tale which, through repetition – through negotiation – is eerily withered and rendered excessive. The syncretic, here, implies both the figuration and abolition of the self as an integrated identity formation. For Jensma any new subject position and consciousness presupposes the forfeiture of stability and the immanence of any negotiation. The self – in the most partial and constructed sense – is a sluice, a conduit, rather than a reified ideal. Refracted rather than whole, the self becomes the syncretic locus in and through which the world is not perceived at a manageable distance but challenged in the immanent moment of perception in which the very meanings and representations that make up the self and the world are revealed as ceaselessly fraught signs.

That Jensma is writing in 1977, under apartheid, is remarkable. Contrary to Sheila Roberts's interpretation, which appears on the back blurb to *i must show you my clippings*, I do not perceive Jensma as 'the first wholly integrated South African' but as a historically charged marker which defers both to a prior – persistent – syncretic dis-articulation and to a radical late-modern variant of it. By pointing to both the past and the present, Jensma ruptures a causal logic, embodied in Roberts's formulation, which supposes a cultural advance and transformation. Jensma's syncretic logic is non-teleological and non-retrogressive. It figures the radical syncretic moment as both continuous and untimely, or, in Bhabha's sense, as narrative negotiation *and* rapture. In shattering the illusion of progressivity and integration, Jensma intensifies an awareness of the dis-articulation and radical heterogeneity of the continuous present moment, a moment that has relentlessly been repressed in favour of a belief in change as a conditional and consecutive movement.

I have already pointed out the loss inherent in this causal conceptualisation of change. Now I wish to point to yet another emergent danger in contemporary South Africa: the danger attendant upon the emergent culture of the self in cultural expression. Having largely given up the ghost of resistance, contemporary cultural expression has elected to focus on autobiography as the locus of expression. In 'Talkin' Loud', a *Mail & Guardian* article on the emergent self in dub poetry, Matthew Krouse concludes: 'Love is in, politics is out. These days struggle poetry entails the struggle for the individual to be heard' (Talkin' Loud p. 1). While I would endorse the emergence of the expressive self, I would also draw the reader's attention to the implications behind the increasingly private and privatised nature of this expression. If this emergence can be perceived as an advance in cultural expression, it can also be perceived as a regression. Perceived negatively, the self sustains the integrity of its agency. Perceived positively, the self de-territorialises every posture of coherence and stability. While both perceptions conceive the self as constructed and syncretic, the former remains the errant and bastard progeny of a Manichean system of constraints and divisions while the latter confounds every attempt to integrate, stabilise or essentialise the self at the expense of the other. Here one should be wary of all reactively syncretic valorisations of the self. I would argue that it is the radically syncretic construction of identity, evident in the poetry of Jensma, which best qualifies and liberates the self's refracted agency. Today it is not a matter of love being 'in' and politics being 'out'. What matters is the reflexive merger, displacement, and transformation of these purportedly separate modalities of being.

Veit-Wild cites Hans Arp as a key influence in Jensma's work. Here one should also note the influence of the Dadaist Tristan Tzara. In a review entitled 'Dada', Tzara proclaims 'Pure Idiocy' and pronounces that intelligent man has become an absolutely normal type. The thing that we are short of, the thing that is interesting now, the thing that is rare because it possesses the anomalies of precious being, the freshness and the freedom of the great anti-man, that thing is the *Idiotic* (*Surrealist Art* p. 30).

Tzara's view complements Bhabha's conception of transformative culture as 'something new and unrecognizable'. Of particular value to the rethinking of culture's agency is Tzara's critique of the normalisation of the intelligent man. In South Africa it is precisely this normalisation, which legitimates the fetish of the self and inures the thinker to radical change, that has assumed a stranglehold over the value and purpose of culture.

Founded on a manufactured unity in difference, or sameness, South African culture has failed to shift beyond its persistently reactive conception of itself as an echo or mirror of a received or projected reality. The problem of course is that the conception of South African reality has, certainly since the mid 1990s, become increasingly more refracted and partial, which is why the Manichean system – still operative in the utopian synthesis of difference – has become all the more difficult to sustain. Today culture is forced to realign itself to the varied powers that define the needs of its interest groups and the individuals that form these groups. The problematic source of this refraction and localisation of interests – along with the ventriloquistic role of culture therein – is democratisation. My insistent view is that while democratisation may appear to have accentuated the possible, it has not in fact shifted the possible towards innovation and transformation, but rather deafened every radically human and aesthetic plea. Hence Tzara's seemingly absurd call for the 'idiotic'. Tzara is not alone in making this plea. Seemingly sober and authoritative thinkers such as J. M. Coetzee and Michel Foucault have also sought to affirm the chastening value of stupidity. Coetzee, in *Life & Times of Michael K*, speaks of an 'idiot light', while Tzara foregrounds 'the anomalies of precious being, the freshness and freedom of the great anti-man'.

Dadaism was no schoolboy prank. On the contrary, along with the best in surrealism, it was defined by an urgent bid to institute a transvaluation of values. If, in the context of South Africa's recent past, Wopko Jensma is perceived as an exemplary syncretic artist and radical who sought inspiration in the incantatory, anaphoric, and strange, he is by no means the last. If, in Tzara's words, Jensma is the 'anti-man', it is because he has challenged the authorised script of what it means to be human in South Africa. A precursor and a looped echo, Jensma captures the aggression and distress that prevails today. In 'Blue 2', which appears in a collection sickeningly entitled *Sing For Our Execution*, we read:

!batter a fences down

enter, i coshed'm down
cup ma head in ya bloodbeat

!fence ya aint no more

baby-black ya eyes a croon
i eat ya, a lashy streak

?fence dont shadow me

aint we nobody's business?
nobody knows da trouble i see

?fence ya aint killin me

days's a down'n out, yea
zombies coon my creoltown

!fence buzz off in a blue

aint ya business, daddy-o?
ya aint foolin me no more

!batter a fences down (p. 7)

If Coetzee's Michael K is the mute allegorised figure of freedom who vaults the prison that would contain him (*Life & Times of Michael K* p. 228), then Jensma is the vocal Nietzschean inmate who refuses to be destroyed by that which seeks to kill him. Caught between the exclamation and the question mark – marks of rage and doubt – 'Blue 2' dramatises the ongoing struggle to shatter the fences that separate people, cathects the individual, and nullifies the quest for a radically syncretic humanity. If one were to still oneself, place the heart in the ear and listen closely, the psychic distress that the poem dramatises would become all the more achingly apparent. What interests me here, however, is the syncretic echoing of a suppressed tongue.

Syntactically, 'Blue 2' conjures the rhythms of the blues. Moreover, the poem anticipates the argot of rap and the rhythms of dub that prevail today. Therefore, while Jensma reveals a debt to the spirit of Dada, he also reveals a potent commitment to a struggle, the psychic, anaphoric, and linguistically expressive root of which also resides in Africa. It is vital to note that I am in no way claiming that Jensma is the son of Negritude, that is, the proponent of a romantically infused return to an originary spirit and tongue. Rather, Jensma's poetry incarnates the syncretic ideal, an ideal shot through with conflicting epistemic and linguistic drives. In the best sense, his poetry embodies a conscious hybridisation of expression. Here a perception by Gilles Deleuze – that Kafka stole the German language from its crib – aptly serves my own perception of the agency that defines the poetic expression of Jensma. Like Kafka, Jensma invokes a disarticulation of the ruling tongue. By rendering expression strange – by framing expression between an exclamation and a question mark – Jensma cancels all sobriety and reaffirms the gravity of his theme and the resistance that is the conditional pretext and ground for its expression.

In contemporary South Africa Jensma's syncretic voice – largely disregarded – lives on. Its most prominent current avatar is Lesego Rampolokeng. Conscious of the transitional period in history in which he lives, a period he largely perceives as a betrayal of the fight for freedom, Rampolokeng has hurled himself into the gaps that others would close and, therein, forged a poetry that uncovers the lies and the hypocrisy that shape South Africa's cultural imaginary.

Long before Sachs's critique of the propagandistic deployment of resistance culture, Rampolokeng challenged a prescriptive vision of culture which, in retrospect, has not only failed to bear fruitage but, tragically, has revealed itself to be nothing more than a genuflection bereft of substance. Dismissive of the nationalist cause, wary of the 'struggle bonus', Rampolokeng has located his vision between and against the dogma of nationalism and its co-conspirator against freedom, international capital. In *Horns for Hondo* he writes:

> my struggle is international
> the radar of my conscience is universal . . .
>
> my fire is unfanned by race
> nor does race hasten my marching pace
> there's nothing black about my action
> for no fog clouds my vision (p. 21)

If Rampolokeng locates his struggle in an international arena, this does not mean that he has lost track of the urgency for change in his native land. Rather, he embarks by refuting all claimants upon his being. Race is not a calling card. The struggle presupposes no bonus. Rampolokeng acutely reaffirms the unresolved and unabated freedom to translate identity 'in a discontinuous intertextual temporality of cultural difference' (*Festivals of Laughter* p. 28). In the context of an appraisal of the writing of Rampolokeng, Bhabha's formulation all the more succinctly describes what I have called a radical syncretism. There, any attempt at closure presupposes a normalisation of an inherently abnormal condition. For Rampolokeng this normalisation, which inures and numbs the truth, is a 'fog' which, like Jensma, he seeks to clear.

In *End Beginnings*, raps 31 and 41, Rampolokeng describes himself as a self-styled 'doctor of rap', 'a surgeon come to operate' (p. 33), who works to expose the diseased core of South Africa's body politic and cultural imaginary. By challenging the calling card of race, by implicating the ANC in the hypocritical and dehumanising deployment of it, by exposing the 'black on black / black attacks' (p. 101), Rampolokeng points to the stunted and deformed nature of the societal and cultural imaginary he challenges and seeks to alter. Ruthlessly critical of the prurience and sentiment that masquerades as concern, Rampolokeng ushers forth a poetic vision that not only indicts the perpetrators of a simulacral consciousness but, like Jensma, trumps and surpasses this indictment with a battery of exclamations and questions.

Syncretism is not a system of answers but a radical form of sophistry, an unabated crossfire of unresolved contradictions. Its purpose is to awaken the dead, and expose abnormality at the root of the seemingly normal. Radical syncretism acknowledges no *a priori* truth, neither does it post its own truth as the answer. Immanent and interstitial, it is an aesthetic and epistemological strategy that, in challenging authorised beliefs and practices, serves to further destabilise public doxa and received authority. The weapons at Rampolokeng's disposal include a hybridised deployment of language and music. Its strength lies largely in its performative power. A litany of injunctions and contestations, Rampolokeng's poetry avows no centre. Rather, in the words of Tony Morphet, it is a poetry that is 'translocative', a poetry 'that crosses the lines of the multiple discourses that are constructing the cultural nodes and spaces of the society' (Cultural Imagination p. 143).

Refracted and vehicular rather than enclosed and sedentary, Rampolokeng's language mirrors the disparate and conflicted interests of a society that remains terribly fractured and inherently unnameable. Like the dervish's trappings, his language is shredded and patched, at best a corrupted and differential intertext. The simulacral strategies of transparency and verisimilitude were never Rampolokeng's objective. His poetry serves not to mirror societal fantasy but to further exacerbate and till its existent ills. One could, if one chose, dismiss its impact as merely pathologically reactive. Rampolokeng is well aware of the conscriptive and nullifying attempts of those who choose to absorb the translocative and evasive contradiction he poses. This contradiction is reinforced in 'Sebokeng Siege', which appears in *Talking Rain*:

> when i'm rapmaster supreme
> war-bomber in the extreme
> i'm called subversive
> when i'm only creative
> i write to fight
> to make a dark light bright
> they say i'm kinky
> when i'm only inky (p. 33)

Here the highly charged reflexivity vital to a radical syncretism is revealed. Rampolokeng emerges not only as the sophist who is able to absorb and contradict every interpellation, but also as a thinker/poet/radical/eccentric. He reveals himself as someone who is able to ridicule and deactivate the very interpellative system that would fix him. Like Dambudzo Marechera, with whom Rampolokeng has found the greatest affinity, he has sought 'to fight the rules set by old men'. The 'liberation' he calls for is a 'liberation [. . .] from anything that oppresses the imagination' (*Festivals of Laughter* p. 32). Marechera himself has stated:

> From early in my life I have viewed literature as a unique universe that has no internal divisions. I do not pigeonhole it by race or language or nation . . . There is a healthy interchange of technique and themes. That Europe had, to say the least, a head start in written literature is an advantage for the African writer: he does not have to solve many problems of structure – they have already been solved. I do not consider influences pernicious (p. 35).

Here Marechera describes the non-doctrinaire rationale that moves a radical syncretism; we find an imputation that echoes Bhabha's notion of a 'discontinuous intertextual temporality of cultural difference'. Here culture is not the property of nations. If

Marechera credits Europe with the burden of having solved narratological and structural problems that he need no longer address, it is because the very problems attendant upon these solutions have become the departure point of his own inquiry.

In his telling critique of the so-called perniciousness of influence, Marechera promotes his own syncretic vision of the intertextual agency of literature. Rampolokeng – after Jensma, after Marechera – has embarked on his own de-territorialisation of linguistic and canonical authority. His objective is not merely to play havoc with the public address system, but, in foregrounding the materiality of discourse, in projecting its pliability, Rampolokeng attempts to invoke a disarticulation of every system of order, be it linguistic, moral, or aesthetic. If he is the rap surgeon come to operate, then it is an operation that aims to liberate cultural expression from its unthinking somnambulism. South African society, as I have suggested, is in a deep and profoundly damaging sleep. Rampolokeng's worst fear is that South Africa may never awaken.

I began this chapter with the cryptic title 'The Navigating Harlequin'. Its source is the most reviewed work in English literature: Joseph Conrad's *Heart of Darkness*. Therein we read:

> His aspect reminded me of something I had seen – something funny I had seen somewhere. . . . Suddenly I got it. He looked like a harlequin. His clothes had been made of some stuff that was brown holland probably, but it was covered with patches all over, with bright patches, blue, red, and yellow, – patches on the back, patches on the front, patches on elbows, on knees; coloured binding around his jacket, scarlet edging at the bottom of his trousers; and in the sunshine made him look extremely gay and wonderfully neat withal, because you could see how beautifully all this patching had been done. A beardless, boyish face . . . [an] open countenance like sunshine and shadow on a wide-swept plain. (p. 122)

This apparition that greets the narrator, Marlow, inspires wonder in the midst of a dark and treacherous journey. It is an apparition that, after Rampolokeng, is curiously 'kinky'. Unlike Chatwin's shredded dervish, the harlequin is strikingly neat, the embodiment of a deliberate syncretic order in the midst of chaos. To this motley and syncretic creature Marlow gifts *An Inquiry into some Points of Seamanship*. It is this gesture that this chapter has sought to re-enact. If we too are caught in a darkness that masquerades as light, then we too need a book on navigation that could point the way forward. If the harlequin is the recipient and our guide, then this harlequin, this guide, is the radically syncretic artist. The book may not prove useful. The syncretic artist may possess no final answer. Yet in a time of distress the radical syncretic artist at least is there to re-route the lost: 'make a dark light bright'.

FIVE

A Life Less Ordinary: The Prosaic, the Sublime and the Queer

It is useful to exaggerate when dealing with emergencies.
— *Friedrich Wilhelm Nietzsche*

If the emergency is South Africa under apartheid, then the exaggeration required will suppose a counter force. But if that counter force merely mirrors the emergency it resists, if the very act of resistance – the fight *against* – chooses an enemy for an ally, and in so doing reveals itself as a strangely collusive act, then that which becomes all the more necessary is the creation of a third term of engagement, a third space that is irreducible to polarisation and collusion. Anthony Appiah arrives at this conclusion when, speaking of Yambo Ouologuem's novel *Le Devoir de Violence* (1968) he notes that the novel resists the conventions of realism because these conventions legitimate the nation. Rather, as Degenaar reports, Ouologuem's purpose is to deligitimate nationalism: to 'reject not only the Western *imperium*, but also the nationalist project of the postcolonial national bourgeoisie' ('How Texts and their Reception will Change' p. 13).

One exaggerates, then, to challenge a naturalised contradiction. In South Africa, a society also caught between a Western *imperium* and a postcolonial national bourgeoisie, one finds an equivalent need for exaggeration. That this exaggeration emerges in the 1980s under the innocuous sign of the 'ordinary' reveals all the more acutely the extent to which the seemingly inconsequential and the everyday was struck from the list of concerns which characterised the resistance movement.

The key proponent and celebrant of the ordinary within South Africa is Njabulo Ndebele, an activist who straddled the contradiction between the *imperium* and the postcolonial nationalist movement. Ndebele's fiction, *Fools*, similarly expresses a wariness regarding the edicts of naturalism and realism, while the role of the ordinary within his critical writing seeks to develop a psychic and epistemic alternative to the binary of oppression and resistance that characterised the struggle. My view is that Ndebele's motivation for and celebration of the ordinary formed a crucial attempt to reappraise the moment of change. That Ndebele ultimately failed to sustain the radical agency resident within the ordinary is another matter. What remains indisputable is that he issues forth a third term, or third space, the critical relevance of which has by no means diminished.

In the words of Graham Pechey, Ndebele's valorisation of the ordinary is one that calls for

> a post-heroic culture of irony, the local, the ordinary: that is to say, a culture, or a literature, preoccupied not with the polar conflicts of 'the people' versus 'the state' but with textures of life which have eluded that epic battle and have grown insouciantly in the cracks of the structures that South Africa's fraught modernity has historically thrown up (The Post-apartheid Sublime p. 57).

Pechey's assessment is notable for the stress it places on the 'textures of life' which, in bypassing the tough binaries and absolute contests, illuminate the 'cracks' that traverse and complicate South Africa's 'fraught modernity'.

The ordinary emerges as a third or supplementary term of critical engagement and perception. The vantage point from which the ordinary speaks its truth may add to the existing debate regarding resistance and change, but as a supplementary logic it does not add up. Kelwyn Sole notes in the unpublished version of his essay 'The Witness of Poetry: Economic Calculation, Civil Society and the Limits of Everyday Experience in a Liberated South Africa' that the ordinary or everyday 'exhibits its referential instability and indeterminacy'. Sole furthers this view by deferring to Lefebvre's 'insistence on the ambiguous, interstitial, dialectical existence of the "everyday" as "leisure and work and private life" coupled with moments "lived" *outside* of culture' (my emphasis).

The upshot of course is that the 'ordinary' as a descriptor or trope is as patently resistant to instrumental intellection as it is to being harnessed to a head-on and prescriptive system of resistance. Indeed, one could argue that the ordinary *resists* resistance, but then in the charged context of apartheid South Africa no act, no matter how seemingly passive or uninvolved, could be conceived as thriving beyond a society founded on conflict and racial strife. As a supplement then, the ordinary remains a political gesture. The question, though, remains: what constitutes a politics of the ordinary?

Ndebele conceived his resistant critical discourse as a politics of the ordinary. The question I will address is to what extent Ndebele successfully sustains his politics of the ordinary as a third space, as a way out of the reductive and collusive impasse defined by action and reaction. That the term emerges in South African critical discourse in the mid-80s – within the very eye of the storm as it were – affirms its indissoluble linkage to an existent resistance culture. But how is the term positioned? I would suggest: apodictically.

Harnessed to a call to freedom, and placed in the service of an imagined civil society, the discourse of the ordinary both pointedly and subtly calls for what Ndebele terms a 'need for governability (of the townships) . . . *rooted in the experience of the people themselves*' (*South African Literature and Culture* p. 108). This formulation – the striking inverse of that which sought to make the townships ungovernable – anticipates the hour when South Africa, as a civil society, becomes normalised. That this hour remains a deferred one does not diminish the desire that drives Ndebele's call to the ordinary.

As a trope for normality the ordinary cannot be satisfactorily understood solely as the counterweight to violence and discord. In keeping with a supplementary logic the ordinary emerges as that which is neither a call to arms nor a call for accord. Instead, as I understand it, the ordinary marks a call to *stillness*, a call for a time beyond a state of siege and unquenched longing, a time outside the riven and churning world. The rediscovery of this time – which, after Benjamin and Bakhtin, I would also describe as a time outside of time: a non-time, or a 'time of the now' – is one that still awaits us.

There is no disputing the increased global preoccupation with the resuscitation or, more pointedly, the recovery of the redemptive moment of the ordinary. For Lefebvre, the time of the ordinary is that which is 'lived' outside of culture. Sole notes that for Felski, it is the figuration of 'broken patterns, non-rational and duplicitous actions, irresolvable conflicts and unpredictable events' (The Witness of Poetry). For Langbauer, who does not conceive the ordinary as a temporal but as an ontological and spacial descriptor, the ordinary is 'the purloined letter': that which is as hidden as it is obvious to see (ibid.). For Lefebvre, the ordinary or everyday elicits a response to the precise degree that it confounds it, because in seeking to make

> the invisible visible, by giving form and content to an experience so vague and *seemingly* natural that part of its significance is that its subjects cannot define it, by defining, or theorizing, the everyday, it is transformed into what it is not . . . (ibid., my emphasis).

Consequently, the ordinary is far *less* ordinary than it would appear, for, as Sole reminds us, the ordinary 'allows us to de-familiarise that which seems fixed and natural in the lives we lead' (ibid.), or, more precisely, the ordinary *resists* the very allowance we assume as a right of perception. The ordinary is not so much perceived as it is that which perception, in the stilled instant, uncovers in spite of itself. This illuminated unfamiliar/familiar moment occurs in the place *between* perception and its putative object. This is the moment – the moment between – which distinguishes the photography of Zwelethu Mthethwa. It is the moment, after Pechey, which signals 'the textures of life which have eluded that epic battle and have grown insouciantly in the cracks of the structures that South Africa's fraught modernity has historically thrown up' (The Post-apartheid Sublime p. 57).

Pechey's summation of the ordinary is highly suggestive. Not only does he allude to Ndebele's valorisation of the local and the everyday in South African cultural practice, he also complicates and thereby develops the claim that the valorisation of the ordinary is a peculiarly local concern. In so doing, Pechey invokes the engagements of De Certeau, Lefebvre and others and figures the rediscovery of the ordinary as a distinctly transnational and minoritarian enterprise. This more inclusive critical vision is implicit in the phrase: 'South Africa's fraught modernity'.

What is it that renders South Africa's modernity fraught? The answer lies in the fact that South Africa cannot conceive of its fate solely within the paradigmatic boundaries of the nation-state, for at every turn its identity is informed and compromised by the continued impact of the *imperium*. The ordinary anticipates this impact to the precise degree to which its resists being co-opted by the counter-hegemonies of empire *and* nationalism. That which therefore gives Ndebele's and Pechey's projects their force is the knowledge that the ordinary and the everyday is a localised and transnational cultural (and non-cultural) concern. The valorisation of the ordinary supposes a post-imperial and post-national logic, a logic which, against these competing and collusive powers, calls for a civil society.

Nevertheless, it is precisely this conception of the ordinary as that which promotes a civil imaginary that has failed to take hold in South Africa. President Thabo Mbeki's State of the Nation Address in 1999 reveals the precise degree to which the country, as Ari Sitas notes, 'drift[s] into a cruel logic of [a] global power-downsize' (Witness of Poetry), a logic which marginalises the needs of the urban and rural poor. Instead of 'encouraging pro-people and pro-poor development', what happens is the betrayal of the ordinary and everyday in the name of market freedom. As Sole's reading of Mbeki's 1999 Address makes blisteringly clear,

> South Africa was in a 'better position than ever before' to face the challenges of mass unemployment and social poverty because South Africa had become 'one of the most attractive emerging markets' through proposed implementation of policies embracing public-private sector partnerships, privatisation of State assets, and the planned implementation of more 'flexible' labour laws to assist the private sector to become 'the rudder of the economy' (Witness of Poetry).

Clearly, the ordinary is destined to have no place, whether in a resistance culture founded on ungovernability or a post-resistance culture founded on the governability of the state and market forces. Hence my conception of the ordinary as a third space or a time of the now that is unrecorded, unheeded, and uncared for. It is this time – at once present and a present absence – which is the focus of this inquiry. I differ from Sitas in that this inquiry into the time of the ordinary is not shaped by the concerns of the disenfranchised, though undoubtedly this loss remains integral and profoundly relevant. Rather, my more *conceptual* address is concerned with the epistemic and psychic veracity of the ordinary as a trope in and through which to institute a redemptive and revisionary ethic. In this regard Ndebele's position straddles my own and that of Sitas. Crudely, it is a position that negotiates the sublime and the prosaic, categories that make for uneasy bedfellows.

To all intents and purposes, Ndebele appears wholly fixated upon the interstitial or hybrid moment within South African culture, in particular its writing. And yet, on closer examination, one sees a set of epistemological influences which impact upon Ndebele's thinking and which are not peculiarly seeded here. If 'local is *lekker*', this by no means presupposes that the local is peculiarly and distinctly South African. Indeed, the very basis of Ndebele's thought is, necessarily, split. As Stefan Helgesson notes in *Sports of Culture: Writing the Resistant Subject in South Africa (Readings of Ndebele, Gordimer, Coetzee)*:

The subaltern subject is shown to occupy a split position between the attempt to redeem an 'African' identity condemned by the Manichean logic of colonial orthodoxy, and the desire and necessity to partake in the 'civilizing project' with its seemingly universal promise of betterment (p. 39).

In attempting to relate these complicit yet incommensurable objectives, we will see that Ndebele is caught in an epistemological deadlock which, as Pechey and Helgesson note, is appeased in his fiction, but which remains intractable in his critical discourse. For the purposes of this chapter, it is the problems resident in Ndebele's critical writing that assume centre stage, in particular the epistemological cogency and viability of his critical trope: the ordinary. For though I may concur that under the sign of the ordinary Ndebele has effected a crucial psychic and epistemic breakthrough, I am also well aware of resistance of this sign to its absorption within Ndebele's theoretical project.

Daphne Read's assessment of the ordinary is seemingly persuasive when she states that, for Ndebele, 'the ordinary is . . . less a rigorous theoretical category than a politically strategic metaphor for the cultural work to be done in building a democratic culture' (Witness of Poetry). Here a nagging doubt prevails: how to conceive the ordinary, which for Lefebvre is always in danger of being 'transformed into what it is not', as something – a concept or ideal – that could further a social and political project? Surely when conceived as 'the invisible visible' the term resists intellection to the precise degree that it resists instrumentality? Sole anticipates this question:

> there is an interstitial, non-institutionalised element of human experience and activity which the purview of 'civil society' cannot encompass; an element that the term 'the everyday' gestures towards more adequately (Witness of Poetry).

For Sole the adequacy of the term belies its very resistance to instrumental and ideational co-option. Therefore, if the term can be said to have an adequacy, then this adequacy must be measured against the realisation that the ordinary or everyday cannot be wholly absorbed and made to speak its truth on behalf of social change. To do so would be to defeat the non-collusive and non-aligned nature of the ordinary. If it fails as a theoretical category, it also fails as a politically strategic metaphor. This failure is also its greatest strength.

This rather austere reading of the agency of the ordinary – one which acknowledges its ceaseless problematisation and deconstruction – is not, however, what distinguishes Ndebele's use of the term. For Ndebele the term's viability is directly linked to an agenda that, as Sole notes, concerns 'the transformation of blacks into the subjects of their own initiatives' (Witness of Poetry). Moreover, Sole adds:

> [Ndebele's] dislike of 'State management culture', his discernment of the 'soul-wrecking' environments in which many blacks still live, his uneasiness with the dictates of the 'rules of the market place', his realisation of the problems limited resources throw up in achieving the goals of reconstruction, his insistence that 'the limits of democratic participation' should be extended in all spheres in the construction of a new society and that pre-liberation 'alternative' grassroots

organisations are possible contributors to this, all demonstrate a strongly democratic impulse in his thought (ibid.).

It is for all of the above reasons that Ndebele's conception of the ordinary has for well near two decades provided a fertile ground for rethinking South Africa's cultural predicament. However, it is also for all these reasons that Ndebele's conception of the ordinary has come to stand for what I perceive as an epistemic and psychic limit, a limit which Sole signals as a 'defining humanism' (ibid.).

What distinguishes Ndebele's humanism is his reasonable and wholly justifiable desire to transform the oppressed 'into the subjects of their own initiatives' (ibid.). Therein and thereby Ndebele locates the inhumanity that fuels his humanism. However, my insistent demurral, after Lefebvre, concerns whether or not the ordinary can be satisfactorily assigned to this project. How to 'giv[e] form and content to an experience so vague and seemingly natural that part of its significance is that its subjects cannot define it'? (ibid.).

Contra Lefebvre, Ndebele goes on precisely to give form and content to the ordinary. In *South African Literature and Culture* we read:

> . . . the ordinary day-to-day lives of people should be the direct focus of political interest because they constitute the *very content* of the struggle, for the struggle involves people not abstractions. If it is a new society we seek to bring about in South Africa then that newness will be based on a direct concern with the way people actually live. That means a range of complex issues involving man-man, man-woman, woman-woman, man-nature, man-society relationships . . . It will be the task of literature to provide an occasion within which vistas of inner capacity are opened up (p. 57).

If Ndebele is un-enamoured with the reflexive exigencies of theory, he is as un-enamoured with the putative impenetrability of the ordinary. Entering where angels fear to tread Ndebele, in a series of compelling though deeply contradictory and problematic essays, compounds the conundrum that Lefebvre addresses. In no uncertain terms, Ndebele conceives the daily lives of the oppressed as the moral 'content' of struggle. Here a 'new society' is invoked. Yet how to conceive the new when its content is not? For if the struggle serves the people, and if the people are by no means 'new' but defined by needs and beliefs as vague as they are immemorial, then how to harness the two? One does so precisely at the expense of the ordinary; one does so, rather, in the name of the society of the spectacle.

In other words, though it appears to be the ordinary that Ndebele is championing, it is rather his collusive relation to that which he would negate – the spectacle – that is the abiding theme of his thought. If Ndebele fails to address the ordinary – the invisible visible – it is because his project of resistance – putatively written in the name of the ordinary – is all the more concerned with the spectacular – the all too visible. Ndebele makes his enemy his ally, and does so at the expense of a suppressed knowledge that the ordinary *resists* any vaunted project of 'rediscovery'.

After Lefebvre, then, what is one to make of the ordinary, or rather, how can one think that which cannot be made subject to thought? Lefebvre's riddle is echoed in Michel de Certeau's *Practice of Everyday Life* and Gilles Deleuze and Felix Guattari's anti-systemic and minoritarian theorisation of emergent cultures. Lokangaka Losambe picks up on this radical agency, which he reads in and through Ndebele's fiction. As Helgesson notes, Losambe draws on Deleuze and Guattari's distinction between the 'arborescent' – the rootedness and firmness of cultural identity – and the 'rhizomatic' – the on-going horizontal connections *between* the social, political and material. Unfortunately Losambe advances nothing more than a gloss. Moreover, he posits the harmonious coexistence of terms which, for Deleuze and Guattari, are irreconcilable (*Sports of Culture* p. 37). The salient point here is not Losambe's problematic conclusion but his initial insight: that resident in Ndebele's fiction, and latent within his critical writing, is the source of a divergent view of cultural practice and expression. This source, though, is not finally nurtured but suppressed in Ndebele's critical writing. It is the drama inherent in this suppression, and its effect on the fate of critical discourse in South Africa, that is the theme of this chapter.

Ndebele both opens and closes the door to a critical insight. What remains to be asked is why? For a critic as insightful as Ndebele to have elected to shut down the radical agency in his own thought surely means that the figure of the subaltern which he sought to liberate remains trapped within and between the dual inheritance of the colonial orthodoxy (the *imperium*) and the civilising project (nationhood) that forms the basis of Ndebele's thought. Ndebele stands at the threshold of the past and the future.

In hindsight of course it is all too easy to dismiss the fraught position that Ndebele, by virtue of his inheritance, necessarily represented. Today, given the ascendance of a transnational and post-imperial conceptualisation of culture, it is inhibiting, if not obstructive, to conceptualise Ndebele's valorisation of the ordinary and the everyday solely within the contradiction and continuum between the orthodoxy of colonialism and the emergent civilising project which, together, have fostered the new nation-state.

Consequently when I speak of 'South Africa', it must be remembered that other than as an indefinitely pronominal descriptor with its own – limited – rhetorical efficacy, the country is not conceived as a historically and geographically bounded and determined site. Rather, 'South Africa' serves as a drifting signifier – akin to Kentridge's conception of sonar – through and in which I hope to assess the epistemological basis for the conceptualisation of traces of an emergent – though beleaguered and repressed – consciousness. In other words: how and why do we think of who and what 'we' are? To what end does the claim to nationhood validate the contiguous and fraught nature of modernity as it is played out at the southernmost point of Africa? How do we think of cultural change both inside and outside the boundaries of the nation? Pechey implicitly raises these questions.

Like Ndebele, Pechey values the textures – the local, the detail, the interstitial. But unlike Deleuze and Guattari, neither Pechey nor Ndebele succeeds in thinking through his otherwise seductive and compelling claims. The flaw in their respective projects resides in the theoretical closures that dog their claims. Neither is able to translate his insights in a manner that is truly immanent for the simple reason that neither can conceive of a changing present – the time of the now – that transmutes the dogma of the past and the fiction of the future. In this sense both remain victims of their inheritance: Ndebele is governed by the civilising mission of humanism; Pechey – as we will see – falls prey to a metaphysical sentiment and conceit. Neither satisfactorily shifts the binary of the people and the state.

If Nedebele's putative project is the rediscovery of the ordinary, and Pechey's the rediscovery of the extra-ordinary (or sublime), there is also a third project and term – one that synthesises and displaces both the aforementioned projects – that I will explore under the descriptor *queer*. In the context of this chapter, this descriptor serves as a catalyst for challenging and refashioning attitudes both inside and outside the community that typically is defined by this nomination. If George E. Haggerty in *Gay Histories and Cultures* defines it as 'a watchword of today' (p. 723) this is because queer challenges the boundaries of the hetero-sexual/homosexual dichotomy and is, at the same time, representative of a move toward greater inclusiveness of all non-heterosexual persons and categories. In this manner, queerness precisely defounds the contraries of man-man, man-woman, woman-woman, by placing each pairing under erasure.

Nevertheless, it is not strictly within the domain of sexually defined identity formation that the term is relevant here. Rather, as Jagose notes, queer – like the ordinary – serves as an 'intellectual model' that 'exemplifies a more mediated relation to categories of identification' (Queer Theory p. 173). For Judith Butler, 'the term . . . emerges as an interpellation that raises the question of the status of force, of stability and variability, *within performativity*' (Critically Queer p. 168). As Donald Morton notes:

> Rather than as a local effect, the return of the queer has to be understood as the result . . . of the (post)modern encounter with – and rejection of – Enlightenment views concerning the role of the conceptual, rational, systematic, structural, normative, progressive, liberatory, [and] revolutionary . . . in social change (Queer Theory p. 173)

It is in this mediated sense that queer emerges in this chapter as a trope which serves as a provisional, contingent, and eccentric corrective to Ndebele's civilising mission and Pechey's more opaque transcendental mission.

While queer can potentially synthesise and illuminate the epistemological drives of Ndebele and Pechey, it more importantly destabilises the constitutive binary that founds their respective thought processes. A rhizomatic conception, queer best expresses the cracks and contradictions in contemporary conceptions of culture in South Africa, cracks and contradictions which Ndebele and Pechey at best allude to, at worst contain. So, while Ndebele's project is undoubtedly critical to a transgression of the absolute contests that have characterised South Africa's historical fate, it finally falls victim to the very determinism it would circumvent. This claim needs, of course, to be proven. The task of this chapter will be to illuminate Ndebele's critical strengths and to foreground the limits to his thinking. Pechey, Ndebele's editor and gentle detractor, offers a compelling inroad towards a re-fashioning of Ndebele's premise, an in-road that I re-fashion yet again. But first let us turn to Ndebele's essays in his collection *South African Literature and Culture: Rediscovery of the Ordinary* (1994). In the conclusion to 'Guilt and Atonement' we read:

> The past is knocking constantly on the doors of our perceptions, refusing to be forgotten, because it is deeply embedded in the present. To neglect it at this most crucial of moments in our history is to postpone the future (p. 158).

To those who have lived under apartheid and who are now making their way through South Africa's phantom democracy, Ndebele's conclusion is a truism. This truism occludes as much as it reveals. At best Ndebele's conclusion forces us to broach the question: to what extent have we in fact weaned ourselves from our brutal legacy? Ndebele's answer: barely, if at all. The past is 'embedded in the present'. The phrase is telling. We are immediately called upon to question the sequential mapping of time. At every turn causation is parasited. The 'past', the 'future', is more affect than fact. So while Ndebele wills a transitive conception of change, he well knows that transition cannot at any point circumvent the immanence of the 'present'. To conceive of change one must address the present. Here the present, as the time of the now, is yet another way of understanding the ordinary. My suggestion, then, would be to rethink the ordinary within the ever shifting present, a critical time which I have noted as strikingly absent within the conceptualisation of change in South Africa.

To reiterate: it is only by assessing change within the present – in which the past and the future are embedded – that South African society will re-imagine and re-image itself. This of course is more easily said than done, which is why the sum of change will never be the sum of words. At best words are affective injunctions, ciphers for what we are and what we must become. If we are bound by our past, then our words are bound too. To think then, to unleash the imagination, words must reflexively admit the intransitive at the core of all seemingly seamless and reflective/teleological addresses. This, I believe, is the pathos that must dog Ndebele's concluding statement to his essay 'Guilt and Atonement'.

Evident in the title, as in the closing statement, is the need for balance. What is occluded is the fact that there is no balance. The conjunction – *and* – does not merely wed a conflictual and transitional dynamic. Rather, as a figure of multiplication the conjunction destabilises and disfigures the dialogue between the opposing terms guilt/atonement. If Ndebele attempts to balance the past with the future, then this balancing act can also be understood as epistemically flawed, for the past and future, as affective temporal signatures, are not understood here as being mutually exclusive and easily weighted, but as incommensurable lodes embedded in an ever-shifting and abyssal present. The question however remains: What present? Whose present?

In his essay 'The Government of Freedom', in *Refashioning Futures: Criticism after Postcoloniality*, David Scott turns us to the dilemma of writing history *within* the present. He refers to Michel Foucault's now 'scarcely . . . controversial' notion that 'the investigation of the past ought to be connected to questions derived from the present' (p. 70). In a sense, this is what Ndebele means when he speaks of the past knocking on the doors of our perception. It is the past that is the visitant, the past that is the house guest. And where does the past reside? Its place – if it can be said to have a place – is *in* the present. This present is by no means natural or inevitable. Rather, the present according to Foucault and Scott is 'assembled contingently and heterogeneously'. It is a history of the present, then, which enables us 'to act – and act *differently* – upon it' (ibid.).

This notion, by now axiomatic, is at the heart of Ndebele's concluding summary. Though what Ndebele fails to admit into his formulation – an absence which Scott also cites in Foucault's historicisation of the present – is that any project of historical (or genealogical) investigation must admit that *in the moment of investigation alterations occur in the present* which, necessarily, compel us 'to alter the questions through which the past is made a resource for contemporary intellectual reflection' (p. 71). Scott rephrases this crucial insight:

> If . . . what we want the past to illuminate for us ought to be guided by the task of understanding the predicament in which we find ourselves, then as that predicament alters what we ask the past to yield up to us has also to alter. Surely the project of writing histories of the present, if they are not to be merely academic exercises, ought to hang on some such focus on a *changing present* (ibid.).

The salient issue is not the *neglect* of the past – which I consider impossible – but the institution of a perspectival appraisal of the impact of the past upon a changing present. If Ndebele appears anxious it is because within him a conscience tolls. This conscience, however, has no residence in the past. Rather, his conscience is expressed within a ceaselessly refracted and attenuated present.

In his seminal collection of essays, Ndebele fashions a vision for a changing country. As the subtitle to the book intimates, Ndebele's project is the 'rediscovery of the ordinary'. The subtitle is alluring and disarming. In a country shaped and marred by the contestation of absolutes, Ndebele's comparative whisper not only plumbs the depths of the everyday but, like many other practitioners in contemporary cultural studies, locates the vocation of meaning and change *within* the ordinary. While the essays are broadly concerned with matters pertaining to South Africa's fate, their focus is more or less restricted to the predicament of the country's culture. I will not go into what culture may or may not mean. Rather, in addressing Ndebele's project directly I will recover – or rediscover – what it is Ndebele forges, and why – given the moral and epistemic strictures which guide and define his discourse – he does not finally forge the critical reflexive turn that Scott regards as key to any history of the present, namely that any project of this nature must ceaselessly *alter the questions through which the past is made a resource for contemporary intellectual reflection.*

It may appear that I am being gratuitously punitive in faulting Ndebele on the basis of the moral and epistemic framework that guides his thought. My point however is that this framework is inherently limiting, even disfiguring, precisely because, while rhetorically persuasive, it does not satisfactorily capture the riddle of what it means to live and act in a changing present. The best approach is to see Ndebele's critical incursion as *a* perspective that is best approached through a critical-interpretive engagement with its project of rediscovery.

Ndebele's first incursion turns on the question of *writing*, in particular black writing. In 'Turkish Tales and some Thoughts on South African Writing', Ndebele notes:

> writing's probings into the South African experience has been largely superficial. This superficiality comes from the tendency to produce fiction that is built around the interaction of surface symbols of the South African reality (*South African Literature and Culture* p. 28).

Ndebele is responding to the reactive and polemical dimension in South African writing, to the absence of interiority, to glib characterisation, to forced dramatic closures. I will not belabour this point. I simply wish to point out the fact that Ndebele is reaching towards the defining humanistic tropes of classical social realism that he finds markedly absent in the fictive execution and telling of South Africa's story.

In 'The Rediscovery of the Ordinary: Some New Writings in South Africa', he approaches the problem more effectively and persuasively. Through an inspired deferral to Roland Barthes's essay on wrestling he draws attention to the 'emptying out of interiority to the benefit of its exterior signs, [the] exhaustion of the content by the form' (*South African Literature and Culture* p. 42). For Ndebele, this self-negating, emptying, or inverting of the processes of expression suppresses the psychic, emotive, and intellective depth of experience in South Africa. While he understands why this comes about – a society of the spectacle begets a fiction of the spectacle – he also promotes the alternative to what he perceives as the life-negating outcome of a society of the spectacle.

What, Ndebele asks, is the root of 'the quintessence of obscene social exhibitionism' in black writing? Why this 'spectacle of social absurdity'? By way of an answer to 'the problematic relationship between art and objective reality' he turns to T. T. Moyana, who writes: 'An additional difficulty for the creative artist in South Africa, especially the black writer, is that life itself is too fantastic to be outstripped by the creative imagination' (ibid.). Moyana's observation is echoed in J. M. Coetzee's 'Jerusalem Prize Acceptance Speech'. Therein Coetzee speaks of 'the *crudity* of life in South Africa, the naked force of its appeals, not only at the physical level but at the moral level too' (p. 99). Clearly, for Coetzee, this burden of crudity is not carried by black writing alone. Irrespective of race (class or gender) 'truth . . . overwhelms and swamps every act of the imagination' (ibid.).

While Moyana and Coetzee concur, what makes Coetzee's formulation the more compelling is that he realises that the crudity of life in South Africa, 'its callousness and its brutalities, its hungers and its rages, its greed and its lies, make it *as irresistible as it is unlovable*' (ibid., my emphasis). Here Coetzee uncovers a truth about what it means to live in South Africa that no redemptive vision of cultural change can easily circumvent. For Coetzee, perversity compels as much as it disgusts. This tug-o-war is the pathological root of cultural expression. Therefore any re-fashioning of our past, our present and our future must inhabit this truth before it can begin to negate it.

To what extent does Ndebele admit the pathological attraction to the very perversion that the writer would vault? And, given the seemingly intractable link between resistance and shame, self-disgust and longing, how does Ndebele access the ordinary? He begins by summarising the limit text of writing under the sign of the spectacular:

> The spectacular document . . . is demonstrative, preferring exteriority to interiority; it keeps the larger issues of society in our minds, obliterating the details; it provokes identification through recognition and feeling rather than through observation and analytical thought; it calls for emotion rather than conviction; it establishes a vast sense of presence without offering intimate knowledge; it confirms without necessarily offering a challenge. It is the literature of the powerless identifying the key factor responsible for their powerlessness. Nothing beyond this can be expected of it (p. 49).

While Ndebele acknowledges that this writing of the spectacle is inherently reactive and pathological, he does not – at any point – account for why it is irresistible, for if he were to do so he would not be as easily able to parse his own relation to South Africa's objective reality into a sequence of neat oppositions: exteriority/interiority; recognition and feeling/observation and analytical thought; emotion/conviction; a vast sense of presence/intimate knowledge. By focusing on Ndebele's favoured terms – interiority, observation and analytical thought, conviction, intimate knowledge – one discovers a paradox. Ndebele wants distance *and* intimacy. This fusion is not the same as Theodor Adorno's notion of distanced nearness.

Ndebele's favoured criterion is no different from that evinced in classical social realism in which the dialectic works to synthesise the relation of the individual to the society. One thinks of George Eliot's notion of character as an unfolding, and of Raymond Williams's notion of the knowable community, that is, of a conceptualisation of characterisation and narrative formation as an indissoluble mirroring of subjective and objective lived experience. Now while this call is understandable, is it in fact feasible within a society such as South Africa? Is it not, rather, Ndebele's humanism – his call for the ordinary in an extra-ordinary world – which is anomalous, given its willed refusal to accept a constitutive perversity – a characterlogical and narratological fragmentedness and excessiveness – as the root of who and what we are? Is Ndebele's call for a rediscovery of the ordinary not in fact an impossible and fantastical appeal rooted in a humanist valorisation of the individual in society, the individual here being both the one who authors the narrative and the agents characterised within the narrative?

What Ndebele finds abhorrent is that 'South Africa . . . is a public society . . . in the sense that its greatest aberrations are fully exhibited' (p. 55). But is this in fact so? If the aberrations are all too visible does this automatically mean these aberrations are transparent: mere surface symbols? I believe Ndebele forces this conclusion in order to forge his claim that the very public nature of South African society exhausts and conceals the myriad integuments of its being. Hence Ndebele's counterpointing of the opposing terms listed above.

As Coetzee has pointed out, the crudity of South African lived experience cannot be so easily parsed. It is insufficient to admit to a 'culture of oppression', Ndebele acknowledges. Culture, to be understood, demands on the part of the writer the provision of a 'compelling context to examine an infinite number of ethical issues which have a bearing on the sensitisation of people towards the development of the entire range of culture' (ibid.). Concluding 'The Rediscovery of the Ordinary', Ndebele affirms that the role of the writer is

> to confront the human tragedy together with the immense challenging responsibility to create a new society. This demands an uncompromisingly tough-minded creative will to build a new civilization. And no civilization worth the name will emerge without the payment of disciplined and rigorous attention to detail (p. 58).

Here again a paradox surfaces, for in the midst of a sovereign and panoptic call to institute a 'new civilization', Ndebele poses the rider that this will be achieved only if the detail – the micrological – is kept at the forefront of the writer's imagination. Again we find a humanist logic at work. Again this logic is modified by a penetrating focus upon that which is irreducible to the structuring of a binary or counter logic. Clearly, then, the uncovering of Ndebele's epistemological project is not as easy as it seems.

In 'Redefining Relevance' Ndebele acknowledges the epistemological limit which shapes South Africa's Manichean condition, 'an epistemology in which reality is conceived purely in terms of a total polarity of absolutes'. These terms are 'entirely understandable', says Ndebele. 'South African society is a highly polarised society. It is understandable that its constituent polarities should dominate the thinking of its citizens' (p. 60). Given this understanding, why is Ndebele reluctant to deepen his own call to change? Why is he unable to admit a radical perversity as a constituent element of any understanding of South African society?

The answer, I think, lies in Ndebele's inability to forego a *moral* response to the dilemma of South African society. For Ndebele it is 'transcendence' (p. 64) that matters, not immanence. While he wills the destruction of 'closed epistemological structures of South African oppression, structures which can severely compromise resistance by dominating thinking itself' (p. 67), the claim Ndebele makes is not matched by a critical discourse which, within its own performative drive, unleashes 'the social imagination' (ibid.). In other words, Ndebele's claim is just but its execution remains problematic. When he states that the creative process must free itself from the laws that bind them, that the perception of what can be written about must be extended to include the means and methods of writing, I wholly concur. Nevertheless, while his 'redemptive approach' admits the liminal and micrological, it does not in itself develop a new epistemological approach to writing and to the re-imaging and re-imagining of a society. Nedebele speaks from an authoritative margin that is generous in its spirit but punitive in its execution.

Here one should remember David Scott's proviso that any theoretical project of historical investigation should 'urge us to alter the questions through which the past is made a resource for contemporary intellectual reflection' (Government of Freedom p. 71). In questioning the epistemological basis of Ndebele's project, I do not merely aim to dismiss it but, more important, to show how the project must be reappraised within the predicament in which I find myself, a predicament which cannot accept Ndebele's founding premise, even and especially when my own seemingly concurs. In other words, Ndebele's resistance to the spectacular blinds him to the extraordinariness of the everyday. The either/or framework that moves his logic must, I believe, be replaced by both/and. If this is not achieved we will find ourselves in the trap which Ndebele knows he is caught, a trap from which he is unable – intellectually – to remove himself.

It is in this regard that the immanence of Homi Bhabha's logic goes a long way to furthering the very social imagination that Ndebele calls for. If Ndebele is ensnared within paradox, Bhabha wills and thrives therein. While Ndebele knows that writing cannot serve as a lesson, while he knows that solutions are not to be found in fiction, while he accepts literature at best to be a

> manifestation of the principle of contradiction . . . that everything involving human society is in a constant state of flux; that the dialectic between appearance and reality in the conduct of human affairs is always operative and constantly problematic, and that consequently, in the representation of human reality, nothing can be taken for granted (p. 69)

he does not move these realisations beyond the epistemological and structural limit of 'irony', a trope which to my mind limits more than it releases; for irony empowers rather than disinvests, mediates rather than disseminates. Irony is the trope of a sovereign intellect, albeit embattled, the province of the controlling – ambivalent – mind. While Ndebele may call for 'an open-handedness in the use of language, a search for originality of expression and a sensitivity to dialogue' (p. 73), surely he must know that this is not possible by means of irony which, elsewhere, he defines as 'self-critical awareness' (p. 78). Is he not therefore 'unconsciously prescribing [his] own containment?' (ibid.).

Ndebele's response to Sol Plaatje will serve as an index of the former's critical vision. What Ndebele values in Plaatje's language is

> the dialectic of ambiguity, of understatement, literary tradition, and subtle, highly suggestive allusion and [Ndebele vaguely adds] other similar things (p. 79).

As I have already pointed out, Ndebele's critical criterion owes much to the tradition of classical realism. There resistance is inferred, the call to change located within the very hegemonic system of power which Ndebele and Plaatje contest. As Plaatje notes in his introduction to *Native Life in South Africa*:

> Mine is but a sincere narrative of a melancholy situation, in which, with all its shortcomings, I have endeavoured to describe the difficulties of the South African Natives under a very strange law, so as most readily to be understood by the sympathetic reader (ibid.).

The economy of reception Plaatje sets up fulfils the implicit and seductive criteria which Ndebele values. Here we are far from the declamatory and vulgar economy of resistance culture that Ndebele abhors.

To what extent though, is Plaatje's strategy necessarily or inherently better? By way of a counterpoint, consider Bhabha's response to Charles Taylor. Taylor – like Ndebele and Plaatje – calls for the 'self in moral space' (*The Location of Culture* p. 213). This, as I have pointed out, is also axiomatic to classical realism. There the self, irrespective of the ambiguity which conditions it, serves to mediate and ultimately control the way the world is seen, received, and represented. Any anxiety must be tempered. Hence Plaatje's 'melancholy situation' demands a 'sympathetic reader'; a reader who is simultaneously distanced and intimately responsive. For Bhabha, however, the very civilisation inherent within this economy of reception is problematic.

Using Charles Taylor's *Sources of the Self* as his foil, Bhabha writes:

> Charles Taylor sets temporal limits to the problem of personhood: 'the supposition that I could be two temporally succeeding selves is either an over-dramatized image, or quite false. It runs against the structural features of a self as a being who exists in a space of concerns' (p. 214).

Bhabha then goes on to counter Taylor's view:

> Such 'over-dramatised' images are precisely my concern as I attempt to negotiate narratives where double-lives are led in the post-colonial world . . . These subjects of study require the experience *of anxiety to be incorporated into the analytic construction of the object of critical attention*: narratives of the borderline conditions of cultures and disciplines. For anxiety is the affective address of 'a world [that] reveals itself as caught up in the space between frames; a doubled frame or one that is split' (ibid., my emphasis).

Now it is precisely this anxiety, critical to the moment in which a changing – postcolonial – present is historicised that Ndebele acknowledges but will not admit into his critical schema. His very critique of the overly dramatic in black South African writing as a sign of the dissipation of narrative complexity implicitly suggests Ndebele's refusal to admit that the post-colonial subject is necessarily caught *between* the spectacular and the ordinary. The one aspect cannot be exchanged for the other, whether at a psychic level or at a level of narrative formation. In other words, the telling of the story of resistance in South Africa *demands* the very over-dramatisation or exaggeration that Ndebele sees as profoundly limiting and disfiguring.

While Ndebele calls for an open-handedness in narrative expression he also advocates a closure. Like Charles Taylor, Ndebele conceives of a 'self in moral space'. Unlike Bhabha – or David Scott – Ndebele cannot admit a constitutive disruption – a splitting of identity and narrative formation – as key to the 'analytic construction of the object of attention'. If, for Bhabha, 'it is radical perversity, not sage political wisdom, that drives the intriguing will to knowledge of postcolonial discourse' (p. 212), then for Ndebele it is the reverse. If Bhabha, like Coetzee, well knows that the crudity of a culture of oppression is as irresistible as it is unlovable, then Ndebele's stance is to call for a redemption founded within a social realist and humanist tradition which at no point must admit the perversity of the over-dramatic, the extra-moral, or spectacular. Rather, Ndebele diminishes the performative power of his thinking by opting for the 'inductive' position of the 'witness'.

In an essay with the telling opposition 'Actors and Interpreters: Popular Culture and Progressive Formalism', Ndebele notes that Plaatje's great contribution to a South African culture of resistance has been as a 'methodical observer and interpreter', that is, the observer and interpreter within a moral space. The question here is whether Ndebele's reading of the perspective, location and agency of Plaatje's writing is correct. What does Plaatje mean when he defines his situation as 'melancholy'? Does this not imply that his subaltern position is disturbed, if not fraught? Why else would he seductively call for the 'sympathetic reader'? Is this not again an indication of a constitutive unease which founds any representation of resistance? And what are we to make of Plaatje's telling description of the 'difficulties' of the South African Natives under 'a very strange law'? Does Plaatje not suggest here that the means of grasping the workings of this strange law necessarily calls for an interpretive project which needs a self-reflexive logic founded on de-familiarisation – the distancing and rendering strange of the seemingly familiar? In that, surely, the surface reality that Ndebele all too easily diminishes is more complex than it initially appears? Is Ndebele not being overly simplistic when he distinguishes surface from depth, the visible symbol from the inner integuments of being? And, if so, then why does Ndebele insist upon the distinction? Surely a more productive approach would be to focus on what Bhabha calls 'the borderline conditions of cultures and disciplines'?

As Ndebele states:

> In order to prevent perpetual random social experimentation, every society will reach a stage where it has to consolidate the existing accumulated social knowledge and, at the same time, create groups whose task it is to observe and experiment under more controlled, more disciplined conditions' (*South African Literature and Culture* p. 84).

Not only is this position reactionary, it is also false. Unlike the positions held by Albie Sachs and Václav Havel, we find Ndebele's terror of perpetual random social experimentation – akin to Bhabha's radical perversity. Here we find the interpreter valorised as a sovereign analyst. Here the passage of historical time is conceived of as progressive, with key events mounting to a critical watershed wherein the past and the future can be over-determined. Clearly what Ndebele cannot or will not countenance is the immanence of history within a ceaselessly changing present. Here civilisation is an act of discipline, the thinker civilisation's servant. Ironically, for all his talk of a redemptive space for the oppressed, Ndebele merely reinforces the very Manichean mechanism which will keep the oppressed shackled to yet another strange law: the law of sequential time in which history is parsed, values located for all eternity, and change conceived as possessing an end in itself. At this juncture Ndebele's logic is profoundly dangerous. Not only is it humourless, it will not accept that change can never be achieved through the sustenance of a master narrative.

At best, then, Ndebele's thought is riddled with contradictions that, unfortunately, are never conceived of as empowering. In the final instance, an overwhelming dialectical logic shuts out the best in his thought. In the end he emerges, in Foucault's words, as nothing more than the bureaucrat of the revolution and the civil servant of truth. This conclusion is severe. While others would affirm the continued currency of Ndebele's critical thought, my own view, in the last instance, is that this cannot be achieved without addressing what Tony Morphet correctly notes as the incoherence of Ndebele and (Sachs's) 'account of the cultural imagination':

> Both founder on the issue of closure. Both appeal to the notion of incorporative irony for the sake of greater range, flexibility, complexity and openness, but *neither is able to relinquish the fixed point of closure* in the framework of social action to which they have committed themselves (Cultural Imagination p. 142, my emphasis).

Graham Pechey counterpoints Ndebele's well-known essay 'The Rediscovery of the Ordinary' with his own, 'The Post-apartheid Sublime: Rediscovering the Extraordinary'. In that Pechey situates himself beyond and between the space opened up by Ndebele, a space he defines as 'a post-heroic culture of irony, the local, the ordinary' which, in eluding the 'epic battle', enables a rethinking of 'the cracks of the structures that South Africa's fraught modernity has historically thrown up' (p. 57). Pechey's position echoes David Scott's in *Refashioning Futures* as well as Homi Bhabha's in 'How Newness Enters The World'. What Pechey aims to do is '[free] a strand of implication [in Ndebele's thinking] that was in any case already there' (p. 58). This strand he discovers not in Ndebele's critical writing, but in his fiction. There, the 'modern and premodern meet', resulting in a 'distinctively modern practice of short story writing' (ibid.).

The story Pechey cites is 'The Prophetess' (*Fools* pp. 30–52). Pechey's conclusion to his reading is that 'it is in the heart of the ordinary that the extraordinary is to be found' (The Post-apartheid Sublime p. 58). This conclusion – echoed in Lefebvre's formulation of the ordinary as 'the invisible visible' – invokes a turning away 'from the fight against apartheid, with its fixation upon suffering and the seizure of power' (The Witness of Poetry). This turning away, while not effectively apparent in Ndebele's criticism, emerges in

> just such stories as these: stories which then open out to transform the victory over apartheid into a gain for postmodern knowledge, *a new symbiosis of the sacred and the profane, the quotidian and the numinous* (The Post-apartheid Sublime p. 58, my emphasis).

For Pechey it is Ndebele's stories which most effectively disfigure the logic of opposing and contestatory terms and which fuse a seeming contradiction into an enabling and revisionary aesthetic. For Pechey, nevertheless, this fusion of the quotidian and the numinous is not the province of fiction alone. Rather, his project of recovery reveals this fusion as constitutive to critical thinking as well. For Bakhtin – Pechey's key theoretical inroad – this fusion of seemingly incommensurable terms is called 'great time' (The Post-apartheid Sublime p. 60). This epochal *and* micrological shift, which Ndebele does not admit in his critical writing, is for Pechey the surest means whereby South African intellectuals may rethink and reinvigorate their methods and processes of conceiving change. The writing for which Pechey calls 'is that which can only by an act of hermeneutic violence be read as being *for* any one proposition and *against* another construed as its opposite' (p. 63).

Here the telling phrase is 'hermeneutic violence', the strategic assimilation and containment of thought within an oppositional logic. This, as I have already stated, is the violence that disfigures the best in Ndebele's critical writing: he falls victim to the very strategy of containment that he purportedly abhors. Having described what the new writing is not, what then does Pechey offer critical discourse? The answer follows pell-mell:

> we are in the presence of writing in this strong sense when the discourse before us has no designs of assimilation upon other discourses; is unimpressed by the monopolistic claims of any one narrative, even its own; and loves the incommensurability of 'phrasal universes' above all else (ibid.).

Pechey then states:

> The polar contest of apartheid and its antagonists needed for its own purposes to compel an infinity of disparate temporalities and identities into a totality. Writing is under no such necessity, and it is the business of post-apartheid criticism to respect this discourse, whose agnosticism where centres of power are concerned is absolute (ibid.).

It is here, within a revisionary conception of critical writing, that this chapter fixes its Medusan gaze. It is here that I wish now to reinforce Pechey's fusion of the quotidian and the numinous, his call to the extra-ordinary, that alternatively I have termed the extramoral, the perverse, the exaggerated, and the spectacular. It is only by admitting these phenomena, which Ndebele recklessly suppresses, that we can begin to effectively and un-slavishly rethink the critical moment in a changing present.

In the concluding paragraph to his essay Pechey notes:

> The literature which South Africa's post-apartheid condition both needs and can deliver is the many-voiced discourse of an *ekstasis* which frees us from the future of hopes and fears and admits us to a sphere of 'unexpectedness', of 'absolute innovation, miracle' (Bakhtin, *Speech Genres* 167). It matters little that the sources of this imagining of the unimaginable – this 'post-apartheid sublime' – are local or global, high-cultural or popular; what language (or silence) it puts to use; or to what genre any one of its texts belongs (ibid.).

Here Pechey eloquently expresses the basis for this chapter. However, where I differ from Pechey is when he concludes that

> it is enough that the writing thus produced should offer from its distance-which-is-not-indifference a model of the ontological priorities appropriate to particular historical phases (ibid.).

The problematic and mock-generous term here is 'enough'. In insisting upon sufficiency, Pechey dissipates an otherwise thoroughly compelling vision of what a revisionary critical aesthetic implies. This gripe aside, Pechey effectively levels the hegemonic structure of critical discourse. More compellingly, he locates the affective and performative project of *ekstasis* at the core of his critical vision. The term, which suggests being outside and beyond oneself, not only undoes a controlling and sage wisdom but, more significantly, also returns us to the unthinkable, the strange, or radically other which cross-sects and shapes so much of current thinking. The term not only questions the efficacy of secular rationality, but opens up the terrain of critical writing as a 'many-voiced discourse'. While Pechey momentarily constrains the radicality of his vision he does conclude with an anthemic call:

> Now that South Africa is no longer an object of the world's scrutiny, and that its writers are under no imperative to report from the ground or rally the troops, they are free to polish and infinitely reposition a mirror from which the formerly scrutinizing communities beyond its borders can join all native South Africans in scrutinizing themselves. The field of South African writing is now in every sense without bounds (p. 73).

The freedom Pechey ascribes to South Africa's current condition is of course conditional and thoroughly dependent upon the 'mirror' one affixes to it. Today it can be said that we have moved from one paradox to the next: from a closed society that was strangely open, to an open society that is strangely closed. In this paradoxical sense we remain bounded. However, this is not what Pechey means when he says that South African writing is now 'without bounds'. The link he is making here is to the affective power of the sublime, a condition that is not reducible to the strictures of mind but which in the Longinian sense – and not the Kantian – is liberating. The epistemic shift that Pechey calls for demands that we rethink the very notion of resistance, the notion of history and our idea of what it means to be free. What, after Longinus, does it mean to be without bounds? And why is it necessary to recover this impulse in order to conceive of freedom?

If Kant, when confronted with the unthinkable, falls back and recovers a recuperative mechanism within the domain of reason in order to understand the sublime, then Longinus refutes reason's sovereignty. What Longinus expresses as the affective potency of being unbounded-in-itself, Ndebele (like Kant) sees as chaos that the mind's civilising mission must control. If Pechey cannot wholly accept this radical *ekstasis*, then neither can he accept Ndebele's strategy of containment. From a negative standpoint, Pechey's vision could be perceived as sentimental. This is certainly the case when we consider his reading of the abolition of the death penalty:

> Instead of the sublime of terror surrounding the hanging we have the sublimity of that momentous judicial decision in which the death penalty, having been declared unconstitutional, is given up for good. The word ending the ending of words in killing constitutes the highest reach of the sublime of justice: nothing less than Law and Justice coinciding in a majestic cancellation of the sublime of terror (p. 62).

But is this cancelling of the death penalty truly sublime? In the next sentence Pechey discloses that it is not. Shifting from the death penalty to the project of Truth and Reconciliation he states: 'Noble as it sounds [State-sponsored Truth and Reconciliation] partakes more of the beautiful than of [the] sublime' (ibid.). In other words sublimity cannot work in the service of government, it can only appear to do so.

The question Pechey begs and does not answer is whether we have in fact weaned ourselves from the sublime of terror, that is, from our pathological attachment to the unthinkable. Are we not, as a society, as thinkers, incapable of washing the blood from our hands? Is the strange law that binds us not darker and more terrifying than we could ever have imagined? Is our conscience, our sobriety, our good will, nothing more than a ruse? And, indeed, will we ever free ourselves from an inner and outer scrutiny that afflicts us at every turn?

If liberation is a chimera, it is because we have been looking for change in all the wrong places. Abolishing the death penalty does not lead to greater freedom. If this conclusion appears fatalistic, it is because it is precisely fatality that continues to condition our life experience. Irrespective of all claims to change, change will not and cannot happen without a key epistemic shift from the dialectic of immorality and morality to the post-dialectical domain of the extra-moral: a domain that is none other than the extraordinary heart of the ordinary.

This, at best, is what I understand to be the post-apartheid sublime. It is precisely this nascent extra-morality that Ndebele at the outset sought to rout out and destroy. This is what he meant when he spoke of preventing 'perpetual random social experimentation'. To counter this threat, which is omnipresent today, Ndebele sought to 'consolidate the existing accumulated knowledge'. Ndebele's gesture is hopeless from the outset. The accumulated knowledge he would amass remains a mere constellation of fragments shored up against our ruin.

If Ndebele turns to a civilising, material, and parochial humanism, then Pechey seeks to harness the sublimity of terror through a saving spiritual metaphysic. Neither truly comes to grips with the unthinkable. Neither can recover an effective fusion of the ordinary and extra-ordinary. The one marred by mind, the other by faith, may call for liberation, but neither is willing to accept the immanence of a psychic and epistemic radicality that must be embraced if one were truly to achieve freedom. Finally, irrespective of reason, irrespective of faith, both thinkers lack the constitutive fearlessness necessary to promote radical change. If each insists upon 'a model of ontological priorities', it is because for both history must continue to be perceived as an incremental shift from one perceptually controlled error to the next. At its root, however, there is no justice to great thinking. Irrespective of what may or may not be said about who and what we are, nothing to date has expelled what Coetzee defines as 'the crudity of life in South Africa, the naked force of its appeals, not only at the physical level but at the moral level too, its callousness and its brutalities, its hungers and its rages, its greed and its lies' (Jerusalem Prize Acceptance Speech p. 99), a crudity of living, of being alive, which makes life lived in South Africa, whether under apartheid or under this phantom democracy, 'as irresistible as it is unlovable' (ibid.).

Finally, it is Coetzee's critical and intractable perception that returns us to the third tropological conceit, queer: a culture of exageration in a state of emergency. This last in the series of conceits has functioned implicitly throughout this chapter. Its ascendant sign has already been evoked in the extra-moral, the spectacular, the perverse, the excessive and the extraordinary. Its philosophical import has compellingly been captured in Bhabha's valorisation of over-dramatisation as key to the double-life as it is experienced in the post-colonial world. Queer signals the 'narrative[s] of the borderline conditions of cultures and disciplines' (*The Location of Culture* p. 214). As an affective and liminal condition, queer attests to the impossible and impermissible division of South African reality, a reality that necessarily accommodates that which it disavows. In this regard, Pechey emerges not as a metaphysician but as a queer theoretician.

Consider, for example, his valorisation of *ekstasis*, a condition which says so much about the borderline of experience in a post-colonial world, a condition which opens rather than closes the world, which opens thinking to the unthinkable, the strange, the radically other. Queer: a 'many-voiced discourse', that levels contradiction and institutes a radical plurality as the basis of any interstitial grasp of a changing present.

As I have stated at the outset of this chapter, queer is not reducible to identities defined by given sexual contracts. Rather, it is ascribed here to a way of thinking that, after Pechey, appeals to an *élan* of mind and a mode of social and cultural engagement that is 'in every sense without bounds'. This is not to suppose that queer, as an 'intellectual model', is wholly sustainable beyond existing psychic and epistemic constraints. Other than Lefebvre's enigmatic conceptualisation of the ordinary, queer emerges as the third term – the third space – which, in foregrounding and enacting a 'mediated relation' to the dominant imperatives of identification, ultimately works towards the deterritorialisation of these imperatives. I address this matter at greater length in the next chapter.

In concluding this assessment of the epistemic validity and agency of the tropological troika – the prosaic, the sublime, and the queer – I wish, finally, to affirm the provenance of the last as the most effective vehicle in and through which to sustain an affirmative cultural imaginary. If this is so, it is because queer, as an intellectual model and socio-cultural agency, reconciles the ordinary and the extraordinary in a manner that does not produce a synthesis, but that further aggravates the *discontinuous relatedness* of these seemingly opposed conditions which Ndebele suppresses and Pechey sublimates. Queer, then, comes to exemplify what Bhabha defines as the double life of the postcolonial subject, a life which constructively perverts existent polarities, which undoes closure and the discretion which founds the separation of terms of engagement, which deliberately over-dramatises the self as that which exists in an extra-moral space, and, against a sage or pious wisdom, celebrates the constitutive perversity of the postcolonial condition as the source of a revisionary agency and not as the marginalised figuration of mere scandal.

A striking cultural manifestation of this revisionary conceptualisation and enactment of queerness is the Cape Town-based Mother City Queer Project. Inspired by South Africa's bigger-better-best constitution, MCQP emerges in 1994 as South Africa's first queer event. An art party, MCQP sought to break the solemnity of resistance culture and institute a culture of play: a culture *as* performance. Those who attended were expected to re-imagine themselves, become something other to the self in moral space.

Against the stern nominality of being, MCQP announced the reflexive and playful innocence of becoming. In a society disfigured by conflict and the attendant allegiances which defined resistance culture, this transmogrifying spirit of play announced a new era in which spectacle emerged not as the figure of oppression, but as the figure of liberation: the liberation of the metaphorical and adjectival, the eccentric, over-dramatic, and unconventional. While the locus for this liberation was sexual and identity politics, it was not reducible to these key concerns. For MCQP it was not the liberated self that mattered, but the liberated collective. The self, conceived interdependently, promoted identity as a cluster formation. Those who attended assumed an eccentric group identity. A de-individualised and collective imaginary formed the key to the MCQP initiative: the double life of the postcolonial subject became a multiple life. In this regard, MCQP effectively accessed a key principle of radical social transformation that Michel Foucault, Gilles Deleuze and Felix Guattari had already provoked as the new – rhizomatic – intellectual model for being.

As the MCQP manifesto attested, queer defined those who lived creatively and critically, who took chances and pushed conventions:

> Although many Queer people are homosexual, not all homosexuals are Queer. Not all heterosexuals un-Queer. In fact, some straight people are Queerer than some gay people. Queerness is not a cut-and-dried definition . . . Queerness is an attitude.

This populist formulation underscores a subversion of received conventions that, I would suggest, is precisely the objective of Pechey's project. Like Pechey, those behind MCQP favour the incommensurability of phrasal universes. They refute the synthesis of 'disparate temporalities and identities into a totality' (The Post-apartheid Sublime p. 63). The difference between Pechey and those behind MCQP, however, is that they do not succumb to, or baulk in the face of, the sublimity of terror. On the contrary, in accordance with Benjamin, those involved in the MCQP project are acutely aware that terror's source is also the source of happiness: that terror and happiness are the inevitable and coeval elements of an act founded on risk.

To play is dangerous, to dream all the more so. Through wit and laughter – sorely lacking in the thinking of Ndebele and Pechey – those involved in the MCQP project would accept terror as a necessary element within the absurdity of lived experience in South Africa. That the project came into being after the HIV-related death of Craig Darlow should affirm all the more the gravity which shaped the will to pleasure, or, in a more radical and unbounded sense, the will to joy, to *jouissance*. If the instigators behind the MCQP project – Andrew Putter and Andre Vorster (Darlow's lover) – are not fatalistic, neither are they sage rationalists. For them beauty is not the inverse of the sublime but its double within an indissolubly contradictory experience of life.

As activists and cultural spin-doctors, Putter and Vorster understand paradox as a locus of play and not as a crucible. For them any anxious or pathological attraction to perversity and to paradox is instantaneously converted into mockery and laughter. For them irony is not a solution but a first step towards the disavowal and deconstruction of the received conventions of sexual, social, and cultural identity. In their apprehension of the world, the prosaic is one with the numinous. This oneness is not a synthesis but a strategic extra-moral trumping of the contradictions that, for far too long, have defined and disfigured the fate of South African identity and its cultural expression.

Could Ndebele have imagined that the spectacle he abhorred would return (did it ever go away?) in a form as affirming and as conceptually challenging as that evinced in MCQP and so many other projects which are emerging each day from the cracks he putatively sought to emphasise, only to seal at the end?

In attempting to civilise the processes of change, Ndebele would diminish his finest insights. In Pechey he has found a thinker gracious and sensitive enough to cherish the finest strands in his thought. Nonetheless, this salvaging process would inevitably be undone by the best that Pechey in turn would offer. If history is never kind, if history hurts, it is because history will never save us from an unforgiving and ever-changing present. If queer is a 'watchword for today', then it is a watchword which, like the ordinary, must embrace its extinction, for thought prevails in spite of the descriptors we affix to it. As Judith Butler notes:

> If the term 'queer' is to be a site of collective contestation, the point of departure for a set of historical reflections and futural imaginings, it will have to remain that which is, in the present, never fully owned, but always and only redeployed, twisted, queered from a prior usage and in the direction of urgent and expanding purposes. This also means that it will doubtless have to be yielded in favour of terms that do that political work more effectively. Such a yielding may well become necessary in order to accommodate – without domesticating – democratising contestations that have and will redraw the contours of the movement in ways that can never be fully anticipated in advance (Critically Queer p. 170).

Like the ordinary, the queer cannot be conscripted into a preconceived system of change. To sustain its life-affirming force, queer must embrace the immanence of its *performativity*. As an exaggeration and critique of normalised systems of contradiction, the queer, like the ordinary, reveals the 'invisible visible'. Therein lies its enigmatic irresistibility as a way of living and thinking the psychic and epistemic impasse of the present moment.

If the conditions that have defined South African history are darkly irresistible and unlovable, as Coetzee has persuasively though problematically proclaimed, does this mean that the conditions which shape South Africa's present are equally so? Then: Yes. Now: Perhaps. In the future? Speaking from this fraught moment in time I would say no. The 'radical perversity . . . that drives the intriguing will to knowledge of postcolonial discourse' (*The Location of Culture* p. 212) is but the pretext to an earth-shattering laughter.

SIX

In Praise of Folly

God look after the wise and look after the strong,
But the fool in his folly will always live long.

– Derek Walcott

In his keynote address at the April 2002 conference at Warwick University entitled 'J. M. Coetzee and the Ethics of Intellectual Practice' David Attwell turns to Coetzee's essay on Desiderius Erasmus's *The Praise of Folly* (1509). Attwell's interest is sparked by

> [Coetzee's] meditation on the public face of the writer-intellectual who distrusts secular rationality, particularly in times of violence when reason seems given over to madness without being aware that the dementia has already set in.

The meditation, Attwell imputes, says as much about Coetzee as it does about Erasmus. Both distrust and write against the grain of secular rationality. Both address 'the difficulties of crafting a position – or perhaps a non-position – from this distrust, a position which resists falling into the dominant rivalries'. Both are aware that any position, even one which stands outside the dominant sphere of contestation and rivalry, is subject to 'the fate of collecting acolytes and detractors who erect it as a new rational standard, so that its legacy traduces what it stands for'. Like Coetzee, Attwell does not accept this co-optation as a *fait accompli*. Rather, the force of his argument, in accordance with Coetzee's, not only challenges the defamation of face perpetrated by those who presume to know, but also signals a line of flight – or epistemological escape route – in and through which the strategies of containment are pre-empted and suspended. This route – after Erasmus – is the route of Folly.

Embodied in Moria, the central figure in *The Praise of Folly*, this line of flight enacts a non-position, which in ceaselessly shifting, both traverses and exceeds the conflicted and irrational positions that are the object of Folly's critique. As Attwell notes:

> [Moria] sees through the madness of those who see themselves as reasonable and self-possessed while giving themselves over to rivalry. Against this madness she positions herself, speaking the truth but mixing it with delight. What is unique about Folly's truth is its *positionality*: it comes

107

'not from the wise man's mouth but from the mouth of the subject assumed *not* to know and speak the truth'.

From the outset, then, Folly must accept and embrace its exilic and extraneous position. Moreover it must convert this position into a non-position, pre-empting traducement by traducing itself. Folly's power must reside in its seeming powerlessness, its conscious elision of the very discursive arena that would either absorb or dismiss its non-positionality. Hence Moria's statement:

> Let none of ye expect from me, that after the manner of Rhetoricians I should go about to define what I am, much less use any Division (*The Praise of Folly* p. 100).

In working to undo and escape an interpellated position, Folly must simultaneously expose the limit inherent in the rhetorical strategies that would contain it. Folly's objective, however, is more than merely deconstructive. In unravelling Folly's agency, Coetzee suggests that Folly's 'truth' comes from

> a kind of *ek-stasis*, a being outside oneself, being beside oneself, a state in which truth is known (and spoken) from a position that does not know itself to be the position of truth (*Giving Offense* p. 95).

Because Folly cannot mirror its truth, given that the truth is shifted in the instant of expression, Folly must inhabit a non-position that is intransitive, evasive, and speculative. What makes the non-positionality of Folly's truth all the more compelling is that, therein and thereby, 'the linear propulsive force of reason gives way to the unpredictable metamorphosis of figure into figure' (ibid.). As a mode of speech or performance, Folly

> yields a bliss that is the object of the desire of those most open to the promptings of desire; and the first manifestation of such bliss is of course laughter, an anarchic convulsion of the body that marks the defeat of the defences of the censor (ibid.).

While Coetzee's conclusion cannot name and contain Folly's agency, it does point to what I will term Folly's radicality. If Folly reacts to reason, it is not motivated by reason. Instead, it is desire – the harbinger of laughter and bliss – that motivates Folly. The motivation is never 'linear and propulsive'. On the contrary, Folly's motivation-as-desire is inherently unpredictable and uncontainable. It is not surprising, therefore, that Folly is the anathema of reason. Folly of course knows this. What is more, Folly knows itself to be reason's repressed conscience. In desiring to desire, Folly threatens reason's sovereignty.

Of particular significance is Coetzee's imputation that Folly is a condition given to *ek-stasis*. Visionary and unpredictable, Folly-as-*ek-stasis* unleashes a value which for those who speculate, those who create, is of incalculable importance. Eschewing the linear and propulsive, Folly constructs its truth as a metamorphosed relay of figurations. This truth, which cannot be known as such, must accept a constitutive dissemblance. Folly's power

– if it can be said to possess a power – must reside in the ruse, the decoy. Parodic and paradoxical, Folly speaks yet does not speak, knows yet does not know.

It is not surprising that Coetzee should turn to Folly. He does so not only because Folly gives offence and confounds censorship, but because without it there would be no freedom for the written word. In the context of this chapter, though, Folly's speculative and creative agency extends beyond the domain of writing. While a reading of 'Erasmus: Madness and Rivalry' will reveal the rigour of Coetzee's inquiry into the veracity of Folly's agency, it would not satisfactorily serve another dimension of this chapter: an inquiry into Folly's veracity in the context of performance art in South Africa. My focus, therefore, builds upon Coetzee and Attwell's respective readings of Folly, and shifts this focus on the public face of the writer-intellectual to the interactive sphere, in particular the art events or 'happenings' devised by Andrew Putter and the performances of Pieter Dirk Uys and Steven Cohen.

My reading here will be schematic. By this I do not mean to diminish their singular impact. Rather, I wish simply to point out at the outset of this chapter that my reading of the engagements of Putter, Uys and Cohen – as well as my reading of Coetzee's *Disgrace* – serve a broader goal, which is a speculative reading of these engagements as figurations of Folly. My principal aim is an inquiry into Folly as a critical – if evasive and non-positional – trope. Through an examination of this trope – one that exposes the paradox of its instrumentality and eschews every strategy of co-optation – I hope to foreground its radical agency as a mode of cultural encounter and transformation.

If Coetzee exposes the hazards of testimony within the public sphere, then Putter, Uys and Cohen, in contrast, are consciously and actively implicated in that sphere. This does not mean that they are wholly caught within the interpellative strategies of reception. On the contrary, their highly public engagements exist as testimonies to the power of Folly to flummox the very economy of reception that chooses to fix them and/or explain them away.

Escape artists caught in the public eye, Putter, Uys and Cohen transform ridicule into laughter. This laughter is not merely mocking and derisive. Instead, following Moria – a performance artist of note – theirs is a laughter, anarchic and convulsive, which splits the axis of madness and bliss. Their penchant for outrage, campness, queerness – all figures of Folly – offers a way out of the dementia that remains resident in secular rationality. In foregrounding this dementia, in stealing and converting its fire, these illicit figurations of Folly do not only de-found power, but, through their *ek-static* agency – through laughter, pleasure, and the convulsive transmogrification of the repressed body – anticipate what Foucault in the first volume of *The History of Sexuality*: *The Will To Knowledge* defines as a 'revolution' (p. 7).

Before turning to the agency of Folly in the works of Coetzee, Putter, Cohen, and Uys – which exist as glimmers of this revolution – I will first restrict myself to an inquiry which deserves further exploration: the non-positionality of Folly. To understand how the non-positionality of Folly emerges, it is necessary to note the contestation of absolutes during the Reformation between the Lutheran reform movement and the Papacy. That this conflict finds its latter-day echo in South Africa under apartheid reinforces all the more the lesson that arises from the impossibility of choosing sides. Famously described by Luther as 'King of the Amphibians, the King of *but*', Erasmus's non-position is the result of his inability and eventual refusal to side with the Lutheran radicals in their fight against the Papacy (*Giving Offense* p. 83). 'Sympathetic to the ideals of reform', Erasmus, Coetzee notes, 'was nevertheless disturbed by the intolerance and inflexibility of the actual reform movement' (ibid.). While he publicly declared that he 'would rather die than join a faction', Erasmus, according to Coetzee,

> deemed the reform controversy insane in its fanaticism. In his view, the escalating violence of their rivalry made the two sides more and more alike, even as they more and more loudly asserted their difference (ibid.).

This striking indifference at the heart of difference, which for Erasmus suggests collusion, leads Coetzee to the following conclusion:

> By refusing to choose sides (one should bear in mind here that to choose sides is not always to choose an ally: it is sometimes to choose a foe), by claiming a position from which to judge (or as he saw it, mediate) the conflict, he only succeeded in drawing the hostility of both factions upon himself (ibid.).

For Coetzee, the 'signal lack of success' of Erasmus's non-position does not diminish its ethical veracity. Rather, Erasmus's non-position, exemplified in *The Praise of Folly*, comes to mark

> a position for the critic of the scene of political rivalry, a position not simply impartial between the rivals but also, by self-definition, off the stage of rivalry altogether, a *non*position (p. 84).

This position, I would suggest in turn, is not only the ethical position of the 'critic' but also of the artist. In the context of this chapter, and in this inquiry in general, this position, which surely echoes Coetzee's own, comes to mark the only way out of the appeal for clemency or sacrificial will that comes with choosing sides. In South Africa it is precisely this choosing of sides that has resulted in the centralisation of a moral conflict at the expense of radical innovation and ethical veracity. If rivalry can be said to be a kind of collusion, then that which was – and is – needed, all the more, is precisely a position which thrives outside or 'off the stage' of contradiction and polarisation. It is this non-position to which Erasmus gives the name Folly.

In *The Praise of Folly* it is Moria, Folly's fictional surrogate and namesake, who imparts Erasmus's judgement on a wisdom that is circumscribed and moderated by a received and disingenuous system founded on allegiance. Dressed in a dunce's cap, Moria challenges all those who mistake her for the embodiment of 'Wisedome'. She claims the very absurdity of her presence as 'the true index of [her] mind'. 'I am no Counterfeit', she says.

[N]or do I carry one thing in my looks and another in my breast. No, I am in every respect so like myself, that neither can they dissemble me, who arrogate to themselves the appearance and title of Wisemen (p. 101).

Erasmus's claim is that Folly is never false. What, then, constitutes Folly's truth? For Coetzee, Folly's truth and appeal lies in its *refusal* to take up a fixed and reasonable position, its *allure* as a figure for a mocking and treacherous desire. Given its treachery and elusiveness, this does not mean that Folly cannot speak on behalf of itself. On the contrary, we find here that Folly has baldly claimed the integrity, transparency, and seamlessness of her non-position. It is the 'wisemen' who dissemble and divide. Folly, on the other hand, mounts critique upon critique, figure upon figure, without in any way attempting to resolve or shut down the critique. While in Erasmus's work each assault is clearly titled and targeted, the target is not the object of the critique but the detour in and through which Folly enacts its unceasing barrage of wit and scorn. As an epistemological strategy, Folly is errant and ceaselessly mobile. It is through a relentless accumulation of wit and scorn, rather than the careful parsing of judgement, that Folly simultaneously tolls and diverts its truth, for Folly hones as it dissipates, focuses as it refracts.

Here Frederic Jameson's reading of Michael Herr's *Dispatches*, a document of war in which movement is key to survival, also befits a reading of the agency of Folly. Jameson goes on to link Herr's understanding of mobility in war – the metamorphic, evasive, and translocatively positional – to the cultural logic of late capital. I will not dwell on this insightful reading. Nevertheless, I do wish to point out a link here with Coetzee's reading of Folly. For Coetzee, propulsion shifts to convulsion. The self experiences identity as a metamorphic figuration. The emergent truth that paradoxically is also a non-truth, since it cannot be known to the deterritorialised subject who speaks the truth, is derived from 'a kind of *ek-stasis*, a being outside oneself, being beside oneself'.

Within the ambit of reason this non-positional state of *ek-stasis* is subject to suspicion, indeed, scorn. After all, from a rational – divisive and propulsive – point of view, what is the good of a truth that cannot know itself? Coetzee's point of course is that it is precisely the vanity of a purported self-truth that remains in question. If Coetzee valorises Folly, it is because Folly destabilises the condition for truth and relativises knowledge and power. In the context of South Africa, a society and culture enfeebled by warring factions and martyred in the abused name of morality, Folly's value is incalculable.

It should, nonetheless, be pointed out, as Attwell has done, that Folly's agency, if permitted to flourish, should in no way be subsumed into a new order of culture and resistance. Rather, in and through engagement, Folly must be permitted its translocative and *ek-static* non-position. Detractors will perceive this claim as a kind of sophistry. Within the ambit of secular rationality, this claim is as inevitable as it is falsely deemed appropriate.

Returning to Coetzee's essay entitled 'Erasmus: Madness and Rivalry', we see that what drives the metamorphosis of figure into figure is 'bliss'. It is 'bliss that is the object of the desire of those most open to the promptings of desire; and the first manifestation of such bliss is . . . laughter' (*Giving Offense* p. 95). Coetzee's observation is critical.

Irrespective of whether a truth is transparent and whether it can be known to the subject who speaks it – in itself a thorny issue which Coetzee plays out through the rivalry between Foucault and Derrida regarding whether or not madness can speak its truth – what matters here is Coetzee's emphasis of a quality that cannot be the quality of the reason. In saying this, Coetzee does not exile bliss from thought – for thought is distinct from reason – rather, that which Coetzee tellingly cherishes is bliss as the 'object' of the desiring mind.

In Coetzee's novel *Disgrace* we find that it is bliss that propels the central figure, David Lurie. An avowed 'servant of Eros' (p. 52), Lurie finds no worth in a life 'cocooned from sense-experience'. Reason – 'the realm of pure ideas' – cannot protect the reasoner from 'the onslaughts of reality'. For Lurie, what matters, instead, is the co-existence of reason and the imagination (p. 22). For Lurie, neither state is pure. Moreover, it is their co-existence that matters the more, for it is the co-existence of these states that allows for bliss, without which life would have no purpose.

In support of this premise, Lurie quotes William Blake: 'Soon murder an infant in its cradle than nurse unacted desires' (p. 69). Here the very extremity of the formulation points to the latent threat inherent in its extremity and cogency. Bliss presupposes risk; bliss is morally dangerous. Then again, without bliss and the disgrace that stalks it, all imagination rots and life becomes protracted and doubly grievous. Disgrace is the disgrace born of bliss, that is, the disgrace affixed to the one who courts bliss, who wills the destruction of the integrity of the self – the self in moral space – in the name of bliss.

Coetzee, like Foucault and unlike Derrida, knows the hazard attendant upon an exploration of this nature, for bliss is akin to madness and subject to judgement. Through the character of Lurie – there are others in his *oeuvre* – Coetzee dramatises the rites of desire and the transfigural and catastrophic nature of bliss. It is critical to repeat here that it is not bliss in itself that is catastrophic but the conditions which, in making bliss impossible, make it all the more desirable. Like Foucault, Coetzee does not banish this madness that is bliss. As a writer-intellectual it has always been this reckless twinning of madness and bliss that has proved the driving force and object of his work. Without this twinning there would be no story and, more essentially, no place for the imagination.

While others have proved insensate, cautious, fearful, and have chosen to remain on the inside of a received morality, Coetzee has irresistibly chosen to focus on the fault-line between the inside and the outside, the knowable and the unknowable, the permissible and that deemed taboo. *Ek-stasis* for Coetzee is the extra-moral dimension of being. The locus of a liberated – if fraught – instinct, *ek-stasis* points both to freedom and entrapment. For the purposes of fiction – which is a kind of truth – *ek-stasis* becomes the crux and prime mover in the game between chance and hazard, a game that, as Mallarmé reminded us, hazard would always win.

This victory cannot, of course, be known to be such, for hazard – another doppelganger for Folly – may have the last laugh, but this does not mean that hazard converts its victory into a transcendent sign of its authority. If hazard or folly can be said to possess a law, then it is a law that deconstructs its sovereignty and power. As a double

negation, Folly does not transform itself into a positive. On the contrary, Folly accepts the incisiveness of its unaccountable and liminal position.

For Moria, Erasmus's narrator, Folly is the marker of passion and pleasure, laughter, foolishness, carelessness, youth, even 'witchcraft' (*The Praise of Folly* p. 109). If Reason is 'confin'd . . . to a narrow corner of the brain', then it is against this narrow corner that the 'masterless' Passions reign. It is 'Anger, that possesseth the region of the heart . . . and lust, that stretcheth its Empire every where' (p. 118). Against 'Modesty' and 'Fear', 'the two main obstacles to the knowledge of things', Moria pits 'Danger':

> Modesty . . . casts a mist before . . . understanding, and Fear . . . having fanci'd a danger, disswades us from the attempt. But from these Folly sufficiently frees us, and few there are that rightly understand of what great advantage it is to blush at nothing and attempt every thing (pp. 135–36).

Moria's point of view is also that of David Lurie in *Disgrace*. In the broader context of cultural practice and engagement in South Africa – in which *Disgrace* has certainly played a critical and controversial role – Moria's view is illuminating. Indeed, one could say that without this view there can be no art.

Here I am once again reminded of Albie Sachs's critique of the instrumentality of South African culture and of his will, akin to Moria's, to bypass, overwhelm, and ignore oppression in the name of an unthinkable and unnameable other space. For Sachs, the 'struggle', when affixed to culture, is never nominative. If it is modesty and fear that compel the naming and shaming of the world, then it is danger and risk, integral to the speculative and creative arts, which allow for knowledge of the world. This knowledge, conceived under the sign of Folly, is invariably double-edged. Sachs calls upon Folly when he states:

> A gun is a gun is a gun, and if it were full of contradictions, it would fire in all sorts of directions and be useless to its purpose. But the power of art lies precisely in its capacity to expose contradictions and reveal hidden tensions – hence the danger of viewing it as if it were just another kind of missile-firing apparatus (Preparing Ourselves p. 20).

Like Moria, Sachs goes on to speak of love and joy and laughter, dimensions of being exiled from the prison-house of the brain, which must create their own empire. However as Erasmus's Moria, Coetzee and Sachs attest, freedom is neither given, nor can it be mastered. Rather, the freedom that is Folly is 'masterless'. In adhering to the treacherous and liberatory rites of Folly it should be remembered that a dissuasive 'mist' shrouds each and every expression of these rites, for every gesture, every word, that runs counter to the edict of Reason is policed. On the other hand, turning to Foucault – who had the gall to give voice to madness – we will discover that Reason's edict is never foolproof, that Folly – like hazard – is never subject to the dice-throw.

Coetzee has spoken of 'bliss' as the 'object of desire'. In the first volume of *The History of Sexuality*: *The Will To Knowledge*, Foucault makes this 'object' his focus. In his opening chapter, 'We "Other Victorians"', Foucault addresses a conjugation that 'the fear of ridicule or the bitterness of history' has prevented: 'revolution and happiness; or revolution and a different body, one that is newer and more beautiful; or indeed, revolution and pleasure' (p. 7). This is Sachs's point, and, implicitly, also Coetzee's, though Coetzee, unlike Foucault and Sachs, would never state that 'tomorrow sex will be good again', or proclaim 'the revelation of truth' (ibid.). Yet if Coetzee may not make such grand claims this does not mean that he refuses to heed their force. To be sure, it is through Erasmus's Folly that Coetzee speaks his abridged desire. Like Erasmus and Foucault, Coetzee too is emboldened by the failure of a repressive power to wholly contain what Foucault calls the 'useless energies, the intensity of pleasures, and irregular modes of behaviour' (p. 9). What perhaps makes Foucault a visionary and a fool – and Coetzee neither – is Foucault's mixing of the provisional with hope. Foucault:

> We must not be surprised . . . if the effects of liberation vis-à-vis this repressive power are so slow to manifest themselves; the effort to speak freely about sex and accept it in its reality is so alien to a historical sequence that has gone unbroken for a thousand years now, that it is bound to make little headway for a long time before succeeding in its mission (pp. 9–10).

What interests me is Foucault's valorisation of Folly in the full knowledge that it is precisely this value – the value of uncensored pleasure and joy – that is the most repressed dimension of human life. Here Foucault echoes Moria. While Foucault is speaking specifically of the repression and traducement of sex, his more nagging focus is on what the fear of sex supposes: the fear of pleasure, joy, and laughter. If we accept Foucault's argument, then Folly remains that which is largely repressed in society. If Folly can be said to thrive, it does so in localised and fleeting ways. Consequently, any ascription of value to Folly must do so in the full knowledge that Folly is always already endangered and that, despite and because of this danger, it must persist in expressing itself. By foregrounding Folly's agency as that which is marked by 'useless energies, intensive pleasures, and irregular modes of behaviour', I wish, all the more, to point to the oppressive powers that would subsume Folly's force, as well as point to the radicality of Folly's agency, an agency which, in order to sustain its freedom, must celebrate its inutility, intensity, and irregularity. It is these states, effulgent yet desolate, which remain the surest manifestations of Folly.

In addition to Folly's links to madness – *folie* – and to a lack of propriety and good sense, there is also a link to the theatrical review – the Follies – which typically comprises a bevy of glamourously and scantily clad girls. This last incarnation has in our polymorphously perverse age undergone yet another transformation. Today this glamorous spectacle, under the signs of drag and camp, has been absorbed into queer culture. Noteworthy examples of this camp metamorphosis of figure into figure are films such as *Priscilla Queen of the Desert, La Cage aux Folles,* and *Moulin Rouge*.

It was Susan Sontag who, in the 1960s, first addressed this strikingly resplendent metamorphosis of Folly. The Cape Town-based Mother City Queer Project (MCQP) is one such initiative that embodies Sontag's reading of camp, a descriptor that I take to be a late-modern variant of Folly. Indeed Sontag's 'Notes on "Camp"' can be read as yet another canny echo of Erasmus's praise of Folly:

[Camp] is not a natural mode of sensibility, if there be such. Indeed the essence of Camp is its love of the unnatural: of artifice and exaggeration . . . It is one way of seeing the world as an aesthetic phenomenon (p. 275).

Now if Moria contests those who judge her position – or non-position – as 'counterfeit', she also trumps this judgement by concluding that 'all things [are] represented by Counterfeit, . . . without this there [is] no living' (*The Praise of Folly* p. 137). Coetzee echoes Moria: 'All human affairs are played out in disguise . . . Without social fictions there is no society' (*Giving Offense* p. 98).

What interests me, however, is not the general validity of this proposition. Rather, I am interested in the relevance of this proposition to the understanding of camp. That which distinguishes camp is the ephemeral, extra-moral, exaggerated, excessive, counterfeit, grotesque, and comic. As a style, affect, or quality of being, camp is precisely defined by its self-conscious avowal of inutility, intensity, and irregularity. Following Foucault, I would argue that these linked conditions and states serve to unlock, unmask, and destabilise the repressive forces that would keep the mind and body – and the free expression thereof – in check. It is as a highly localised and culturally specific phenomenon that I have chosen to read camp: firstly as another name for Folly, and secondly as an example of a highly reflexive and radical cultural agency that – potentially – could serve to foster Foucault's more general view of a future conjugation of 'revolution and happiness; or revolution and a different body, one that is newer and more beautiful; or indeed, revolution and pleasure' (p. 7). This 'revolution', I would argue, cannot be achieved without Folly. If this is so, then what I propose is a strange revolution indeed. In and through Folly, what I am invoking is a 'revolution' founded on paradox, a revolution that embraces the radicality of perpetual change, the endless metamorphosis of figure into figure.

It is reasonably argued that no one can endure revolution of this nature. After all, it is asked: what use is a non-position? What good is endless change? As for joy and laughter, surely these are the predilections of children? Perhaps here one may do well to modify Foucault's call to revolution. Surely the word is too grievous, too stern, and, as such, at odds with Folly? This is certainly Hendrik Willem van Loon's caution in his introduction to *The Praise of Folly*, when he states:

Far from being an appeal to revolution, [*The Praise of Folly*] . . . merely called attention to certain intolerable conditions which demanded the attention of competent authorities (p. 14).

While acknowledging its persuasiveness, I remain unconvinced by Van Loon's judicious response. If Erasmus is at odds with authority that, through Moria, he both mocks and judges, then how can he in turn present himself as a counter-authority? Surely the very condition of Folly is one that is unauthorised? An unauthorised revolution, then? A revolution that cannot be known to be such? If Foucault's conjugation of revolution and laughter, revolution and pleasure, is as absurd as it is incommensurable, is this not a most remarkable declaration of Folly?

Reconsider Sontag's 'Notes on "Camp"':

> Camp is art that proposes itself seriously, but which cannot be taken altogether seriously because it is 'too much' (p. 284).

> What is extravagant in an inconsistent or an unpassionate way is not Camp. Camp is the glorification of 'character' (ibid.).

> What Camp responds to is 'instant character'; and, conversely, what it is not stirred by is the sense of the development of character (p. 286).

> Camp taste turns its back on the good-bad axis of ordinary aesthetic judgement. Camp doesn't reverse things. It doesn't argue that the good is bad, or the bad is good. What it does is to offer for art (and life) a different – a supplementary – set of standards (ibid.).

> Camp refuses both the harmonies of traditional seriousness, and the risks of fully identifying with extreme states of feeling (p. 287).

> The whole point of Camp is to dethrone the serious. Camp is playful, anti-serious. More precisely, Camp involves a new, more complex relation to 'the serious.' One can be serious about the frivolous, frivolous about the serious (p. 288).

> Camp proposes a comic vision of the world. But not a bitter or polemical comedy. If tragedy is an experience of hyperinvolvement, comedy is an experience of underinvolvement, of detachment (ibid.).

> Camp taste is by its nature possible only in affluent societies, in societies or circles capable of experiencing the psychopathology of affluence (p. 289).

Sontag's summation will serve as a means to prise open the conundrum of Folly. Central to the concept and enactment of camp is the moderation of seriousness. Camp not only challenges the propulsive and linear construction of character but supplants this with a conception of character as instantaneous and simulacral. Camp does not merely reverse or invert existing binaries but adds to and substitutes existing binaries. A supplementary logic and agency, camp deterritorialises existing norms of behaviour and cultural practice. Camp's objective – if it can be said to possess an objective – is to scramble the code of received values. This gesture – for it can be nothing more – must dethrone its own seriousness. Here laughter and wit are perceived as the antidote and the cure. Through laughter – bliss and/or pleasure – camp challenges 'the worm of complacency at the heart of sincerity' (*Giving Offense* p. 5). This formulation, Coetzee's, exposes the hypocrisy which camp culture seeks to flee. This hypocrisy, to which we have grown accustomed – a horror that Coetzee names sincerity – is also marked by traits more scorching: guilt, shame, and punishment. It is these traits that for Moria are the markers of fear. And it is precisely this fear which camp culture renounces.

It is important to note that this renunciation is not posted as such, for camp is not merely a reactive condition. Rather, camp deftly displaces, forgets, and metamorphoses every condition that inhibits its freedom of expression. Hence Sontag's focus on camp's supplementary agency and her formulation that 'camp involves a new, more complex relation to 'the serious'. One can be serious about the frivolous, frivolous about the serious' (p. 288). This paradox, as Moria avers, is integral to Folly's agency. If high-seriousness is akin to tragedy, then – under the sign of camp – Folly's mock-seriousness provokes 'a comic vision of the world'.

In 'Taking Offence' Coetzee notes:

> Life, says Erasmus's Folly, is theatre: we each have lines to say and a part to play. One kind of actor, recognizing that he is in a play, will go on playing nevertheless; another kind of actor, shocked to find he is participating in an illusion, will try to step off the stage and out of the play. The second actor is mistaken. For there is nothing outside of theatre, no alternative life one can join instead. The show is, so to speak, the only show in town. All one can do is go on playing one's part, though perhaps with a new awareness, a comic awareness (p. 15).

It is the first actor, the one who embraces illusion and spectacle, who possesses 'a comic awareness', to whom I would ascribe the descriptors of Folly and camp. It is this selfsame actor who will conceive of Folly as an antidote and a cure in the full knowledge that any remedy is suspect. This actor understands that life itself is theatre. The question however remains: what theatre? Theatre to what end? None, one could say. For an actor of this kind there can be no end in sight. An end enacted in the instant that it is deferred. An end as laughable as it is pressingly serious. An end metamorphosed from one figure to the next. An end that is not an end, but the ceaseless enactment and reinvention of desire.

In a psychically marred and oppressive society such as South Africa – a society defined by neat endings and poor beginnings – it is precisely this actor who emerges as life's victor. This victory cannot, however, be achieved without passing through oppression which, at every turn, is never easily dispelled. For it is oppression that makes a mockery of illusion, oppression that demands illusion all the more. The actor, who is illusion's servant will know, after Foucault, that Folly is 'alien to . . . historical sequence . . . and . . . inimical to the intrinsic mechanisms of power' (p. 10). He or she (the pronouns are reversible and have no gendered fixity) will know, besides, that history and power are never foolproof, that the one domain that is difficult to police – which is why it is policed all the more – is illusion. It is in this domain – the domain of signs – that Folly's double-agency emerges.

A stellar example of an actor who activates Folly's double agency is Pieter Dirk Uys. Uys has mobilised his liminality as a gay activist and performer to challenge existing values as well as promote the salience of others. His national AIDS awareness campaign and Ballot Bus are cases in point. Of greater relevance to this chapter, however, is his theatre, in particular his show *Dekaffirnated* in which Uys not only reflexively toys with the various masks he assumes – his lip-smacking P. W. Botha; his white male with a beer-boep; his fag-hag, Vanilla Uys; his irreverent Tutu; his AWB buffoon with a swastika; his Ouma Ossewania Poggenpoel; or, most famously of all, his Evita

Bezuidenhoudt, who is as politically incorrect as she is laughable – but, rather, radically deconstructs his amphibian personae. What is most telling about this deconstruction that occurs in *Dekaffirnated* is that it does not reinforce a split between the simulacral and the real, but heightens an awareness of their interpenetration. It is in *Dekaffirnated* – Uys's performative highpoint – that we find the deactivation of prejudice and reactivation of consciousness. Therein truth – dissembled/deconstructed/dissembled again – gives the lie to power.

As a cultural practitioner Uys occupies a unique position. Endorsed by capital and by the state, he is a curious metamorphic figure who – under threat of being perceptually rigidified and turned into a standard of alterity and reflexive critique – still manages to convert the jester into the insurgent. The response Uys invokes is not merely that which Coetzee in *Disgrace* defines as 'catharsis', in which 'all the coarse prejudices brought into the light of day [are] washed away in gales of laughter' (p. 23). As a figure of camp and Folly, Uys, more than any other South African theatrical performer, has explored the freedom and danger implicit in this figuration.

Uys well understands camp and Folly as a perilous procedure. He well knows that oppression cannot be dispelled with a flamboyant wave of a bejewelled hand. Instead, critical engagement must be perpetual and the outcome accepted as unknowable. Both censor and libertine, Uys – through his many incarnations – exists under erasure. The critical point, here, is that camp-as-Folly can occupy no other position: hence, the attestation of Folly's non-position.

If Folly will have its acolytes, it will also have its detractors. There are those in the majority who will perceive Folly as eccentric and pathological. This perception is inevitable since no culture – including one that champions an extra-moral non-position – can be said to exist wholly outside of judgement. The question then is: to what extent has camp culture sustained its supplementary standard? Furthermore, given Sontag's final statement, to what extent is camp culture marked by 'the psychopathology of affluence'? This last point is of particular relevance when addressing the Mother City Queer Project, an initiative that, despite its initial radicality, has come to embrace its own glamorous ghettoisation.

In a recent interview with MCQP's initial creator and spin-doctor, Andrew Putter, the refrain 'Queer is gone' signalled Folly's co-option and deactivation. Queer, as an intellectual model and way of life, has fallen victim to 'reification', says Putter. In the space of three years – between 1994 and 1996 – 'the project conceptually fell apart'. 'Now', Putter adds, 'no one knows what I'm talking about'.

If, as Putter attests, queer (as camp, as Folly) is failing, then what is the source of the failure? For Putter the answer lies in a deficient critical reflexivity. Today camp is largely an affect of style rather than an eccentric agency of the imagination. Initially conceived as a collective culture, camp has increasingly become a narcissistic fabrication of the self. If MCQP's primary initiative was to 'deform' an existing order, supplant sameness and celebrate difference – 'the differences between people and the difference of one's identity in relation to itself' – then today this initiative has been supplanted by 'lame domestications of desire' (Jamal, Interview with Andrew Putter). We are very far here from Coetzee's notions of *ek-stasis* and bliss, notions that are central to Putter's vision of cultural change. If Putter's initial objective was to 'redeem art from itself, to liberate creativity and artfulness from art', then today what is increasingly evident, according to Putter, is the withering of this critical vision.

Like Pieter Dirk Uys, Putter continues to sustain his personal vision in the full knowledge that it remains 'a utopian ideal'. This phrasing is instructive. If utopia supposes no place on earth, it also supposes a kinship with Coetzee's notion of *ek-stasis*. A state in which one is outside and beside oneself, *ek-stasis* signals a flight from entrapment. As I suggested earlier, this flight is momentary. If Putter has cast a retrospective pall over MCQP, this pall not only suggests the failure of Folly but also supposes that the seed for this failure was always present. Read thus – that Folly inhabits its own risk – then Putter's critique is not merely a marker of pathos, but the marker of an *a priori* danger.

Given the strictures that contain the flight of Folly, it is not surprising that as a quest for freedom Folly would at some point find itself caught. As Foucault has stated, 'it is in the nature of power . . . to be repressive, and to be especially careful in repressing useless energies, the intensity of pleasure, and irregular modes of behaviour' (*The History of Sexuality* p. 9). Camp – or queer – culture, given its avowed celebration of this trinity of deviations, was always already subject to censorship both within and from the outside. Therefore, reading against the grain of Putter's pessimistic conclusion, one could argue that Folly – given its anomalous, spectacular, and other-worldly agency – has had, in the midst of its excessiveness, to assume the cloak of the clandestine. As a revolutionary act, then, camp cannot be known as such. Better to have its seeming frivolity monitored than to have its radical agency exposed. Better to have its deeds perceived as the signification of nothing.

Given this perspective, it is impossible to attest to Folly's failure. Certain initiatives which are undertaken in the name of Folly may waver and fail, but Folly, because it is always already outside and beside any mechanism of power that would entrap it, has as a consequence learnt to subsume every failure and enact its own mock-death. Therein lies Folly's resilience.

In a country such as South Africa, Folly's agency is all the more a necessity, all the more vulnerable. It is this imputation that defines the narrative seam of *Disgrace*, a novel that dramatises a sequence of misadventures, which are as absurd as they are grave. What makes the sustenance of Folly in South Africa precarious and all the more necessary is that the demands placed upon the conscience of its citizenry are relentless. South Africa demands allegiance with the same intensity that it compels outrage, frustration and protestation. Culture, as a consequence, is placed in a position in which it cannot wholly distinguish itself from society's claims. The performance art of Pieter Dirk Uys and the writing of Coetzee – in markedly different, though, I would suggest, connected ways – point to the burden that culture in South Africa must carry.

Given this burden, the inutility I ascribe to Folly may appear all the more suspect. Nonetheless, it is important here to reiterate that I do not see inutility in a pejorative sense. Instead, in Foucault's sense, I am pointing to inutility as a kind of reflexive agency through which culture's seeming uselessness becomes its most incisive and most critical property. In the case of *Disgrace* it is that which is *not* done, that which cannot be remedied which, all the more, reinforces the psychic resonance of inutility: of superannuation and uselessness. In this regard David Lurie, too, emerges as a figure of Folly, a figure immoderate and unmoderated, who, in his resistance to the prurience that masquerades as morality, reveals precisely the inhuman and impossible burdens and prescriptive demands which are placed upon South Africa's hapless and alienated citizenry.

Yet another – markedly different – cultural expression of superannuation and redundancy is Steven Cohen's performance 'Nobody Loves a Fairy when she's Forty'. The title of the piece signals the high premium placed on youth in gay culture: hence, the uselessness a 'fairy' may feel on having passed his/her sell-by date. Through a transgender link, an equivalent sell-by date afflicts women of the same age. What makes Cohen's performance all the more compelling is his deconstruction of the code of fashion. With lilac gloves, tight bodice, frilly tutu and sequined purple high heels, his face masked with an acreage of foundation, eyes and lips a lavish purple too, Cohen appears as the archetypal camp queen or sex worker.

Masked and brazen – the tutu is thrust up and out, revealing a naked rump – Cohen both distances and begs invasion. A further dimension, the most important, is that he does not strut the streets but crawls on his hands and knees. This is no absurdist plea for forgiveness, no mock act of atonement shot through with the 'current of desire', for those who may recall this moment in *Disgrace* (p. 173). On the contrary, Cohen is on his hands and knees because the heels of the shoes he wears are absurdly long, making the shoes impractical, though of course by no means useless. Sponsored by British Airways, Cohen travelled from Johannesburg to Cape Town, the journey between airspace completed on his hands and knees. 'I wanted to see if I would be discriminated on a gender basis or a disability basis', says Cohen. Furthermore, Cohen sought to expose 'how fashion, taken to the logical extreme, makes life impossible' (Jamal, Steven Cohen: Waitress Tells All p. 18).

The challenge is layered. Here pathos meets absurdity, the polarities of male and female are crossed, and fashion targeted as a breach of the possible. It is precisely the general absence of the reflexive acuity of Cohen's stunt that Putter mourns. Here camp is not a depoliticised phenomenon, but a means through which to question the valorisation of youth, the internment of age, the victimisation of drag, the censorship of sexuality, and the imprisonment of life by fashion. In every way 'Nobody Loves a Fairy when she's Forty' is an act of Folly. Like many of Cohen's performances, the artist's detractors have dubbed it as 'toilet theatre' (ibid.). However, Cohen's performances are not reducible to their purported obscenity and absurdity. Obscenity and absurdity are absorbed into the work and made to speak its truth. The objective of the performance is not to define what is good against what is bad, but in Sontag's sense, 'to offer for art (and life) a different – a supplementary – set of standards'. The laughter Cohen invokes may be more acrid than that invoked by Pieter Dirk Uys; still, it is a laughter that is forged in and through the crucible of oppression in South Africa, which of course is not to say that the work of either artist does not have relevance elsewhere. Yet what makes the work of Uys and Cohen compelling is that each conceives of Folly as a projection that is bound by the obscenity of the lived world in which they find themselves. A world in which they must, like Coetzee's David Lurie, speak truth to power.

If mythridisation supposes the internalisation of a poison the better to monitor a sickness, then Folly mixes derision with laughter, the censorious with the libertine, pain with pleasure, seriousness with its mockery, and reason with madness, the better to reveal the impossible that negates and confounds the possible and the probable. Given the heightened seriousness of our time, Folly may thrive only in passing, but when that seriousness is unveiled and revealed for what it is – a fear of life's theatre – then Folly's reign – a reign forged through laughter and pleasure and the paroxysmal transfiguration of our blunted minds and bodies, whether pleasurable or not (then again pleasure is a kind of pain) – will come to pass. It is then that Foucault's testimony will emerge as Folly's last and first laugh. That the deferral of this testimony prevails attests to laughter's degradation – a degradation that feeds prejudice – and the condemnation that is seriousness. As David Lurie fatally remarks: 'After a certain age, all affairs are serious. Like heart attacks' (*Disgrace* p. 42).

SEVEN

Faith in a Practical Epistemology: On Collective Creativity in Theatre

> to trust in the inauthentic, the contingent, the practical
> as a way of arriving at meaning
>
> *— William Kentridge*

All plays are workshopped affairs. If concerted efforts have been made to distinguish an individually scripted play-text from one culled in a rehearsal room, this has been to reinforce a distinction between the product of an auteur and that produced through a group. However, theatre necessitates collaboration if it is to achieve its destined fruition on the stage. While the insistence upon a play as the product of a singular creator may serve to authenticate its textual authority, it cannot satisfactorily explain its affect and agency in and through the processes of production and reception. As Loren Kruger points out in *The National Stage: Theatre and Cultural Legitimation in England, France, and America*, theatre as a hybrid form exposes 'the limits of legitimacy' (p. 22). This seeming weakness, Kruger argues, is also the primary source of the strength of theatre. Kruger's argument, though, extends beyond the privative valorisation of singularly authored plays versus those that are collectively made. In attempting to problematise and render erroneous this distinction, Kruger 'challenges the authority invested in the textual object in which the band of impure autonomy continues to mark and to mar the legitimacy of theatre studies in the shadow of the monument of the literary academy' (p. 187). Because it is

> at once more and less than art, theatre straddles the disputed border country between the aesthetic state and the political and provides the stage on which the contradiction in theatrical autonomy enables the construction of theatrical nationhood as at once a cultural monument to legitimate hegemony and the site on which the excavation and perhaps the toppling of that monument might be performed (ibid.).

For Kruger, it is precisely theatre's illegitimacy, its 'persistent impurity', which allows for its figuration as 'an exemplary sign of the heterogeneity and heteronomy of theatrical nationhood' (ibid.). Furthermore, theatre serves as an index of the functional duplicity of disciplinary autonomy, in which the historical and contemporary marginalization of theatre studies is a function of its perceived lack of autonomy vis-à-vis literary study and its apparent failure to live up to the autonomous standards of that larger and more self-evidently legitimate discipline (ibid.).

Kruger raises a number of inter-linked issues regarding theatre's liminal status and agency, its corruptibility as an art form, its double-edged capacity to reinforce the concept of national unity and to de-found this concept, and its capacity to develop a cultural imagination – national or otherwise – which, more than any other art form, restores the agency of the collective.

While the focus of Kruger's *The National Stage* is restricted to theatrical and cultural legitimation in England, France and America, the strength of her argument also pertains to theatre's agency in South Africa. Liz Gunner echoes Kruger's view. In 'The Struggle for Space', her introduction to *Politics and Performance: Theatre, Poetry and Song in Southern Africa*, Gunner reiterates the value of a play as performance:

> [W]hile writers such as J M Coetzee, Etienne van Heerden, Chenjerai Hove and Tsitsi Dangarembga are part of the brilliant mosaic of Southern African culture, those written forms must, in the African context, coexist and interact with the other myriad forms of performance culture which are constantly being produced and reworked and are part of the indigenous discourse (p. 2).

More forcefully, Gunner goes on to affirm the value of performance – and its relation to empowerment, space, voice, identity, nationalism and gender – as a means of cultural expression which, unduly neglected, could pave the way towards an 'emancipatory' aesthetics and politics. At the point when *Politics and Performance* is released – 1994 – this emancipation remains emergent. What has come to pass is a marked shift from 'the crisis of legitimacy' to 'a crisis of identity' (p. 1). This perceptual shift, conceived in accordance with the historical shift from oppression to a nascent democracy, remains problematic: legitimacy does not precede identity. Instead, the modalities coexist. Moreover, legitimacy and identity are not inviolate givens, but 'impure' syncretic fields of contestation that mark a continuum in an ongoing struggle.

What makes Kruger's argument the more compelling is that she strikes the blow at the heart of legitimation and, by exposing the crisis there – that legitimation is always already embattled – points to theatre's illegitimacy – *the illegitimacy of performance* – as a key to any transforming society. If Gunner seeks to redress a received imbalance between the authorised text and the unauthorised performance, then Kruger returns us to a founding illegitimacy that subsumes and, implicitly, topples this distinction. Like Gunner, Kruger continues to pay lip service to 'the monument of the literary academy'. What makes Kruger's argument the more forceful is that she persists in thinking against the grain of the academy's perceived authority and thereby exposes the 'functional duplicity of disciplinary autonomy'. Kruger counters this built-in duplicity with the duplicity of theatre, which by virtue of its 'persistent impurity' reinforces the impossibility of autonomy and the conditionality of legitimacy. Theatre, then, serves as the succinct figuration of a crisis that dogs every art form.

For Kruger, what makes theatre compelling is that, despite its co-option as 'a cultural monument to legitimate authority', theatre can also serve to break down this authority. Its very hybrid and marginal status – 'at once more and less than art' – and its canny occupation of the 'border between aesthetics and politics' allows theatre to stage the contradiction between these states and – potentially – to effect the emancipatory power that resides in the fusion of these states. Here Gunner and Kruger concur. As Kruger notes:

> The intersection of political, economic, and aesthetic spheres in the institution of theatre as well as the ambiguity of these relationships makes theatre an exemplary site for investigating the complex and contradictory relationships among the discourses and practices sustaining cultural hegemony (*The National Stage* p. 13)

Malcolm Purkey's seminal reflection, '*Tooth and Nail*: Rethinking Form for the South African Theatre', provides a further inroad into understanding theatre's agency in social transformation. Like Kruger, Purkey is interested in the duplicitous and impure role theatre performs in the representation and expression of nationhood. Set against 'the onset of hard-nosed negotiations' of 'post 2nd February, 1990', Purkey sets up a series of key questions pertaining to theatre. These questions, conceived as a supplement – as that which adds to but doesn't add up – cannot be answered without first addressing an anterior and constitutive dilemma which, after Sachs, reads as follows:

> How do we move beyond the reactive apartheid critique? How do we transcend the stock response and the slogan, and begin formulating a comprehensive cultural response to the times? South African society is in a state of the most rapid and complex transition. As apartheid cracks up, and the possibility of a new order based (we hope) on the will of the majority, emerges, oppositional theatre makers face profound questions (p. 155)

These are:

> As apartheid gives way to a new form of government, can theatre makers protect and increase their hard-won relative autonomy, allowing theatre to maintain its responsive and critical role, which has been so central to its particular quality, or will theatre be expected to be subservient to the new order of things?

> Can oppositional theatre maintain its vibrancy and strength, even as its traditional subject, apartheid, finally shows signs of crumbling?

> Is such a thing as objective partisanship possible? That is, can theatre be involved in the struggle for transformation, reconciliation and national unity, and strike a necessary critical distance at the same time?

> Is the so-called, and to my mind narrowly named, 'Protest Play' finally exhausting its meaning and potency?

Can we move from a 'protest' to a 'post-protest' literature? Can our literature and theatre become *pro*active rather than *re*active?

Can we rethink form and find new content for the new South African theatre? Can we build on the remarkable developments of the last four decades?

How do we prepare to make a theatre that contributes to a post-apartheid society? (pp. 155–56)

The questions Purkey poses have proved the seam of ongoing cultural inquiry. Like Kruger, Purkey recognises theatre's 'relative autonomy' in the sphere of cultural production. Like Kruger, Purkey also valorises theatre's 'necessary critical distance' and questions the capacity of theatre to assume an 'objective partisanship'. Purkey also assigns theatre a critical role in the development of a national imaginary. This role, which cannot be prescriptively posted, demands a form of theatrical engagement which, in and through a critical ambivalence, sustains and develops the conditions for protest. Clearly, for Purkey, the period of transition out of which he writes is not a period in which to down tools; on the contrary, it is a heightened and intensively reflexive period in which to nurture the very impurities that make for the finest theatre. Through the collaborative work *Tooth and Nail* (1989–1991) Purkey goes on to answer the questions he poses. But before addressing *Tooth and Nail* – a production which superbly demonstrates the indissoluble relation between politics and aesthetics, and which does so by re-figuring the form and agency of protest theatre – I will firstly ramify the link that joins the critical vision of Kruger to that of Purkey.

Like Purkey, Kruger does not conceive the role of theatre in the construction of a national identity as an indisputable fact but as an 'object of speculation' (*The National Stage* p. 3). The root of Kruger's inquiry is 'the problem of making a nation out of an audience, citizens out of spectators, two key issues whose relationship seems at once natural and hotly in dispute' (p. 4). Kruger goes on to pose the following 'crucial' questions: 'Is the audience spectator or participant? Incoherent crowd or mature nation? And conversely, does mature nationhood call for participation or simply assent?' What is at stake here, Kruger adds, 'is the legitimate role of the people as agent or audience of national representation and the resolution of the persistent tension between agency and audience, revolution and reconciliation' (ibid.).

Like Purkey, Kruger does not perceive the resolution of this tension as given. Rather, she locates theatre's highly charged and ambivalent agency at the root of this tension. For Kruger, it is precisely the fact of theatre's marginalisation – as an art form, as a means of radical inquiry – which allows theatre to deconstruct the very conditions for hope that it seeks to sustain. In the context of South Africa, Purkey articulates theatre's role in sustaining this hope. In 'Twenty-Something Inches Square: Landscape, Mind and Representation', a paper presented at SOAS in 1993, Purkey states: 'The voices that have been hidden by apartheid and oppression must be heard in their own accents, idiolects, concerns and content' (Introduction: The Struggle for Space p. 3). This excavation of hidden stories presupposes their *a priori* silence, a silence conditioned by apartheid, which the conditions for protest could not admit. The rider is how, through theatre, are these hidden stories to be expressed? Given the ethnic, linguistic, and regional diversity of an emergent nation, how is it possible to produce a national cultural imaginary founded on collective assent? My answer is that this collective cultural imaginary remains fraught, if not impossible. Hence the importance of Purkey and Kruger's searching questions. Collective hope, I would suggest, can never be sustained in and through a national imaginary. This, of course, does not dispel the force of a collective imaginary. Instead, the collective imaginary remains sustainable through a constructive embrace of theatre as a liminal, partial, critical and speculative response to the objectivity of nationhood. As Kruger reminds us:

> Notions of 'the people' . . . offer no stable ground or ruling principle on which to erect the nation or the nation's theatre, but rather a battleground of intersecting *fields* on which the legitimacy of national popular representation is publicly contested (*The National Stage* p. 6).

The combative tone of Kruger's argument qualifies and reinforces Purkey's rhetorical question: Whether or not the 'Protest Play' has finally exhausted its 'meaning and potency'. Some may, today, speak of the post-nation and, as a corollary, the post-protest play; yet, given the resilience of the enlightenment ideal of nationhood, an ideal which, as Kruger points out, is the product of 'the functional duplicity of disciplinary autonomy', there remains no way out of the continued examination of a national ideal and the cultural representation thereof. If Purkey's questions still have cogency today, it is because he has factored into them the complexity of human need and its expression through theatre. In this regard Purkey is by no means a solitary voice.

Theatre analyst Ian Steadman also echoes the speculative and reflexive power, that Purkey ascribes to theatre. In his essay 'Collective Creativity: Post-apartheid Theatre', Steadman refers to the Winterveld squatter camp where 'theatre was used to educate a community: not only to extend awareness, but also to provide skills for acting upon that awareness' (p. 312). At once inductive and productive, theatre for Steadman not only 'shows the community how to survive in a system, [but] . . . shows the community how to mobilise resources in order to confront the system' (ibid.). For Steadman, theatre is 'an analogue for social action' and an 'analogue of group experience' (ibid.). Steadman goes so far as to assert that it is this conceptualisation of theatre as a group experience which best qualifies its success. He then makes the compelling suggestion that it is precisely this collective expression that is 'perhaps homologous with a sense of the demise of liberalism':

> Has the emergence of popular democratic politics signalled the emergence of collective creative work and the end of a situation where an individual progressive artist is allowed to speak on behalf of the oppressed? Has the cult of individualism, of personality – with all its implications regarding a 'star' system – begun to fray at the edges? (p. 309).

Given the emergence of a *laissez-faire* culture in South Africa today, a culture marked by the 'cult of individualism', one could pre-empt further inquiry and flatly say no. Nevertheless, holding fast to the collective agency of theatre, I would suggest that Steadman's searching claim is still cogent. If autobiography is emergent, this by no means distinguishes the phenomenon from a collective imaginary. If the hegemonic afflatus of the self can be deemed ascendant, this does not mean that the myriad hidden stories – stories affixed to no star system, with no inherited or manufactured ballast – will not be told. Rather, when speaking of a 'shift' from a crisis of legitimacy to a crisis of identity – in the full knowledge that they are coeval – it is vital that this latter crisis be conceived in the plural. As Steadman insistently reminds us, the non-representation or misrepresentation of the oppressed is not a distant memory, a pathology one excavates by turning to the annals of history; rather, it is a pathology that continues to exist today:

> While some South Africans are celebrating the death of apartheid, the theatre continues to signify the exploitative relations of social life which will long continue to be the heritage of apartheid (p. 86).

In answer to Kruger's question on whether the audience is spectator or participant, Steadman's response would be both. For Steadman it is critical that theatre not reinforce a divide. On the contrary theatre, in order to sustain the ongoing struggle for social, political, and cultural transformation, must sustain in and through its imaginary a double-edged vision of revolution *and* reconciliation. This double-edged agency of theatre is succinctly expressed in Jane Taylor's formulation that theatre is about 'the making of meaning and the meaning of making' (Taking Stock). It is precisely the cogency of this formulation which forms the seam of Kruger's study of the agency of theatre. Because of its formal hybridity and its liminal impurity in relation to the other arts, each of which theatre absorbs in order to make itself, theatre is well placed to expose the contradictions which threaten a projected national unity, while, at the same time, providing a way forward. This way – the way of theatre – is the way of the shadow play. Theatre projects as well as protests, intuits as well as states, dreams as well as concretises. Figural and literal, total and partial, theatre necessarily straddles a contradiction. It is this contradiction that is the root of theatre's 'impurity', an impurity which, for Kruger, marks and mars all claims to legitimacy, be it the legitimacy of the people, the authorised nation, or the legitimacy of contesting fields of cultural inquiry that would pronounce the theatre dead, the better to enliven those art forms that dissimulate a seamless integrity.

It should be noted here that I am not counterpointing what J. M. Coetzee calls 'the mystique of orality' (The Novel in Africa p. 9) with the dead hand of writing. Rather, both fields of expression are conceived as corrupted. If Gunner's tellingly titled introduction to *Politics and Performance*, 'The Struggle for Space', suggests this valorisation of the voice – and Purkey, whom she quotes, certainly confirms this – then it is vital, at the outset, to deconstruct this binary and demystify an oversimplified faith in the voice – as 'accents, ideolects, concerns and content' – as the surest and most 'pure' means of conveying Africa's emergent narrative. As Coetzee suggests, there is no font of speech that could redeem Africa. Voice is yet another compromised notional essence 'in these anti-essential days, these days of fleeting identities that we pick up and wear and discard like clothing' (The Novel in Africa p. 7). If theatre is the space of the spoken word, then it is the space of the compromised and corrupted word. What this awareness achieves is the de-familiarisation, the rendering strange, of the mystique associated with voice. Such a formulation certainly flies in the face of the acculturated conception of Africa as the cradle of orality and, by extension, performance. The implication which underpins this bald contradiction is that theatre is not a platform for the sustenance of this mystique, but a constitutively contested site in which voice – among other variables – reflexively foregrounds and challenges its putative truth. That this mystique prevails, that popular opinion persists in perceiving voice as the locus of truth, in no way diminishes my critique of it. Voice is not *quite* the 'dark essence of the body', just as Africa is not 'a continent where people share' (p. 5). What has increasingly become a matter for dispute, therefore, is the originary primacy of the voice and of the collective. In the context of this inquiry both are necessary, and both are makeshift. If this is so, it is because Africa, and Africanness, does not constitute 'a special identity, a special fate' (ibid.). Rather, Africa is made and remade. The role of theatre, there, is not to speak its truth, to bear witness and give testimony, but to understand the limits and impossibility inherent in these acts. If in Africa there is no 'shared fiction of the future', if 'the creation of the past seems to have exhausted . . . collective creative energies' (p. 3), then, all the more, one needs to rediscover – in these anti-essential days – the means to rethink the jaundiced logic of the collective, and, by extension, the theatrical role of the voice. To not do so would be to fall precisely into the trap of mysticism, a trap that ensures that theatre replays the past at the expense of an incommensurable present and unthinkable future.

This resistance to acculturated truths, we will discover, is what distinguishes the theatre of Malcolm Purkey, William Kentridge and Brett Bailey. While they understand the importance of witness and testimony, they also understand that in and through theatre this witness and testimony is necessarily impure and partial. In the work of each there is no fourth wall and its attendant illusion of transparency. Presence, voice, meaning are the symptoms of a ghosting: phenomena thwarted in the instant of their enactment. This process is not understood as a failing, but as attempts to dramatise and manifest a constitutive indeterminacy. Against a culture of resistance which, for decades, has reduced theatre to a moral polemic, Purkey, Kentridge and Bailey have in singular and connected ways sought to convey an immanent, non-discursive and unresolved struggle with the making of meaning as an act of change. Their theatre has, as a consequence, foregrounded the limit *and* openness of theatre-making. For Purkey, Kentridge and Bailey, theatre's strength lies in its illegitimacy, and it thus emerges in Kruger's words as 'an exemplary site for investigating the complex and contradictory relationships among the discourses and practices sustaining cultural hegemony' (*The National Stage* p. 13). So while each seemingly engages with the necessity for witness and testimony, they also know that this necessity cannot be fulfilled without a redefinition of the very form of theatre, a redefinition which, in the name of truth, must challenge and undermine truth's transparency.

The Junction Avenue Theatre Company's play *Tooth and Nail* is a case in point. For Purkey, *Tooth and Nail* best exemplifies an answer to the questions he poses above. Created over six months in 1988 and presented at the Market Theatre in February 1989,

Tooth and Nail pre-dates and anticipates Sachs's inquiry into the development of a radical cultural imaginary. A pointedly collaborative work comprising puppetry, music, movement, oratory and dialogue, *Tooth and Nail*'s objective, through improvisation, was to 'critically reflect the mad world of apartheid in all its manifestations' (*Tooth and Nail* p. 156). While influenced by an international commitment to collective expression, *Tooth and Nail* was also infused by 'a vital additional element': the creation of 'a space where South Africans [could] momentarily leave the monster of apartheid behind them and meet as equals, without prejudice, to work creatively together' (ibid.). Here it is the very ideal of collective creativity that is momentary and aberrant.

Amongst theatre practitioners in South Africa, Purkey's testimony is a familiar one. As William Kentridge also attests:

> The vital part of workshop theatre in South Africa in the 70's and 80's, was that it was a practical and workable and successful strategy for overcoming one of the factors of apartheid, which was to make different people completely ignorant of the details of the lives of large sections of other groups in the country . . . The workshops and those play situations in which those different parts of the world were able to come together were a basic information-sharing strategy (An Interest in the Making of Things p. 145).

For Purkey, Kentridge and Steadman, the workshop was a vital arena in which to overcome psychic entrapment and isolation under apartheid. Furthermore, it was in and through collective creativity that the 'monster' could be confronted and exorcised. That the workshop continues to thrive not only proves its continued currency as a means of making theatre, it also reinforces the fact that the 'monster' that separates people and renders a desired unity unassailable persists.

In 'South African Perspectives on Post-coloniality in and through Performance Practice', Miki Flockemann points to collective creativity as a continued constant in theatre. Today the monster of apartheid is being torn apart bit by bit, the visceral and abstract threat refracted, localised and particularised. Flockemann notes the emergence of

> 'minor' voices, as woman, gay, coloured . . . can be seen as attempting to construct a 'new' space from which to speak, often in one-man/woman shows which claim subjective experience previously subsumed in public political narratives (pp. 235–36).

These voices, while subjective, remain linked to the 'cultural minorities' from which they stem. Hence autobiography remains a product of the collective, and the collective, in turn, the key to unlocking the agency of theatre in South Africa. Steadman's insistence that South African society continues to be marked and marred by 'the heritage of apartheid' all the more reinforces the currency of theatre as a means through which to confront the past, contest the present, and construct the future. Matthew Krouse, in 'My Life in the Theatre of War: The Development of an Alternative Consciousness', reinforces Steadman's conclusion. 'It is strange,' Krouse notes,

> but official homophobia appears to be replacing official racism and fear of communism. The banning of political ideas is being replaced by the banning of already otherized sexual identities.

... This is alarming because it indicates, to me, that in many ways the struggle for human rights is far from over in South Africa. If the freedom to love is indeed part of the struggle, then perhaps ours has just begun (p. 114).

Given the continued struggle for human rights, evident in the emergence of 'minor voices', it is clear that Purkey's vision of the theatre workshop as a place where the divided can meet 'as equals, without prejudice' remains a necessary – if utopian – one. Nevertheless, theatre is not merely a stage upon which to enact a moral corrective. Instead, theatre is the stage in and through which the forms and languages that give breath to this corrective can be *discovered*. Protest needs a shape. Conceived non-reactively, protest through theatre emerges, after Kentridge, as 'a faith in a practical epistemology' (The Crocodile's Mouth p. xii).

For the Junction Avenue Theatre Company, working in the late 1980s, this shape – or practical epistemology – initially constituted 'a strong concept of character development and narrative structure . . . indebted in part to a kind of social realism and in part to the theories of Brecht' (*Tooth and Nail* p. 158). This shape, largely defined by the oppressiveness of the lived world in which the Junction Avenue Theatre Company found itself, would be transformed by the company's exposure, via tours through America and Europe, to the work of Kantor and Pina Bausch, 'Oh La La Human Steps' and Carbon 14, and other leading experimental companies from the USSR, Eastern Europe and Latin America. Through this exposure the company confronted an internationally 'emergent theatre language [that was] highly complex, sophisticated, imagistic and abrasive' (p. 159). As a consequence, the initial formal orientation governed by 'simple dramatic through-lines and straight forward narratives, even when broken up with Brechtian interventions' (p. 160) no longer seemed enough. The challenge that Purkey and others in the company now faced was how to reconcile the radical theatrical experimentation that they encountered with the blighted and oppressive world to which they returned. The challenge would prove not to be as difficult as it seemed. On the contrary, Purkey was to discover that an experimental theatre language was the surest and most effective way to reflect and engage with political unrest. The palpable media imagery of oppression and resistance,

the upturned cars on fire and burning bodies . . . the Zola Budd and the Casspir, new police and riot police uniforms, gas masks and riot helmets, wooden replicas of AK 47's, and the dreaded necklace with its connotations of witch-craft and burning at the stake [provided artists in general with] a subject of the most powerful and devastating sort (ibid.).

In answer to the madness and unrest, the Junction Avenue's response was to fragment and refract the narrative. In *Tooth and Nail*, the first production in which the company would fuse a radical aesthetic to an oppressive situation, the narrative structure was broken into 70 fragments, each forming a 'fleeting' image or aspect of South African life. The formal language that defined the respective fragments included 'song, dance, chant, imagery, obsessional repetition, fictional language, opera pastiche and puppetry' (*Tooth and Nail* p. 161).

In keeping with Eisenstein's ideas about collision in the cinema or the theories of the Surrealists, each fragment was intended to derive much of its meaning from juxtaposition with other fragments. Each fragment was conceived of as very short, some only lasting thirty seconds and most lasting no more than a minute or two. The overall effect we wanted to create was one of a barrage of contradictory statements and pictures, abstract sound, cold ideas and impenetrable flashes of meaning that somehow threw light on the deeply confused historical moment we found ourselves in (ibid.).

Here it is critical to note Purkey's resistance to transparency, his insistence on contradiction, and his valorisation of theatre's syncretic impurity. Purkey's eventual rejection of the influence of Brecht's Epic Theatre and his embrace of Eisenstein's logic of montage and the Surrealist's more insistently unresolved and syncretic fusion of differences is telling. If Brecht constructed a meta-aesthetic in which history is told as a series of non-sequential but ultimately sustained and containable movements, then the aesthetic that governed *Tooth and Nail* sought to shatter every strategy of containment. Rather, meaning, according to Eisenstein's logic of montage, was forged through an instantaneous concatenation of fragments. This meaning was never prescribed or anticipated, but discovered in the instant of perception. Because of the rejection of a single point of entry and exit and the cancellation of a central figure that could be said to narratologically or psychologically mediate the work, the audience was forced to accept its own immanence, it own agency, as another dimension of a larger – abrasive and dislocated – intensity. At once empowering and disempowering, *Tooth and Nail* cut to the core of an aesthetic and political revolution in process. This revolution, as Steadman, Krouse, and others attest, is by no means over. And, as Purkey reminds us: 'We are no longer fighting against the state in a broad anti-apartheid struggle. We are now faced with the complex task of what we want to fight for' (p. 161).

In this regard surrealism has proved a critical influence. As an aesthetic that in Alexandrian's words 'set out to liberate the workings of the subconscious, disrupting conscious thought processes by the use of irrationality and enigma, and exploiting the artistic possibilities of terror and eroticism' (*Surrealist Art* p. 7), surrealism proved a compelling aesthetic vehicle. If Steadman ascribed a positivist agency to collective creativity, then Purkey and the Junction Avenue Theatre Company sought to break this positivist deployment of the collective and, through irrationality and enigma, to sustain a more complex inquiry into theatre's possibilities. In this regard, Purkey's 'fight' is by no means over.

If I have chosen to address the strength of collective creativity by focusing on *Tooth and Nail* it is because it is the surest index of a theatre that ramifies a radical politics with a radical aesthetic vision. That the play was workshopped in 1988, a period of stringent internal repression and boycotts, is all the more remarkable. The influence of this first experimental theatrical engagement finds its latter-day echo in the works of Brett Bailey and William Kentridge, dramaturges who have similarly sustained theatre's pre-eminent value as a liminal, syncretic, and impure art form. Like Purkey, Bailey and Kentridge have contested an issue-driven theatre defined in a restricted way by social realism. In so doing they have not only extended the appeal of theatre, but reinforced the complex veracity that conditions the making of theatre. Each in their own way sustains the critical and aesthetic edge that Kruger describes as the 'border between aesthetics and politics' (*The National Stage* p. 187), a border, which, in and through the enactment of a play, is ceaselessly galvanised, torn, and contested. Reflecting on the aims and objectives that defined *Tooth and Nail*, Purkey notes:

> We wanted aspects of our work to be difficult and opaque, for we wanted to make a theatre, which was not easy to co-opt. On the other hand we wanted to make a play as popular and populist as our previous work. Theatre for the majority implies popular and accessible forms, but the then current theatre seemed bankrupt to us. We wanted our work to be new and difficult and popular all at the same time (*Tooth and Nail* p. 163).

While Purkey challenged Brecht's conception of Epic Theatre, he was not averse to learning from Brecht's critique of Lukacs:

> We must not derive realism as such from particular existing works, but we shall use every means, old and new, tried and untried, derived from art and derived from other sources, to render reality to men in a form they can master . . . New problems appear and demand new methods. Reality changes; in order to represent it, modes of representation must also change (ibid., Brecht, *Aesthetics and Politics*, 81).

However, a key difference between Brecht's vision and that of Purkey persists. If Brecht valorises mastery, then Purkey – given the extremity of the 'barrage' of contradictions that defined *Tooth and Nail* – produces an aesthetic and political vision that cannot, finally, be mastered:

> We embarked on a project to radically change our modes of representation, without successfully rendering reality in a form available for mastery. Many found the play [produced at the Market Theatre in January 1989] too difficult and inaccessible, though many others were deeply excited by the new form and the challenging ideas. By the time we had reworked the play by invitation for the 1991 Grahamstown Festival it seemed much less opaque. History had caught up (*Tooth and Nail* p. 163).

The upshot of this telling reflection is that the radical role and agency of theatre is not derived simply through the construction of a transparent and immediately digestible truth. On the contrary, it is theatre's encrypted and refracted concatenation of intensities, its construction as a linked series of defamiliarised and surreal evocations, which allows for a 'new' thought, a 'new' feeling.

Here it is important to remember that Purkey's primary political objective was to institute the new on behalf of a human struggle for freedom. This proviso will become all the more urgent as we forge ahead. As Kruger, after Sacvan Bercovitch, has also pointed out: '[T]he ground for radical dissent' should not 'redefine radicalism as an affirmation of cultural values' that confirm 'patrician domination' (*The National Stage* p. 28). If I reiterate this proviso, it is because theatre in South Africa has largely failed to sustain the aesthetic complexity and ontological intensity manifested in *Tooth and Nail*. Its failure to imagine itself as a practical and, more forcefully, a radical epistemology, has resulted in a diminished conception of how, through theatrical experimentation, one achieves social transformation. All too often, and all too predictably, theatre has emerged as a pale pretext for a plea for human rights. As Miki Flockemann has noted, what has become dominant within the South African theatrical imaginary is a host of 'nostalgic evocations of the past, particularly in musical dramas which attempt to reconstruct lost communities' (p. 236). This mimetic and workmanlike revisionism has resulted, all the more tellingly, in

> reruns or reworkings of older productions, perhaps most notably early works by Athol Fugard . . . [which] can be seen as even more pertinent in the post-revolutionary period than when they first appeared as 'transgressive or resistant cultural acts', for the way they perform the construction and far-reaching effects of the diseased body politic (ibid.).

Here Flockemann echoes Krouse and Steadman. Here, more troublingly, Flockemann locates the continued, indeed ascendant, dominance of an aesthetic founded on transparency and verisimilitude: worlds remembered, repeated, that reinforce a historically produced psychic disfigurement which, while it persists, is not matched by theatrical forms that could transfigure or critically reflect on the disfigurement.

Against this distanced and mediated return to – and re-run of – a seemingly transparent pathological imaginary, Flockemann points to the work of Brett Bailey and William Kentridge as salient alternatives of theatrical expression. In speaking of Kentridge's *Ubu and the Truth Commission* (1997), scripted by Jane Taylor and involving the Handspring Puppet Company, Flockemann notes the deployment of 'eclectic performance styles and traditions' the better to 'represent the unrepresentable, or to say the unsayable concerning the atrocities of the past which have come to light through the Truth Commission testimonies' (p. 236). What Flockemann neglects to point out, though, is the reflexive rigour, which governs Kentridge and Taylor's exploration of what truth may or may not be. Like Antjie Krog, who tracks the Truth Commission in *Country of My Skull*, Kentridge and Taylor point to the evasiveness of truth and to the corrupted ground that founds truth's expression. As Krog observes:

> Every narrative carries the imprint of the narrator. And if you believe your own version, your own lie – because as narrators we all give ourselves permission to believe our own versions – how can it be said that you are being misleading? To what extent can you bring yourself not to know what you know? Eventually it is not the lie that matters, but the mechanism in yourself that allows you to accept distortions (p. 197).

Krog's critical reflection succinctly articulates the basis for, and the processes involved in, the making of *Ubu and the Truth Commission*. Indeed, her observation cuts to the core of Kentridge's oeuvre. In an interview with Carolyn Christov-Bakargiev, Kentridge counters the dominant aesthetic and ethic founded on transparency and verisimilitude with 'the *unwilling* suspension of disbelief' (In Conversation with William Kentridge

p. 19). Like Krog, Kentridge challenges the veracity of aesthetic and ethical forms which, in the repression of their constructedness, belie the fact that truths are made and remade. In addition, what interests Krog, as it does Kentridge, is the *mechanism* which allows one to make up a given truth. As a mechanism, then, theatre sustains a constitutively restless and provisional relation to truth. Hence Kentridge's 'polemic':

> Mistrust of Good Ideas in the abstract. Mistrust of starting with a knowledge of the meaning of an image and thinking it can be executed. There is for me more than an accidental linguistic connection between executing an idea and *killing* it (The Crocodile's Mouth p. xii).

The basis for Kentridge's mistrust is not scepticism. Rather, it marks an other faith, one that is not defined by the suspension of disbelief, but which, in its paradoxical faithlessness, returns both thought and deed to an originary discontinuity and unsettlement. For Kentridge there can be no art that can change life without this constitutive unsettlement, which is why, like Krog, Kentridge conceives of truth under erasure, and promotes 'trust in the contingent, the inauthentic, the whim, the practical, as strategies for *finding* meaning' (p. xiv, my emphasis). As a 'practical epistemology', then, theatre emerges as 'one of many possible ways' (ibid.) of dealing with the making of meaning.

As stated at the outset, what distinguishes theatre is its 'persistent impurity'. A domain caught between the factual and the fictive, theatre either suppresses the duplicitous condition for its being or chooses to foreground this duplicitousness. Kentridge has chosen the latter position. Together with Jane Taylor and the Handspring Puppet Company, Kentridge has, in *Ubu and the Truth Commission*, elected to dramatise and to frame the *question of truth*. There the machinery of theatre-making is deployed as a reflexive tool and as a thematic means through which to tell the story of truth. This strategy allows Kentridge and Taylor to stand both inside and outside truth, thereby exposing its 'functional duplicity'. The conceit is a consummate one, for while it gives the lie to truth, it also informs us that the lie – another name for theatre – is also a kind of truth.

Reflecting on a play about the Truth Commission, *The Story I am About To Tell*, which was made by a support group for survivors of apartheid atrocities, and which was performed by 'the three "real" people [who] give their testimony' (The Crocodile's Mouth p. xiii), Kentridge notes that despite its apparent authenticity, the play remained 'a partial solution to the questions raised by the Commission. Because what the "real" people give, is not the evidence itself, but performances of the evidence' (ibid.). Kentridge goes on to note: 'the most moving moment . . . was when one of the survivors (survivor of three years on death row) had a lapse of memory'. 'How could he forget his own story?' Kentridge asks, then adds: 'but of course he was in that moment a performer at a loss for his place in the script' (pp. xiii–xiv). Between memory and memory's loss, lies theatre. Furthermore, within memory and its loss lies what Kentridge calls the paradox that is 'half testimony, half performance' (p. xiv). If Kentridge insists upon the insufficiency of both, it is not because he wishes to insist upon a lack at the expense of truth, but because he wishes to affirm the lack – or lacuna – which inhabits truth. His very 'faith' as an artist and thinker is marked by an attenuated and deeply felt ambivalence: a resistance to the seamlessness and transparency of meaning. His is a resistant faith, a faith attentive not only to the fact that meaning, in the first and last instance, is incommensurable, but that meaning, as a ceaseless project of making, can only know itself by *surprising* or *alarming* itself.

Ubu and the Truth Commission, like its aesthetic and ethical precursor *Tooth and Nail*, serves here as an exemplary instance of the best that is reflexive and impure in theatre. In Kruger's sense, the production exemplifies the exposure of 'the functional duplicity of disciplinary autonomy' (*The National Stage* p. 187). It is not only the disciplinary autonomy of the Truth Commission itself that is in question, but also the autonomy of a cultural institution that could co-opt the production in the name of aesthetic excellence and, by implication, aesthetic truth. For Kentridge, the very pairing of aesthetics and truth is a contradiction in terms. In 'An Interest in the Making of Things', speaking of his film *Johannesburg Second Greatest City after Paris*, Kentridge pointedly remarks:

> I didn't start off saying, well, I want to do a film about two men and their rather distant relationship to each other which is mediated by the view of a starving crowd in front of them. It started as much less precise and impure (p. 143).

While Kentridge is interested

> in the area in which meaning comes, it's not something that's just storyboarded and scripted in advance, it's between programme and it's also obviously not complete chance (p. 144).

For Kentridge the creative act cannot be rationally over-determined and neither is it subject wholly to chance. Instead, the act – an act of making – is necessarily caught between knowing and unknowing. If knowledge is a compatriot it is also an enemy. An equivalent logic, as I have pointed out, pertains to the meaning and making of truth. If Kentridge defers to the unconscious, and suggests that 'one's unconscious is a step ahead', he is clearly ascribing a dimension to theatre-making that is not hard-and-fast and literal. The fact that he describes his more recent production, *Confessions of Zeno*, as a 'dream' further reinforces the importance of wonder in the reflexive instant in which wonder is materially constructed. Mary Lynn Mather reports him as saying 'It's almost like seeing a dream and how the dream *works*' (Cue, p. 2, my emphasis).

Flockemann points to a similar material reflexivity and preoccupation with the unconscious in Brett Bailey's *Ipi Zombi?* (1996). Like Kentridge's dramas, Bailey's are ensemble works. If Kentridge and Bailey are presented as auteurs, they, in turn, reiterate the power of the collective that comprises and produces the work. What links the works of these dramaturges is the syncretic combination of elements, an interest in repetition and ritual, and a commitment to the artistic possibilities, which an exploration of irrationality and enigma and terror and eroticism afford. In Bailey's play *Ipi Zombi?* the 'true' story that is told happened in August 1995 near Kokstad in the Eastern Cape, where 12 boys were killed in a combi-taxi accident. Subsequent accusations of witchcraft resulted in the brutal murder of two women.

> Perceived as one of the most controversial aspects is the way the work simultaneously performs the 'constructedness' of the claims, but also presents us with the 'reality' of the existence of the zombies: 'this is a hungry story', the audience is told, 'we live in hungry times, the roads are eating our children (South African Perspectives p. 237)

Flockemann's reading of *Ipi Zombi?* echoes my reading of *Ubu and the Truth Commission*. In both works, the audience is positioned within and outside the 'truth'. In both works, this shift allows for a more flexible deployment of the mechanics of staging the enigma that dogs a received truth. One of the striking characteristics of an emancipatory politics and aesthetics is that it heightens the subjectivity of truth and challenges its hegemony as an *a priori* law or value. The downside of the increasingly speculative, relative, and immanent grasp of the truth is that, in dethroning the authority and established power of a unified resistance culture, it has enabled the very liberalism that Steadman pronounced dead, to thrive. Hence Kruger and Bercovitch's caution that radicalism not be redefined as an affirmation of cultural values which confirm a patrician domination.

Kentridge's production of *Confessions of Zeno*, is an interesting anomaly since it precariously tracks the fault-line between theatre's radical agency and its conscription into a received set of values. Inspired by Italo Svevo's pre-First World War novel, *Confessions of Zeno* pivots on a curiously negligible *ménage à trois*. At the centre is Zeno, effete, bored, inactive, who struggles to give up smoking, is oppressed by a dead father he cannot renounce, a wife he does not care for, and a lover whose charms only further aggravate his boredom. The theme seems to reproduce the traits of the bourgeois drawing room drama. In so doing, the current preoccupation with the self or private life is emphasised. The story is slight, easily digestible, and often amusing. Its enactment, though, comprises a boldly congested mix of animation, shadow-puppetry, recursive and monotonic music (by Kevin Volans), opera, monologue – in short, all the ingredients one associates with a Kentridge production. However, unlike in previous works such as *Ubu and the Truth Commission*, there seems to be no in-built reflexive critique, no critical distance that forces the audience to mediate the drama. It is as though Kentridge has intuited a cultural exhaustion, a sense of ennui that has shorn society of its reflexive power and left it as naked and perplexed as Zeno, the central figure who embodies this intuition. Taylor's libretto reinforces this sense. Her text, featured on a LED, is repetitive, obsessive, often fragmented, and non-sequential, suggesting a psychology that is neither propulsive nor depthful. If *Confessions of Zeno* embodies the current fascination with the emergent self, then it is an exhausted and pointless self, bereft of a reflexive and critical power. The question is whether Kentridge's production merely reproduces this current fetishisation of the self, or whether by foregrounding it he in fact is once again a 'step ahead'?

It is clear that while Kentridge utilises an aesthetic and culture familiar to Western theatre goers and TV viewers – 'a flawed, sympathetic, and usually private protagonist with whom the bourgeois audience can identify' (*The National Stage* p. 18) – the means through which he produces this reading is insistently strange. Does this mean that Kentridge exposes 'the contradiction within bourgeois society between public relations of apparently inescapable domination and the suffering that is identified as essential[ly] private and thus not the province of public social action'? (ibid.). Here I confess that I cannot finally state – either with certainty or with a productive uncertainty – whether Kentridge is a part of the problem or a ravishing and subtle critic thereof. What remains undeniable, nevertheless, is that the very absence of conflict and controversy in and around the play, and the deafening applause at its close, all the more silences the private story: that of Zeno and society at large. A paradox emerges: Zeno confesses yet does not confess. Prattle corrupts meaning. There are in fact no asides and no privacy. On the contrary, under the glare of footlights, the self which South African society champions today emerges as a husk, a late-modern gasp of a high-modern catastrophe. If anything, *Confessions of Zeno* poses a warning. If Kentridge describes the work as a 'dream' then it is a dream from which we must awake.

Returning to Gunner's formulation that South Africa has shifted from a crisis of legitimacy to a crisis of identity, we now find that this crisis is the very seam of Kentridge's drama. What is interesting is that the crisis is not presented as such. Instead, through a repetitive and often non-sequential script, through an eerily apocalyptic projection of puppetry and video imagery, the lulling dance of cigarette smoke and the explosions of war, through projected though unspoken words, the audience is drawn into a dilemma which the drama cannot or will not speak, and that dilemma – the dilemma of the play and the dilemma of the society that contains it – concerns the reason for being. As I understand it, *Confessions of Zeno* suggests that there is no reason, and worse, no being. Hence the husk that defines the play's characterisation, its haunting and abyssal music, its stripped scenography, its making of itself as a withered spectacle. Therefore, my horror at the applause, applause as resounding as it is utterly meaningless.

As a collective exploration of the emptiness of self-obsession, *Confessions of Zeno* marks a new chapter in South African theatre. If Bailey explores *ek-stasis* through ritual, then Kentridge, in *Confessions of Zeno*, has explored a society inured to the crisis that drives it. Today, it seems, there is no fight: no understanding of what it is one must fight *for*. Today the radical integrity of Purkey's vision touches a barren eye and a barren ear. Which is not to say that the struggle for which Purkey has fought is over. Rather, it would seem that the struggle has been lost, mislaid, that it has forgotten itself and exists in a vacuum between testimony and performance. If *Confessions of Zeno* could be said to exemplify this vacuum it is because it is both a symptomatic manifestation thereof and its most compelling critique. One discernible reason for this vacuum is the enervation of collective creativity, an enervation, which Coetzee, in 'The Novel in Africa', interprets as symptomatic of a society exhausted by its past and incapable of anything other than *enduring* the present. The future, he says, is 'a structure of hopes and expectations . . . [which] resides in the mind [and] has no reality' (p. 3). It is, I think, an equivalent exhaustion, impasse, and impossibility, which defines both the theme and enactment of *Confessions of Zeno*. There the collective energy – the energy and brilliance of Kentridge,

Taylor, Volans, and the Handspring Puppet Company – revolves around a corpse, and that corpse is the intransitive and un-housed self. The warning here, a warning I ascribe to *Confessions of Zeno*, is that we tread very carefully when expounding the value of the emergent self in South African culture. Moreover, that in the context of theatre – which I have argued to be the site of the most incisive exploration of a collective cultural imaginary – we continually re-examine the conditions that make life possible or impossible. If Kentridge has foregrounded the ascendance of ennui and fatalism – embodied in the figure of Zeno – it is because he must post the danger that awaits those who would renounce collective agency in favour of the aborted and subtracted agency of the self. If Kentridge has sought to show the workings of a dream, it should be added that he has also shown the workings of a nightmare. Today, in South Africa, there remains no triumph of the self. Rather, the self emerges as yet another endgame: yet another inauthentic and improbable probability. Zeno speaks. On the screen we read:

> I became artificial, so that my natural self came out
> in strange and unnatural bursts that struck me as false.

EIGHT

An Extremely Vexed Occupation: Writing South Africa

> . . . nothing is
> But what it is not
>
> — *William Shake-*
>
> *speare*

Porter tells us that when Giuseppe Verdi wrote his opera of *Macbeth*, premiered in Florence in 1847, his aim was to show 'effects with causes' (Effects with Causes p. 20). At the forefront of his interpretation of Shakespeare's play was A. W. Schlegel's *Lectures on Dramatic Art and Literature*. 'In the progress of the action, this tragedy is altogether the reverse of *Hamlet*,' wrote Schlegel.

> [I]t strides forward with terrible rapidity. . . . All designs are scarcely conceived but they are put into action . . . as if the drags were taken from the wheels of time, and they rolled along without interruption in their descent (ibid.).

If the moral lesson of Shakespeare's play and Verdi's opera is clear, what mattered the more was the inexorable *descent*. A drama about evil, both secular and supernatural, the opera would be suppressed in Papal Rome. That Verdi felt compelled to assure the Florence impresario that the content was not 'political' (this after the crushing of the 1848 revolution), and that the opera was a faithful rendition of 'a tragedy that is one of mankind's greatest creations' (ibid.), reveals precisely the play's unnerving quality.

It is not surprising, then, that in South Africa in 2002 Brett Bailey would take up the challenge which Verdi's opera presents. Not for him the cerebrality and introspection of *Hamlet*; better the excrescence of a drama about evil that no happy ending can satisfactorily contain. Bailey shifts the drama to darkest Africa, the continent which, 'after the pyramids', Hegel declared, 'World spirit leaves . . . never to return' (Kentridge, Faustus in Africa! p. 128). No matter how high-handed one may find Hegel's riposte, no matter how one may demur or protest, there is no dispelling the fact that the philosopher's view has become common global knowledge. Africa: place of unreason, place of the mad; un-evolved, unworldly, superstitious and immoral. Not a place for the 'World spirit' but a place for the damned, a place where effects exist *without* causes.

In 'African Modes of Self-Writing' Achille Mbembe reflects upon this view of Africa in the global imaginary. Instead of countering it, Mbembe explores how Africa has internalised and domesticated this pathological reading. The 'state of war in contemporary Africa should in fact be conceived as a general cultural experience that shapes identities, just as do the family, the school, and other social institutions,' says Mbembe. It is war that defines Africa as a 'zone of *indistinction* . . . a space set outside human jurisdiction, where the frontiers between the rule of law and chaos disappear, [in which] decisions about life and death become entirely arbitrary, and everything becomes possible'. It is this 'descent into indistinction', the 'spread of terror' defined by torture, mutilation, and mass killing, which 'fragments inhabited space, blows apart temporal frames of reference, and diminishes the possibilities available to individuals to fulfil themselves as continuous subjects'.

It is this axiomatic view of Africa – part prejudice, part truth – that informs the theatre of Brett Bailey. The inverse of a moral or redemptive vision – typified in the theatre of Athol Fugard – Bailey's theatre precisely explores what Mbembe calls the 'descent into indistinction'. Bailey's Africa, after Mbembe, renounces the moral imperative: 'a debt owed to life'. Against causation and the conception of subject-hood as continuous, Bailey's theatre re-enacts what Mbembe terms 'the exercise of charisma (which authorises the practice of oracular pronouncement and prophecy, of possession and healing); the logic of sacrifice (mourning and funerals); and . . . the domain of the miraculous (. . . the belief that anything is possible)'. It is these key psychic and epistemic formations that, after Mbembe, come to mark a theatre 'sculpted by cruelty', a theatre which marks the 'new African practices of the self'.

Mbembe's reading of Africa echoes Schlegel's reading of *Macbeth*. For what compels and disturbs Schlegel is that the drama advances with an uncontrollable and 'terrible rapidity', that it possesses a design that is 'scarcely conceived', that it hurtles onward 'without interruption in [its] descent'. A play defined by mutiny, betrayal and insurrection, *Macbeth* comes to embody present-day Africa. Given its Dionysian violence and its traffic in the charismatic, the sacrificial, and the miraculous, it is not surprising that the play was banned in Papal Rome. In unruly Africa such censure falls away. Though Africa may yearn for faith and reason – evinced in the call for a renaissance – this cannot be achieved without addressing the critical renunciation of the debt owed to life, a renunciation that, for Mbembe, 'marks the limit of the principle of utility – and thus the idea of the preservation – in the service of a community'.

Caught between a yearning for faith and reason, and its impossibility, Mbembe does not wholly yield to the prevailing perception of Africa as a zone of indistinction – 'of nonsubstantiality, instability, and indetermination' – but, by passing through this axiomatic perception he restores, after Fanon, a conception of change from the standpoint of time:

Because the time we live in is fundamentally fractured, the very project of an essentialist recovery of the self is, by definition, doomed. Only the disparate, and often intersecting, practices through which Africans *stylise* their conduct and life can account for the thickness of which the African present is made.

It is precisely here that Mbembe activates a reflexive turn that at no point is allowed to rigidify. Stylisation becomes the means through which Africa embraces its indeterminacy. And it is here that Bailey's theatre emerges as an innovative response to the contradictions that, necessarily, define the making of Africa. Stripped of a morality that is incommensurate with the truth of living in Africa – of being African – Bailey chooses, rather, to explore the parodic quintessence of existing prejudices about Africa. That his theatre is also a brilliant critique of these prejudices is another matter. Eschewing faith in redemption or craven reason, Bailey elects to explore the zone of indistinction in an enabling way. Critically, his drama does not conveniently parse prejudice and reflexive critique; rather, it tills and twists the unease and indeterminacy that dogs the perception of Africa within the global imaginary.

Robert Greig's review in the *Sunday Independent* foregrounds the unease that Bailey exacerbates. Greig begins by noting the attendant hazards that come with the transposition of Verdi's opera to 'postcolonial Africa', an Africa that exists after imperialism, after the World spirit, after . . . but also before.

Bailey's production is not one that is made for the royal court of England or the opera houses of Florence and Paris. There is nothing smug or effete, no craven last compromise – unlike Shakespeare, who wrote the play for the court of King James and ensured that the play's inversion and perversion of power would be staunched at the close by the restoration of power's rightful authority; unlike Verdi, who despite his compulsive attraction to the drama's irrevocable descent would still seek a cause within its dark effects. Bailey, in Greig's words, would 'chop into Verdi's score with all the vengeance of the Macbeths themselves, hacking the opera down to about 90 minutes, and centre[ing] it very much on the drama' (Horrific and Funny Product p. 10).

For Bailey there would be no final reintegration, no final authorisation of justice. It is this refusal – a conscious elision of the reactionary premise that founds the conclusion of the play – that makes it all the more compelling and ultimately disturbing. It is this disturbance, measured through Greig's response, which has triggered this concluding inquiry into the dark veracity of South African culture, a veracity and complexity which finds a brilliant psychic, ethical, and aesthetic correlative in Bailey's *Macbeth*.

In keeping with the syncretic logic of postcoloniality, Greig notes that Bailey 'mingles allusions to different times and places – for Bailey artistic purity and consistency are yesterday's notions' (ibid.). The driving power of the production, we learn, is not textual but visual. The implication is that the story of *Macbeth*, by virtue of being a school set text, is already thoroughly inscribed into the cultural DNA of the audience. A further implication – which challenges the capacity of words to stand in the place of imagery – points to Bailey's preoccupation with visualisation and movement as the dominant markers for contemporary meaning, markers which have become increasingly more trenchant and pervasive in cultural production.

Today we watch more than we listen. Meaning largely resides in the eye. Hence Greig's observation that Bailey's production emphasises 'multimedia action rather than music' (ibid.). Both music and words become secondary. 'Bailey thinks in the images of a painter who has been saturated in the darkest of black magic and Hieronymous Bosch' (ibid.). This prioritisation of the visual – and its linkage with the occult – produces yet another structural de-territorialisation: that of the stage. There is no proscenium arch, hence no 'resultant safety for the audience'. On the contrary,

> the cavernous State Theatre has been cut in two. The audience sits on the stage in a V-shape. A playing area is between the seats and the orchestra, which is shoved up against the opposite wall . . . As you come into the theatre, you move between life-sized statues of sangomas and warriors: at first, not looking properly, you imagine the figures are live human beings . . . Bailey places the action of his work in an indeterminate zone between life and death (ibid.).

Following Greig's reading, a disturbing logic unfolds: having placed the ear under erasure, fixated and haunted the eye, then refracted it through movement, having undermined the audience's capacity to mediate the action by splitting its focus, Bailey has shifted the established co-ordinates of reception. To what end? Greig points to the answer when he notes that Bailey 'places the action of his work in *an indeterminate zone* between life and death' (ibid., my emphasis). This placement, the key to Bailey's oeuvre, brings me to the core of this inquiry: an examination of indeterminacy as the condition for the representation of culture in South Africa, a condition that Leon de Kock describes as an 'extremely vexed occupation' (Introduction: South Africa in the Global Imaginary p. 272).

The source of this vexation is incarnated in Bailey's *Macbeth*, a production in which, according to Greig,

> [d]ivisions between life and death, good and bad are entirely eroded. . . . a production that has a consistent vision of evil as a state of no boundaries (Horrific and Funny Product p. 10).

If Shakespeare and Verdi post a triumphal and concluding good, then Bailey, unhampered by a teleological commitment to the righting of a collapsed order, chooses – or is compelled against choice – to shift his focus or fixation to the unresolved moment in the battle between good and evil when evil assumes dominance. Whether or not in that moment Bailey *chooses* to prioritise evil is open to question. To maintain that he does is, I believe, to ascribe sovereignty and control. Bailey, I would suggest, resists the notion of total control. Greig, in turn, qualifies his claim:

> The sheer originality of Bailey's vision is arresting. It is steeped in a sense of the otherworldly but also – and this is what makes it eerie – in a slightly Edwardian notion of juju and darkest Africa. It is as if Bailey views Africa bi-focally, combining two perspectives and living with the contradictions. He relishes the contradictions, using them comically, anticipating criticism and deflecting it. You cannot take *Macbeth* entirely seriously because it includes so many devices

that draw attention to its theatricality and artifice, but the thoroughness of his imagination and the consistency of images create an unignorable atmosphere of horror (ibid.).

Greig concludes:

> Bailey works in a universe where nothing is either/or and everything is both/and. His Macbeth is horrific and funny. His characters are absurd and deeply serious. His action is luridly melodramatic and powerfully dramatic. What one sees is ultimately meaningless and so saturated with significance it is claustrophobic. Watching demands involvement and also distance. This does not rely so much on balances – it is as if Bailey pushes his vision and directing so far, it bursts through the usual categories into a soupy realm devoid of morality and whose characters have no choices (ibid.).

What makes Greig's review of Bailey's production of *Macbeth* a worthy point of departure for this inquiry into the crisis of representation is that his reading compellingly informs cultural production in general and the figuration of South Africa's destiny in particular. Bailey's choice of Verdi's opera (and Shakespeare's play) is fitting not only because it allows him to continue a theatrical exploration into ritual murder, exorcism, and the occult, but because, by focusing on the liminal moment in the drama, he is able to foreground a more far-reaching exploration of this liminal moment in South Africa's cultural history. Furthermore, in affixing an extra-moral dimension to this moment – a moment between and *beyond* good and evil – Bailey challenges the play's received closure.

It is this challenge, a challenge that Greig succinctly articulates, which today has come to shape the inquiry into culture in South Africa. This inquiry, in which my own writing plays a part, has been compelled to express or dramatise itself reflexively. If Bailey's production could be said to incarnate this engagement, it is because it serves as a telling cipher for a host of contradictions that afflict and shape cultural production in general. Greig has deftly forged a summation of some of these constitutive contradictions. These include a destabilisation of an authoritative perspective, the implication of reason in the irrational, the daemonisation of sense and the senses, the imbrication of seriousness and laughter, the refraction of integrated characterisation, the uneasy blending of the familiar with the horrific, the melodramatic with the dramatic, and, most important, the manifestation of an aesthetic and ethical *resistance* to balancing these coeval and incommensurable positions.

If Bailey 'bursts through the usual categories' (ibid.) it is not only because he chooses to play fast-and-loose with these categories – through a reflexive play and heightened theatricality – but because his aesthetic and ethical vision, while caught in the binaries he attempts to dissolve, also points to an extra-moral and a-categorical realm, a realm that bursts and renders fluid all categories and which, always nascent, has emerged in and through his production to challenge a hegemonic and moral drive to categorise, divide, and rule.

Another suggestion thrown up by Greig's review is that this emergent extra-moral and a-categorical agency was always already a part of the psychic fabric of the society which colonialism and apartheid sought to suppress. The allusions to 'juju', 'black magic', and the 'interzone between life and death' point to an irrational or pre-rational dimension to cultural expression: the emergent return of the repressed. This Dionysian dimension has always been an integral part of Bailey's theatre. In *Macbeth* it finds the perfect vehicle. Bailey has been condemned and celebrated for this exploration in his work. His exploration serves as a clue to the realisation that the very desire for control and division means the suppression of extra-moral and a-categorical drives – drives which not only pose a threat to this desire for control and division, but which thrive despite the putative threat ascribed to them by a dominant, though ceaselessly embattled, power. By conjuring these repressed drives, Bailey's production not only challenges the continued dominance of a system defined by division and rule, but also poses an invitation to those who seek to restore these repressed drives and factor them into an alternative conception of the agency of culture.

Leon de Kock, while avowedly more 'vigilant' and more 'skeptical' than Bailey, has taken up this invitation. De Kock begins his introduction to the critical anthology *South Africa in the Global Imaginary* with a quotation from Breyten Breytenbach's *Dog Heart* (1998):

> What I want to write about is the penetration, expansion, skirmishing, coupling, mixing, separation, regrouping of peoples and cultures – the glorious bastardisation of men and women mutually shaped by sky and rain and wind and soil. . . . and everywhere is exile; we tend to forget that now. The old ground disappears, expropriated by blood as new conflicting patterns emerge (Introduction p. 263).

From the outset we see that de Kock, via Breytenbach, has embarked on an exploration of South African history and culture marked by a foreknowledge of inter-penetration and bastardisation. If 'the old ground' has disappeared, it is not because that ground supposed a fixed and pure order, but because the penetrations, expansions, skirmishings and couplings which were already under way allowed for 'new conflicting patterns' to emerge. Here Bailey's *Macbeth* serves as an index of the new that is also the old, for, like Breytenbach, Bailey consecrates no pre-given 'purity and consistency'.

Focusing his inquiry upon the terrain or 'field' of South African cultural studies, de Kock discovers the inverse of Breytenbach and Bailey's fascination with 'the dangerous fluidity of categories' (p. 278). De Kock notes a well nigh pathological suppression in South African cultural studies of a vision that could inhabit and sustain Breytenbach's conception of history and culture. The objective of de Kock's study is to discover the reason for the suppression, and, more compellingly, to inquire why it has consistently failed to succeed.

De Kock begins by asking the question: 'If cultural heterogeneity is nothing new or surprising in a context of globalization', then why does cultural heterogeneity in South Africa remain 'to this day a scene of largely *unresolved* difference'? (p. 264). The emphasis is telling. Irresolution, we will discover, is the key to de Kock's alternative reading of South African history and culture. It is also this irresolution that, for Greig, forms the defining characteristic of Bailey's production of *Macbeth*.

For de Kock, who develops Greig's observation, we find that the continuance of *'unresolved* difference' is symptomatic of the incommensurability of lived experience in South Africa. Contrary to Breytenbach's celebratory immersion in difference, de Kock argues that the proponents of cultural studies have striven to mediate difference, and to do so from sovereign and authorised positions. Even self-critique in the instant of mediation, de Kock notes, has failed to justify the insistence upon difference. It is difference – as the other, known or unknown – which the South African cultural analyst has valorised and rendered 'totemic' (p. 265). I will not detail the various examples de Kock provides in order to demonstrate this reification of an unresolved and constitutive difference that defines South Africa's cultural imaginary. Instead, with de Kock and Breytenbach, I will address the emergent conflicting patterns that define cultural inquiry within and on behalf of South Africa today.

Stephen Gray anticipates this emergent focus. In 'Some Problems of Writing Historiography in South Africa' (1989), cited in de Kock, Gray charts a vision of culture that could bypass the endemic polarisation that continues to define cultural analyses and engagement. 'The writer', says Gray,

> is always forced into a position of having to negotiate between extremes, into crossing the language-colour barrier; he or she can only be a syncretist and hybridizer. And *therefore* the basic act of writing is one of carrying information across one or other socio-economic barrier, literally of 'trading' . . . I propose, thus, a new identikit portrait: the writer exists at any of several boundaries (*not* at the centre of one self-enclosed group); his or her act of making literature is part of transferring data across that boundary, from one audience to another – an act which in its broadest sense may be termed 'translation' (Introduction pp. 268–69).

What is interesting here is not only the nature of the cultural engagement Gray promotes, but also the counter-engagement that prohibits it. Clearly Gray's values and vision are in accordance with Breytenbach's in that both champion syncretism and hybridity. The enunciation of their vision, though, is markedly different. There is in Gray's promotion a tentative, provisory quality that hems in the thrill of the epistemic possibility he advocates. Gray, as I read this passage, implies that cultural translation through syncretism and hybridity presupposes a stain: something illicit. The word 'trading', with its suggestion of clandestine sexual exchange, further ramifies the taboo that Gray wishes to break. However, the tentative and curiously apologetic nature of Gray's bid all the more attunes the reader to the hegemonic dominance of a 'pure' position from which to mediate and read South Africa. Gray's suggestion of a new identikit portrait – one that challenges a prescribed subject position and self-enclosed group – in a macabre way echoes the pass-book that ensured the policing and division of South Africa's citizenry. This echo is of course unintended, since Gray opposes the splitting of South African society into neat ethno-linguistic boxes. Nonetheless, such is the nature of the beast of oppression that in the very moment that Gray calls for a 'new identikit portrait' he reprises the insidious logic of the separable and cellular. That Gray is writing in 1989 – on the eve of South Africa's germinal democracy – all the more reinforces the shadow of oppression and the trenchant nature of unresolved difference in South Africa's cultural imaginary.

De Kock roots this unresolved difference in colonialism and apartheid, systems of 'violent representation' which 'tended to compromise all identities' either in the name of God and England or God and the Volk. Nevertheless, de Kock argues, all attempts to 'order difference' have failed to overcome its constitutive heterogeneity, which 'has tended to defeat the various statist models of social organization attempted so far' (p. 272). For de Kock, it is this constitutive and unresolved heterogeneity, celebrated by Breytenbach and Bailey, and tentatively broached by Gray, which points the direction of current critical and cultural inquiry. As de Kock notes:

> Unresolved heterogeneity has long been evident in the sense of crisis attendant upon writing about 'South Africa,' whose very nature as a signifier has been slippery and recalcitrant. Ironically, in a country where engagement with poststructuralist paradigms has been belated and grudging, 'South Africa' itself remains a sign under erasure – the question, who 'speaks' for South Africa? – is as vexed today as it ever was (p. 273).

It is this crisis, this vexation, which characterises Gray's position. Ten years prior to his advocacy of critical and cultural translation through syncretism and hybridity, Gray, in his study *South African Literature: An Introduction* (1979) likened his field of research to an 'archipelago':

> The islands with their peaks protrude in set positions, even if one does not readily see the connections between them beneath the surface. Like most archipelagos, it is related to adjacent landmasses: in this case there are three of them – most importantly, the mainland of English literature, by language and historical circumstance; diminishingly, the British Commonwealth; and increasingly, the continent of Africa which gives it its actual nourishment (Introduction p. 269).

The cartographic metaphor is a remarkable one. Not only does it allow Gray to pinpoint the hegemonic influence of empire – which persists, albeit it in a different guise – but because the archipelago also points to the hidden life that blurs or eliminates difference 'beneath the surface'. In 1979, in 1989, Gray sustains an ethical commitment to rethinking South African cultural studies in a way that could release that which has been repressed and/or hidden. Given the affliction of self-enclosure that defined white supremacy in the 1970s, it is all the more remarkable that Gray would point to the continent of Africa as the destined point of 'actual nourishment'. Whether this nourishment, in 2002, has been achieved is debatable. Whether, given the impact of globalisation, exterior forces have diminished, is equally debatable. My argument, in accordance with de Kock's, would return us to the interstitial, ceaselessly compromised, and unresolvedly heterogeneous condition which continues to define South African culture, a condition which Gray sought to cross by alerting us, paradoxically, to the realisation that 'beneath the surface' this condition *had already been crossed*.

It is this paradoxical hidden truth – seemingly small, given the overriding dominance of divisive forces that remain actively engaged – which is exemplified in Breytenbach's words and Bailey's dramatisation of *Macbeth*. It is this hidden truth, which de Kock calls a 'secret life', and which I in turn perceive as the suppressed cornerstone or allegory for a culture at once resistant and post-resistant since it is a culture – defined by the dangerous fluidity of categories – that we already possess, even though we may declare that we do not.

To suggest that South Africa as a culture does not know itself, is to foreground the immense suppression of a hidden truth that lies beneath the surface. The role of art has been to access this repressed and disfigured truth. Bailey's *Macbeth* is a case in point. What I wish to draw the reader's attention to is the suppression of an *a priori* miscegenated consciousness and culture, which no denial and no suppression can successfully destroy. The question is what to make of this miscegenated consciousness and culture? How to express this miscegenation in a way that is not pathological and repressive? How to foreground this *connectedness* that lies beneath to the surface?

These questions are more easily posed than answered. Indeed, as we will discover, the answers that have arisen are all the more damaging, for while they seem to cherish this connectedness, they have all the more suppressed the power of its impact. As de Kock notes, the greatest threat to this miscegenated consciousness and culture – another name for hybridisation, creolisation, and syncretism – is 'unity in difference' or 'sameness' (p. 287). Informed by nationalism and globalism, these 'metatropes' cancel the depth charge that distinguishes this syncretic or hybrid connectedness. For, as I understand it, this connectedness, this secret life beneath the surface, does not diminish the agency of heterogeneity, but hones and clarifies its conflicted condition. De Kock's claim that South Africa, irrespective of its purported unity, in fact remains a hornet's nest of unresolved, heterogeneous, and conflicted states, and Gray's call for a position that crosses boundaries, remain cogent propositions. In pointing to the violence perpetrated under colonialism and apartheid as being 'epistemic', de Kock makes the following compelling observation:

> The crisis of the sign . . . belongs as much in the country's history of suffering as it does in university seminar rooms, and an exploration of South African signifying economies appears essential to an understanding of its literary and cultural production (p. 273).

What makes de Kock's argument persuasive is his emphasis of the epistemic as intrinsic to, and not a supplementary aspect of, an unresolved and differentially constructed culture. Greig, in his review of Bailey's *Macbeth,* similarly suggests that Bailey's aesthetic and ethic does not presuppose an inviolate, intact, and opposed position. His is a non-position, a position that absorbs difference and relativises its impact. The 'indeterminate zone between life and death' is matched by other indeterminacies: between here and there (South Africa and the Europe of Shakespeare and Verdi), self and other, reason and madness, good and evil, and so on. For Bailey these indeterminate extremes are not advisedly mediated; on the contrary, they must be traversed, rendered all the more fluid.

To do so Bailey must speak from within the unresolved heterogeneity of South African culture. In doing so Bailey cannot wholly claim the validity of this inner position, or inner voice, hence the strikingly fraught and hysterical reflexivity of his position. Bailey, therefore, must traverse yet another binary – that between the inner and the outer – the better to express a new conflictual pattern.

If I claim non-positionality as the constitutive matrix for Bailey's aesthetic and ethic it is because, like the country that is its generator, Bailey's production exists under erasure. Hence his refusal to emphasise *Macbeth*'s accepted ending, and with it a resolution of the drama's contradiction on behalf of the good and the just. Indeed, the very unresolved heterogeneity of Bailey's production of *Macbeth* can be said to serve as an aesthetic and ethical response to, and reinforcement of, de Kock's conclusion that any resolution of South Africa – its people and its cultures – in the name of unity is an 'ultimately quixotic attempt to bring a certain order of composure, of settlement, to a place of profound difference' (p. 274).

If Greig, in his review of *Macbeth*, perceives this profound difference – a marker for the absence of closure, the refusal of settlement – as a kind of 'evil', it is not because the erosion of closure and settlement is in itself evil, but because the thematic of the drama, left unstaunched, begs this reading. A less fearful review, or one more attuned to the production's ethical extremity, would ask why the characters in Bailey's play 'have no choices', and why evil emerges as the compelling force that drives the production.

An answer to these linked questions could lead us a step farther in this exploration of unresolved heterogeneity. If profound difference could be read as evil or immoral, it is because the fear of profound difference is kin to the fear of the loss of self, the loss of a definable group, the absence of settlement, in and through which one believes that one mediates the world. It is this oppressive and acculturated belief in a homogenised self and 'self-enclosed group' which Gray bravely believes can be circumvented through syncretism, hybridity, and translation – though, as I have pointed out throughout this inquiry, this is an extremely vexed occupation. In doing so one forfeits as one gains. The decision to follow the journey of syncretism or hybridity or translation is never a moral one. As the Italian idiom *tradurre e tradire* suggests: translation is betrayal. Following de Kock, one could argue that it is precisely morality – and the socio-economic, political, and cultural machinery that sustains it – which has produced the incommensurate and paradoxical faith in unity-through-heterogeneity that defines South Africa today. For de Kock, the homogenisation of heterogeneity is tantamount to 'erasure': another kind of betrayal (p. 274). In contrast, the erasure which Bailey produces is an erasure that stalls conclusion and settlement: it is an erasure that invigorates and foregrounds 'the crisis of the sign' the better to show the unresolved conflict that persists.

De Kock believes that 'it is the *representational* dimension of cross-border contact that has received relatively short shrift in South African studies' (p. 277). What de Kock gestures towards, and valorises, is a critical and cultural discourse that reflexively points both to the construction of difference and its erasure. This position must eschew objective mediation, the positivist construction of knowledge of a given 'contact zone'.

Such a position would not cancel a critical distance; rather, it would reconcile distance with an immanent and subjective engagement.

This is the position Greig finds himself in when, confronted with Bailey's *Macbeth*, he says: 'Watching demands involvement and also distance' (Horrific and Funny Product p. 10). More tellingly, Greig notes: 'the work lurches from horror to humour within the space of a breath' (ibid.). The shift is infinitesimal. To endure a production that shifts with such rapidity, one needs critical subtlety and emotional intensity, for it is not only the production that exists under erasure, but the audience.

De Kock, in a broader though equivalent sense, calls for an epistemic engagement with the question of South Africa that demands a perceptual and emotive dexterity comprised of shifts that are instantaneous and canny. He focuses this engagement in the sphere of 'representation', of signs. Likewise, he locates the canny reading of these signs not only in the halls of academia, but on the suffering minds and bodies of the victims of history. The sum of these minds, these bodies, is each and every one whose history, whose sense of being and place, is defined by the ubiquitous sign: *South Africa.*

Important for de Kock, South Africa – as a system of representation – cannot be objectified as an 'order of differences', a procedure 'intrinsic to the gesture of colonization' (Introduction p. 278). This gesture, de Kock argues, is deployed

despite – perhaps even because of – the observable fact that, on the ground, identities increasingly were becoming hybrid and mixed. Such dangerous fluidity of categories were countered by the establishment of a foundational order of representation in which ironclad binaries operated as metatropes in the long and arduous process of inducing new forms of subjectivity in colonized people (ibid.).

If these 'metatropes' persist today, which they do – indeed, they have sustained their hegemonic dominance – then they do so because of, and in spite of, the processes of erasure which, in foregrounding heterogeneity, have done so without deferring to 'a foundational order of representation'. As I have insisted, Bailey's *Macbeth* is a case in point. Works of this nature remain comparatively unique. The 'dangerous fluidity of categories' which marks the innovation of Bailey's production also sets it apart in a society and a culture driven by the fear of heterogeneity, even in its current paradoxical manifestation as a unity-in-difference, as sameness. As de Kock points out, it is this much-vaunted sameness which 'in the guise of equal civil opportunities as a citizen of empire, a pseudo-universality of being' has resulted in 'the colonized African subject . . . willingly forego[ing] claims to cultural difference' (p. 280).

Against this national and globalised logic of sameness, which bypasses rather than engages with the unresolved heterogeneity of South Africa, de Kock repeatedly points to the agency of an epistemic engagement with the signifying economy of cultural production that turns on what he calls the 'seam':

a 'junction made by sewing together the edges of two pieces . . . of cloth, leather, etc.; the ridge or the furrow in the surface which indicates the course of such a junction.' The *seam* is therefore the site of a joining together that also bears the mark of the suture . . . it needs to be noted that

> [the] postulate of a crisis of inscription is characterized by a paradoxical process: on the one hand the effort of suturing the incommensurate in an attempt to close the gap that defines it as incommensurate, and on the other hand this process unavoidably bears the mark of its own crisis, the seam (p. 276).

It is this double logic of the seam to which Greig implicitly refers when noting the 'indeterminate zone' that characterises Bailey's production. In pointing to the self-awareness of Bailey's theatricality, Greig, furthermore, points out the work's indeterminacy as a reflexive suturing of unresolved difference. What, for de Kock and Bailey, is gained through this syncretic merger? By way of an answer, de Kock turns to Homi Bhabha's essay 'Sly Civility' and locates the logic of this essay – the doubled logic of the subaltern – in Sol Plaatje. According to de Kock, Plaatje,

> a mission-educated subject, who was nonetheless a proto-African nationalist, was thus enfolded in the colonial seam along which difference had been pressed into an uneven alignment with a pseudouniversal model of singularity. The only means open to him to legitimate claims to equal treatment for his people was via an appeal to the foundational 'civil' virtues of empire that had been so closely aligned, by missionaries, with the universal reign of God. At the same time, however, Plaatje's appeals are embedded in an implicit knowledge of the colonial 'grammar of differences' – he was at the same time also campaigning against the notorious Land Act of 1913, whose basis was racist and exclusionary. This is a crucial point to keep in mind when considering the possible meaning(s) of statements by black subjects of missionary education (p. 280).

Having charted Plaatje's 'markedly strained position', de Kock goes on to argue that it is this strained position that is

> typical of the poetics of the seam in South African refractions of identity, an example of how the first-person singular begins to seek ways of slipping across or into the seam joining it with the first-person plural. The process, though, manifests a crisis of inscription. In seeming to foreclose the African subject's difference in an appeal to universal Christian virtue, Plaatje is in fact seeking an assurance that he and his brethren will not be *differentiated against*; in other words, his very act of claiming oneness carries with it the knowledge of doubleness, a doubleness that is the defining quality of the representational seam in which Plaatje is caught (ibid.).

De Kock's canny reading of the slippage that marks Plaatje's position, a position convicted and shifted by its double, is later developed as a position from which to read against the indifference that is the sum of the contemporary culture of sameness. One speaks, today, from both within and outside the hegemonic domination of oneness, the better to retrieve the value of heterogeneity, a value deemed secondary to national and global unity.

Once again, Bailey's production of *Macbeth* returns as an exemplary incarnation of de Kock's thesis. Because of its reflexive foregrounding and erasure of the seam that figures difference, Bailey's production draws the audience's attention to the constructedness of meaning at the same time as it cancels the privative binary that founds this constructedness. Significantly, this reflexivity is achieved not only because of theatricality and artifice; rather, its more 'eerie' agency lies in is commandeering of reflexivity in the name of the unconscious and the unsaid: Gray's hidden world and de Kock's secret life. Thereby, the 'crisis of inscription' becomes a crisis whose source lies not only in representation but also in what representation does not, or cannot, say.

As Greig has noted: 'Bailey's vision . . . is steeped in a sense of the otherworldly but also – and this is what makes it eerie – in a slightly Edwardian notion of juju and darkest Africa' (Horrific and Funny Product p. 10). In other words, by simultaneously showing and concealing – or evoking that which cannot be revealed – Bailey constructs a doubled space of representation and its shadow. In so doing he implicates the familiar in the strange. The result is a de-territorialisation and reinvigoration of the signifying economy of cultural production. This de-territorialisation and reinvigoration emerges as a dramatisation of what de Kock has called the 'poetics of the seam'. This poetics cannot at any point be self-evident. It is a poetics that is defined by a resistance to what Louise Bethlehem calls the 'rhetoric of urgency': a rhetoric characterised by 'a persuasive attempt to weld signifier to signified, to bypass the fraudulent contingencies of the sign and seek a place where things mean what they say' (Introduction p. 284).

As we have noted, it is precisely this vaunted transparency between signifier and signified which Bailey has challenged. The paradox with which he infects the singularity of meaning is, for de Kock, critical to any contemporary reading and expression of South African culture. De Kock's postulate is as follows:

> [A] crisis of representation has been endemic to the geographical and cultural conjunction that has become South Africa and that 'it', the country conceived as a third-person singular entity, is a seam that can be undone only at the cost of its existence. Its very nature, its secret life, inheres in the paradoxes of the seam (ibid.).

In no uncertain terms de Kock has posted a warning to those engaged in cultural analyses and production who refute 'the crisis of the sign' that is South Africa, and who refuse to engage cannily and reflexively with its 'interstitial identity', its 'doubleness and representational crisis' (ibid.).

Speaking specifically of the South African writer – though here one could include those who *write* South Africa in and through other media – de Kock notes that any engagement in representation 'in the full sense requires imaginative inhabitation of the seam as a deep symbolic structure' (ibid.). Once again we find the emergence of the hidden, secret, inner world that founds South Africa's unresolved heterogeneity. De Kock points to the writing of J. M. Coetzee as an exemplary instance of an imaginative inhabitation of this inner world. I, in turn, have pointed to the work of Brett Bailey. All the same, what makes de Kock's valorisation of the crisis of the sign and his perception of the 'paradoxical divisiveness of the seam as a site of self-constitution' all the more compelling is that its agency extends the domain of cultural production to include 'the most everyday acts of identity formation' (p. 285). The crisis of the sign, he says, is 'endemic':

> The country, in all of its various guises as a collective 'state,' has been dogged by a crisis of naming, either a naming of people as other than what they might conceive themselves to be or a naming of oneself in a constitutive (oppositional or identificatory) relation to others (p. 286).

Today, under the metatrope of sameness, a marked shift has occurred, a shift which, for de Kock, may appear redemptive but which remains caught in a repression and denial of an ongoing and unresolved heterogeneity. Today, de Kock notes, the country is characterised by

> an overwhelming desire . . . for a unitary political identity and for the *suppression* of difference. This desire has been formally translated into the new South African constitution, which does indeed enshrine equality for all regardless of race, gender, or class, does make us all the 'same' legally and constitutionally (ibid.).

Nonetheless, as an imaginative inhabitation of a new symbolic structure, this juridically endorsed metatrope of sameness remains patently out of sync with reality 'on the ground', as well as the reality defined by a 'deep symbolic structure'.

> Racial and class cleavages persist. Political rivalries of the past, with accompanying atrocities, continue to emerge. Debates about affirmative action and employment equity cannot but mobilize racial particularity as a category of identity (ibid.).

As a consequence, therefore,

> [w]e are . . . still fully in the seam, still restaging our identities in a place of converging difference – a place where neither oneness nor difference can be maintained without reference to the knowledge of its double, its constitutively cross-hitched character. In such a context representation must bear the strain (pp. 286–87).

Given an episteme that is divisive in the same instant that it is self-constitutive, de Kock advocates the cultivation of selfhood and nationhood – in and through representation – that is ceaselessly mobile and fluid. If we do not take up this call – a call exemplified by the doubled or non-positionality expressed variously by Plaatje, Coetzee and Bailey – then we will remain subject to a 'teleology of liberal justice, which seemingly culminated in the democratic elections of 1994, holding us to oppressive fixations of oneness and sameness' (p. 288).

In the light of de Kock's conclusion it is not surprising that Bailey should render the drama of *Macbeth* inconclusive. Clearly, for Bailey, the righting of an unresolved, unbalanced, and heterogeneous society and culture would be premature. Better then to sustain a dangerous fluidity. Better to post the crisis that dogs order. After Breytenbach, better to let old and new patterns of conflict emerge. The 'soupy realm devoid of morality' is not merely the sign of a willed and gratuitous foreclosure of hope, but an incisive and deft response to a culture that has by no means overcome the crisis of meaning and value that remains its abiding core. 'Profound difference' prevails. 'Let doubt return,' de Kock concludes.

> Let the tatty, patchwork 'rainbow nation' (in Breyten Breytenbach's description, a 'pot of shit')
> become once more, in representation, the normal thing that it is in the streets, the shacks, and
> the bloody intellectual parlors of the old 'new' South Africa (p. 290).

If de Kock has not pointed a way out of our conflicted and interstitial cultural identity,
he has, all the same, made a strident case for a mobile selfhood and a highly charged and
reflexive critical engagement with the crisis of meaning and value in South Africa.

At an international colloquium on the theme 'Living Difference: Towards a Society
of Communities' held at the University of Witwatersrand in Johannesburg in August
1998, de Kock was struck by the notably foreign commitment – that of Richard Rorty,
Nancy Fraser, and Jörn Rüsen – to 'a master narrative [or] governing motif that would
frame everyone's energies within the miraculous new nation' (p. 289). As a counterpoint,
and to the 'dismay' of the international guests, 'South African speaker after speaker, black
and white, expressed disillusionment with or sounded warnings about precisely the new
master narrative the assembled global academics were pressing on them' (ibid.).
Confronted thus, 'Professor Rüsen thundered, "It is imperative for us that you
succeed!"'. Within this emotive outburst 'lay the key'. 'For many reasons', de Kock
reminds us,

> it is imperative for *others* that South Africans succeed at the democratic, multiracial miracle that
> *they* (the non-South Africans) have yet to see realized in their own countries. South Africa must
> carry this burden of moral example, just as in earlier times it carried the burden of having to be
> a moral pariah of the larger world (ibid.).

De Kock's blisteringly acute observation returns us to the question of culpability: who is
responsible for what and for whom? What is at stake in the furtherance of the dream of a
unified nation, a dream that, today, remains in search of an objective correlative? What
are the implications that compound the continued belittlement of a poststructuralist
critique of an unresolved heterogeneity that knows no end? What, in that case, must the
perspective, location, and agency of culture be?

As I have attempted to demonstrate throughout, the perspective, location and
agency of this inquiry must, necessarily, turn not on a chimerical hope but on a
speculative engagement with South Africa's cultural predicament. The job of cultural
analysts and practitioners is not to feed a national and global desire for a simulacral
truth, but, rather, its interstitial and vexed objective should be to resuscitate the canny
and invigorated value of 'doubt'. By doubt I do not only mean the adoption of a 'vigilant
skepticism' to which de Kock subscribes; rather, I mean the commitment to the enabling
power of questions aligned to an openness to the unconscious and unthinkable; spheres
of being that form an active part of cultural production, as Bailey, Breytenbach, Gray and
de Kock have attested.

The answers to the propositions I have made in this inquiry still await us. Caught in
shadow and in glare, the stories that we tell, the critical narratives and the theatre that we
make, remain the unfinished fragments of an inconsolable and unresolved reality. As
long as this unresolved heterogeneity persists – and if de Kock is correct, then thought

and culture have a vested interest in sustaining this irresolution – then the story of South Africa will never be told in its entirety.

'Introductions to South African literary culture conceived as an entity have a peculiar trademark', de Kock observes:

> They apologize for attempting to do the impossible and then go ahead anyway. This gesture, ranging from rhetorical genuflection to anxious self-examination to searing critique of others who have dared to undertake what should not be attempted lightly, reveals a significant fault line of South African literary studies (p. 263).

De Kock defines this fault line as a need for a

> minimal convergence in the domains of origin, language, culture, history, and nationalism (contested or not) to become, in some sense, cohesive and inter-referential. But in the South African case each of these domains fragments into heterogeneity the moment one looks more closely at the literary objects at hand (p. 263–64).

While de Kock is speaking specifically of the construction of cultural identity through literature, his point presupposes the impossibility of synoptic totalisation with regard to the analysis of South African culture in general. Hence the liminality and partiality of my own critical inquiry under the rubric: *Predicaments of culture in South Africa.*

A 'difficult, unpleasant, or embarrassing situation', the notion of a predicament succinctly captures the uneasiness that characterises the mood and enunciation of this inquiry. With its attendant association with shame and disgrace, it further posts an examination of the error or stain that forms the constitutive root of an unresolved and heterogeneous society. My objective has been to galvanise and transmute this error or stain – this difficulty, unease, or unpleasantness – by harnessing it to an affirmative, though non-positive, reading of cultural change. At best this reading has been an 'inquiry', though here, against the dictates of the *Concise Oxford Dictionary*, my inquiry is by no means an 'official' one. Instead, I have elected to align my thinking with the thinking of those who, in embracing the critical and cultural margins – in invoking the strange, unstable, hidden, secretive, occult, or deep – have sought not merely to contest a putative centre, but to further invigorate an inquiry into culture conceived in a manner unconstrained by the canonical, hierarchical, secular and rational. It is my anxious hope, furthermore, that this inquiry has demonstrated and sustained a culture forged in the name of human freedom and the imagination. Inquiry would mean little, if nothing, if it were not forged by this maddening and seemingly impossible ideal.

In 'That Other World That was The World' Nadine Gordimer writes:

> Only through the writer's explorations could I have begun to discover the human dynamism of the place I was born to and the time in which it was enacted. Only in the prescient dimension of the imagination could I bring together what had been deliberately broken and fragmented; fit together the shapes of living experience, my own and that of others, without which a whole consciousness is not attainable. I had to be part of the *transformation of my place* for it to know me (p. 130).

If I conclude with this moving passage, it is because it affirms my own exile from the source of its truth. Raised and schooled abroad, separated from the place of my birth, I too have sought to cohere a fragmented life. However, unlike Gordimer, I have attained no 'whole consciousness'. For me there has been no mirror that could fuse my being with the mysterious world all about me. After Gilles Deleuze, mine remains an orphan line of thought and culture.

On returning to South Africa in December 1989, I too sought to play a part in the country's 'miraculous' journey. Though, unlike Gordimer, I have not been transformed. I remain

> The one who belongs nowhere.
> The one who has no national mould.
> (Camus, in *Writing and Being* p. 120)

It is with this bracing knowledge that I began this inquiry, turning first to the writings of Theodor Adorno and Homi Bhabha and finding in them the means through which to think the exilic and restless condition in which I found myself, a condition, I would discover, that was part of a larger, insistent, and unresolved heterogeneity that formed the troubled seam of my native land.

A witness to the changes between 1991 and 1994, I did not, like Gordimer, perceive these years as 'the grand finale . . . when South Africa emerged amazingly, a great spectacle of human liberation, from double colonization' (p. 114). On the contrary, as this inquiry attests, I have witnessed a continued bondage, and a continued and complex fight for freedom. The interregnum is by no means over. Indeed, I wonder whether the term ever possessed the capacity to reflect truthfully a psychic disfigurement born of empire and racial strife. Today it remains in and through this disfigurement, implacably recorded in J. M. Coetzee's 'Jerusalem Prize Acceptance Speech' that culture, *against* Coetzee's inconsolable vision, will sustain its transforming and life-affirming quest.

CODA

immune

It is one thing to die for liberation:
it is something entirely different to live with freedom.

– Andre Brink

In 'Reimagining the Real' Andre Brink notes the consequences of a sad militancy on white South African writing in the 1970s and 1980s. This sadness resides not in 'the urge for freedom' but in the moment 'when "freedom" becomes, entirely unwittingly, synonymous with "death": death as the ultimate utopia, the ultimate peace, the ultimate escape-from-it-all' (p. 150). Brink duly notes 'a morbid proliferation of apocalyptic fiction' distinguished by attempts to 'counter history with eschatological fervour, through the prophetic revelation of an end to present misery and the advent of a divinely inspired new world order' (pp. 150–51), a desire to renounce history and invoke the new results in a tellingly inward gaze which 'explore[s] the agonies of the private conscience *within* a context of a society falling apart' (p. 151).

It is this turning inward, this devolution of the self from an active agent of change to one that reactively reinforces the pathology it would renounce, in the instant that it proclaims a leap into a redemptive world beyond, which comes to mark the failure of the imagination in South African cultural production. Furthermore, it is this very inward gaze – the gaze of the hermit crab – which, in the aftermath of change, has assumed dominance over the imagination.

Falsely perceived as a marker for a new-found liberty, this ascendant preoccupation with the inward gaze affirms the continued estrangement of the self from a changing world. Today freedom remains a deferred and impossible desire that is compromised at every turn by an unwitting – or witting – morbidity or affirmation that has parasited the self, ramified an ongoing state of siege and left the will to dream the unthinkable within the present, and become that which is other to the self, enfeebled.

We live, today, not within a utopia or a dystopia, but in a middle space – a space between the dead and that which is powerless to be born – which Roland Barthes defines as an 'atopia' (p. 152). Akin to what Jane Taylor describes as a 'vacuum', this space possesses the insidious merit of allowing one to believe in a present that has wrested itself from the past. However, as I have suggested throughout this inquiry, this belief is illusory. The past continues to impact upon the present. This impact, however, has largely not been addressed with an imaginative reflexivity. Instead, what has proved ascendant is the displacement of a fundamental reckoning with history and, more disturbingly, a suppression of an unacknowledgeable desire to embrace the body of Africa.

Exiled from itself, the South African imaginary has chosen, rather, to embrace a negatively liminal position, which has ensured the continuance of its marginality as an outpost of empire. Unfree, enslaved, the South African imaginary has, with an eerie and deft capacity, learnt to accept its simulacral relation to the real. Therein and thereby, freedom is deferred and the imagination kept in thrall.

Against this enervated condition I have sought, after Sachs, to sustain a value and a belief in the possibility of freedom and a liberated imagination that could shift the psychic axis away from continued enslavement. South African culture need not remain a bonded economy. There remains an incalculable value to living with freedom. This value, I have stated, is as much a source of terror as it is a promise of happiness. That the South African cultural imaginary has chosen to suppress this critical and life-affirming paradox reveals, all the more thoroughly, the extent to which it has elected to betray itself. Within the sphere of cultural production – the sphere that Sachs affirms as the endangered source of liberty – I have persisted, against all hope, in maintaining the veracity of this paradox. Without it, I have argued, there can be no art; without it, thinking becomes impossible. Which certainly is why South African culture has largely failed to move beyond the 'ghetto' and the 'gulag'.

That the entire world has elected an equivalent confinement – born of fear and terror – does not bode well for the cultural vision I have sought to sustain. Today it is not liberty that is sought but a genteel mode of indenturedness. Here South Africa's perverse gift to the world – a gift exemplified in the writing of J. M. Coetzee – is a gift that knows itself as that which stems from a poisoned well. It is the gift of *ressentiment* – the gift of those who must renounce liberty the better to enshrine the idols of pain, of guilt and shame. It is the gift of those who, in not knowing better, or, in knowing better, have chosen to make a mockery of faith.

It is against this mockery, then, that I alighted upon Albie Sachs's paper, 'Preparing Ourselves for Freedom'. In it I found the seed of a 'new consciousness' which, like the desire that spurred it, has been utterly thwarted. That Sachs should return at the conclusion of this inquiry – an inquiry that has been made in his name – is not only fitting but also illuminating. Until my e-mail correspondence with Sachs I could not have known the depths he had plumbed in order to draw the sustenance he so desperately needed in order to thrive. Like many, I knew of the bomb that had destroyed the fullness of his body, but beyond imagining, I could not have known the immensity of the struggle for recovery. Much more than this, I could not have known that in 'recovering from the bomb [he had] felt free free free free, immune to fate and criticism' (personal communication).

Where others would turn their pain to fear and hate, Sachs emerged from the devastation of that 'particular moment' a man who, for the first time, could call himself 'free'. No longer a victim of fate, no longer wholly subject to an oppressive moral and ideological vision, Sachs experiences, at the heart of terror, an elation for which he can find no other word than freedom.

Within this devastating moment – indissolubly linked with the 'fracturing of [his] body' – Sachs begins to discover the visionary seed that had driven his quest. He speaks of 'Preparing Ourselves for Freedom' as an act forged in 'delirious moments of recovery' (ibid). Here, in the hybrid moment between that which is not yet concept, not quite experience – how does one 'experience' an act of terror inflicted upon one? – Sachs fashions a saving insight that could not have been known prior to the delirium from which the insight emerged. Not knowledge, then, not the unknowable either, but something other, something that could not have been seen or felt until that delirious and ripe moment. In the most brutal yet most affirming sense, that which Sachs experiences is a negative moment of apprehension, a moment that is also an allegory of hope.

That many have never found this moment is their loss. That Sachs has chosen not to remind the stunted multitude of their loss reveals, all the more, his understanding that it is a moment that cannot be regulated or enforced. At best, those who have grasped this life-changing moment must tread softly. Which is why 'Preparing Ourselves for Freedom' emerges in the way that it does: out of the blue, without fanfare, and with little certainty. An expression of immunity to fate and criticism, Sachs's paper, in its highest and most delirious moments, has come to exemplify a radicalism that is unconscripted and unscripted. From delirium, knowledge dawns.

Sachs experiences 'the duality and tension between comrades in a very African struggle. And the grave, heavily pained and ultimately disempowering expressions to be found in . . . various forms of art and culture' (ibid). It is this estrangement of culture, its inward and mortified gaze, which Sachs declares not as false but as ominously limiting. For Sachs it is the culture of the dead and dying, a paroxysmic culture, which cannot imagine a world beyond its own beleaguered and fearful, or fantastical, record. Here, the distinction between the one who records and the one who acts is palpable. What Sachs, in turn, achieves is the merger of these worlds: 'The paper pre-supposes a protagonist, someone totally immersed in the struggle, willing to give his or her life to it, yet torn between loyalty to the thought, structures and discipline that connected him or her to the process of change and the vitality, impulses, dreams and internal harmonies that registered all the time in daily life' (ibid.).

These quotidian harmonies are not those that Njabulo Ndebele mistakenly valorises in the name of the 'ordinary'. Rather, these harmonies are a product of the 'extraordinary'. They are the glimmers that have painfully been both cherished and thwarted in the name of sacrifice. That they re-emerge within the delirious moments of recovery – a recovery, lest we forget, from a violent horror – should all the more poignantly remind us that these gentle moments could not have existed outside of and at the expense of the spectacular.

Rather, Sachs recalls: 'We had lived through extraordinary personal emotions and experiences in Mozambique that were undetachable from our being there as part of the struggle, yet intensely personal, passionate, deeply felt and intimate. The stories of our lives were filled with greater wonder, surprise and richness of the experience than any book, film or piece of music' (ibid).

This qualification is a critical reminder to those who address themselves as the recorders and makers of culture. To think, then, to begin to feel, one must abolish vanity and self-possession, vanquish the fetish of pain, break apart the sage wisdom that would keep the imagination in thrall and begin . . . then begin again. It is not pain that is the harbinger of liberty, but that within pain that is not pain. It is this saving insight that South Africans must learn to recover. This recovery, Sachs reminds us, can never wholly be a conscious act, and neither will it merely stem from openness to the unknowable. Rather, this recovery arises from a psychic and epistemic rupture, from a place within rupture called love: a place that is immune.

BIBLIOGRAPHY

Abrahams, Lionel. 'Retreat.' *A Dead Tree Full of Live Birds*. Claremont: Snailpress, 1996.

Adorno, Theodor. *Minima Moralia*. London: The Gresham Press, 1974.

—. *Prisms*. London: The Garden City Press, 1967.

Alexandrian, Sarane. *Surrealist Art*. Trans. Gordon Clough. UK: Thames and Hudson, 1970.

Ammons, A. R. 'Corson's Inlet.' *The Norton Anthology of Poetry*. Third edition. Ed. Alexander W. Allison et al. New York and London: WW Norton, 1983.

Attwell, David. 'Dialogue and Fulfilment in J.M. Coetzee's *Age of Iron*.' *Writing South Africa: Literature, Apartheid, and Democracy, 1970–1995*. Ed. Derek Attridge and Rosemary Jolly. Cambridge: Cambridge University Press, 1998.

—. 'Interview with Homi Bhabha.' *Current Writing* 5.2 (1993): 101–113.

—. 'The Life and Times of Elizabeth Costello: J.M. Coetzee and the Public Sphere.' Keynote address at the conference on J.M. Coetzee and the Ethics of Intellectual Practice. Warwick University. Unpublished, 2002.

—. 'The Problem of History in the Fiction of J.M. Coetzee.' *Rendering Things Visible: Essays on South African Literary Culture*. Ed. Martin Trump. Johannesburg: Ravan Press, 1990.

—. 'The Reflexive Turn in Black South African Fiction.' Unpublished, 2002.

Bailey, Brett. 'Looking for Big Dada.' *Mail & Guardian* 1–7 June 2001: 2–3.

Bakhtin, Mikhail. 'From the Prehistory of Novelistic Discourse.' *Criticism and Theory: A Reader*. Ed. David Lodge. London: Longman, 1988.

—. *Rabelais and His World*. Trans. H. Iswolsky. Cambridge, Mass.: MIT Press, 1968.

Balme, Christopher B. *Decolonizing the Stage: Theatrical Syncretism and Postcolonial Drama*. Oxford: Clarendon Press, 1999.

Bedford, Emma. 'Confessions of Zeno.' *Art South Africa* 1.1 (Spring 2002).

Bertelsen, Eve. 'Phasing the Spring: Open Letter to Albie Sachs.' *Pretexts* 2.2 (Summer 1990).

Bethlehem, Louise. 'A Primary Need as Strong as Hunger: The Rhetoric of Urgency in South African Literary Culture under Apartheid.' *South Africa in the Global Imaginary. Poetics Today* 22.2 (2001): 365–89.

Bhabha, Homi. 'Aura and Agora: On Negotiating Rapture and Speaking Between.' *Negotiating Rapture*. Ed. Richard Francis. Chicago: Museum of Contemporary Art, 1996.

—. 'Culture's in Between.' *Multicultural States: Rethinking Difference and Identity*. Ed. David Bennet. London and New York: Routledge, 1998.

—. 'Editor's Introduction: Minority Maneuvers and Unsettled Negotiations.' *Front Lines/Border Posts*. *Critical Inquiry* 23.3 (1997): 431–59.

—. 'Narrating the Nation.' *Nation and Narration*. London and New York: Routledge, 1990.

—. *The Location of Culture*. London and New York: Routledge, 1994.

—. 'The Third Space.' *Identity: Community, Culture, Difference*. Ed. Jonathan Rutherford. London: Lawrences & Wishart, 1990.

Boehmer, Elleke. 'Endings and New Beginning: South Africa Fiction in Transition.' *Writing South Africa: Literature, Apartheid, and Democracy, 1970–1995*. Eds. Derek Attridge and Rosemary Jolly. Cambridge: Cambridge University Press, 1998.

Brecht, Bertolt. *Aesthetics and Politics*. London: Verso, 1980.

—. 'Alienation Effects in Chinese Acting.' *In Politics and Performance*. Eds. Lizbeth Goodman and Jane de Gay. London: Routledge, 2000.

—. 'Theatre for Pleasure or Theatre for Instruction.' *Twentieth Century Theatre Sourcebook*. Ed. Richard Drain. London: Routledge, 1995.

Brink, André. 'Interrogating Silence: New Possibilities Faced by South African Literature.' *Writing South Africa: Literature, Apartheid, and Democracy, 1970–1995*. Eds. Derek Attridge and Rosemary Jolly. Cambridge: Cambridge University Press, 1998.

—. 'Reimagining the Real.' *Reinventing a Continent*. London: Secker and Warburg, 1996.

—. *The Novel: Language and Narrative from Cervantes to Calvino*. Cape Town: University of Cape Town Press, 1998.

Bristow-Bovey, Darrel. 'Little Winkers and Young Duffers Evoke the Teeming Glory of Love.' Hot Medium. *Sunday Independent* 1 Dec. 2002: 10.

Butler, Judith. 'Critically Queer.' *In Politics and Performance*. Eds. Lizbeth Goodman and Jane de Gay. London and New York: Routledge, 2000.

Chapman, Michael. *Southern African Literatures*. London: Longman, 1996.

—. 'The Aesthetics of Liberation: Reflections from a Southern Perspective.' *Current Writing* 10.1 (1998): 1–16.

Chatwin, Bruce. *Anatomy of Restlessness*: *Uncollected Writings*. Eds. Jan Borm and Matthew Graves. London: Jonathan Cape, 1996.

—. *The Songlines*. London: Picador, 1988.

Christov-Bakargiev, Carolyn. 'In conversation with William Kentridge.' *William Kentridge*. London: Phaidon, 1999.

Clifford, James. *Routes: Travel and Translation in the Late Twentieth Century*. Cambridge, Mass. and London: Harvard University Press, 1997.

—. *The Predicament of Culture: Twentieth-century Ethnography, Literature, and Art*. Cambridge, Mass. and London: Harvard University Press, 1988.

Coetzee, J. M. 'Ali Mazrui, *The Africans*.' *Stranger Shores*. London: Secker and Warburg, 2001.

—. *Disgrace*. London: Secker and Warburg, 1999.

—. *Giving Offense*. Chicago: University of Chicago Press, 1996.

—. 'History of the Main Complaint.' *William Kentridge*. Ed. Carolyn Christov-Bakargiev. London: Phaidon, 1999.

—. 'Jerusalem Prize Acceptance Speech.' *Doubling the Point: Essays and Interviews*. Ed. David Attwell. Cambridge and London: Harvard University Press, 1992.

—. *Life & Times of Michael K*. London: Penguin Books, 1983.

—. 'The Novel in Africa'. Doreen B. Townsend Center for the Humanities. Occasional Papers. Berkeley: University of California, 1999.

—. *White Writing: On the Culture of Letters in South Africa*. New Haven and London: Yale University Press, 1988.

Colleran, Jeanne. 'South Africa Theatre in the United States: The Allure of the Familiar and of the Exotic.' *Writing South Africa: Literature, Apartheid, and Democracy, 1970–1995*. Eds. Derek Attridge and Rosemary Jolly. Cambridge: Cambridge University Press, 1998.

Concise Oxford Dictionary. Tenth edition. Oxford University Press, 2001. s.v. 'syncretism'.

Conrad, Joseph. *Youth, Heart of Darkness and the End of the Tether*. London: J.M. Dent & Sons, 1974.

Cooke, Lynne. 'Mundus Perversus, Mundus Inversus.' *William Kentridge*. New York: Harry N. Abrams, 2001.

Critchley, Simon. *Very Little . . . Almost Nothing: Death, Philosophy, Literature*. London and New York: Routledge, 1997.

Davis, Geoffrey V. and Anne Fuchs. 'An Interest in the Making of Things: An Interview with William Kentridge.' *Theatre and Change in South Africa*. Amsterdam: Harwood Academic Publishers, 1996.

Degenaar, Johan. 'How Texts and their Reception will Change in the Post-apartheid Era.' *Current Writing* 4 (1992): 10–14.

de Kock, Leon. *Civilising Barbarians: Missionary Narratives and African Textual Response in Nineteenth-century South Africa*. Johannesburg: Witwatersrand University Press and Lovedale Press, 1996.

—. 'Introduction.' *South Africa in the Global Imaginary. Poetics Today* 22.2 (2001): 263–98.

Eisenstein, Sergei. 'A Personal Statement' and 'The Montage of Attractions'. *Twentieth Century Theatre Sourcebook*. Ed. Richard Drain. London: Routledge, 1995.

Erasmus, Desiderius. *The Praise of Folly*. Introduced, illustrated and trans. Hendrik Willem van Loon. Roslyn, N.Y.: Walter J. Black, 1942.

Flockemann, Miki. 'South African Perspectives on Post-Coloniality in and Through Performance Practice.' *In Politics and Performance*. Eds. Lizbeth Goodman and Jane de Gay. London: Routledge, 2000.

Foucault, Michel. *The History of Sexuality*. Vol. 1. *The Will To Knowledge*. Harmondsworth: Penguin Books, 1976.

Gordimer, Nadine. 'That Other World That Was the World.' *Writing and Being*. Cambridge, Mass. and London: Harvard University Press, 1995.

—. *The Essential Gesture: Writing, Politics and Places*. London: Jonathan Cape, 1988.

—. 'The Idea of Gardening.' *New York Review of Books* 2 Feb. 1984.

—. *Writing and Being*. Cambridge, Mass. and London: Harvard University Press, 1995.

Graham, Lucy. '"Yes, I am giving him up": Sacrificial Likeness with Dogs in J. M. Coetzee's Recent Fiction.' *Scrutiny* 2 7.1 (2002): 4–15.

Gray, Stephen. *South African Literature: An introduction*. 1979.

Greig, Robert. 'History's Icons Wither Under Evita's Icy Glare.' *Sunday Independent* 21 Feb. 1999.

—. 'Horrific and Funny Product of a Darker Vision: Brett Bailey's *Macbeth*.' *Sunday Independent* 14 July 2002: 10.

—. 'Roll up for a Relentlessly Feverish Vision of Amin's Circus Maximus: Brett Bailey's *Big Dada*.' *Sunday Independent* 8 July 2001: 10.

Gunner, Liz. 'Introduction: The Struggle for Space.' *Politics and Performance: Theatre, Poetry and Song in Southern Africa*. Johannesburg: Witwatersrand University Press, 2001.

Haggerty, George E. *Gay Histories and Cultures*. Garland Publishing, 2000.

Havel, Václav. 'Six Asides about Culture.' *Living in Truth*. London: Faber and Faber, 1986.

Helgesson, Stefan. *Sports of Culture*: *Writing the Resistant Subject in South Africa (Readings of Ndebele, Gordimer, Coetzee)*. Doctoral thesis in Literature submitted to Uppsala University, 1999.

Heyns, Michiel. 'Houseless Poverty in the House of Fiction: Vagrancy and Genre in Two Novels by J.M. Coetzee.' *Current Writing* 11.1 (1999): 20–35.

Isaacson, Maureen. 'Speaking for Women who have been Silenced: Interview with Andre Brink.' *Sunday Independent* 2 Oct. 2002: 17.

Jagose, Annamarie. 'Queer Theory.' *Fruit Salad: A Compote of Contemporary Gay and Lesbian Writing*. Australia: Random House, 1997.

Jamal, Ashraf. 'In a Field.' Online: Chimurenga 2. http://www.chimurenga.co.za. Also in *The Shades*. Howick: Brevitas New Fiction Series, 2002.

—. Interview with Andrew Putter. Cape Town. 21 April 2002. Unpublished.

—. 'Kentridge under Erasure.' *Art South Africa*, O2, Dec. Ed. Sophie Perryer. Cape Town: Bell-Roberts Publishing, 2002.

—. *Love Themes for the Wilderness*. Cape Town and Johannesburg: Kwela Books and Random House, 1996.

—. 'Music of Silence: The Art of Lien Botha.' *Lien Botha*. Ed. Karen Press. Johannesburg: David Krut Publishers, 2002.

—. 'Small Acts: The Location, Perspective, and Agency of Theory in South African Cultural Studies.' *Theoria: A Journal of Social and Political Theory* 100 (Dec. 2002): 64–81.

—. 'Stagings.' *Senses of Culture: South African Culture Studies*. Eds. Sarah Nuttall and Cheryl-Ann Michael. Cape Town: Oxford University Press, 2000.

—. 'Steven Cohen: Waitress Tells All.' *Doenit* 10 (Sep./Oct. 1999): 18.

—. 'The Third Space: Adorno and Bhabha on Restlessness and Redemption.' *Current Writing* 14.1 (2002): 106–21.

—. 'Zero Panoramas, Ruins in Reverse, Monumental Vacancies: Contemporary Perceptions of Landscape in South African Art.' *Collection of Contemporary South African Art: The Gencor Collection*. Ed. Kendell Geers. Johannesburg: Jonathan Ball Publishers, 1997.

Jensma, Wopko. *i must show you my clippings*. Johannesburg: Ravan, 1977.

—. *Sing For Our Execution*. Johannesburg: Ophir/Ravan, 1973.

Kentridge, William. 'An Interest in the Making of Things.' *Theatre and Change in South Africa*. Eds. Geoffrey V. Davis and Anne Fuchs. Amsterdam: Harwood Academic Publishers, 1996.

—. 'Art in a State of Grace, Art in a State of Hope, Art in a State of Siege', 'Fortuna: Neither Programme nor Chance in the Making of Images', 'Felix in Exile: Geography of Memory', 'Faustus in Africa! Director's Note', 'The Body Drawn and Quartered'. In *William Kentridge*. Ed. Carolyn Christov-Bakargiev. London: Phaidon, 1999.

—. 'The Crocodile's Mouth.' *Ubu and the Truth Commission*. Jane Taylor. Rondebosch: University of Cape Town Press, 1998.

Krog, Antjie. *Country of My Skull*. Johannesburg: Random House, 1998.

Krouse, Matthew. 'My Life in the Theatre of War: The Development of an Alternative Consciousness.' *Theatre and Change in South Africa*. Eds. Geoffrey V. Davis and Anne Fuchs. Amsterdam: Harwood Academic Publishers, 1996.

—. 'Talkin Loud.' *Mail & Guardian* 14–20 June 2002: 1.

Kruger, Loren. 'Black Atlantics, White Indians, and Jews: Locations, Locutions, and Syncretic Identities in the Fiction of Achmat Dangor and Others.' *Scrutiny 2* 7.2 (2002): 34–50.

—. *The National Stage: Theatre and Cultural Legitimation in England, France, and America*. Chicago and London: University of Chicago Press, 1992.

Langa, Mandla. 'In our history and in our blood.' Online: Financial Mail Millenium Issue. http://secure.financialmail.co.za/report/millenium/gd.htm. Accessed: 4 Sep. 2002.

Lucia, Christine. 'And yet, and yet . . .: Confessions of Zeno.' *Cue* 4 July 2002: 1.

Magogode, Kgafela oa. 'High Art Low Fart.' Interview with Lesego Rampolokeng. Chimurenga 3. *Biko in Parliament*. 2002.

Marais, Sue. 'Ivan Vladislavić's Re-vision of the South Africa Story Cycle.' *Current Writing* 4 (1992): 41–55.

Mather, Mary Lynn. 'Creating Shadows of Doubt: Interview with William Kentridge.' *Cue* 4 July 2002: 2.

Mbembe, Achille. 'African Modes of Self-Writing.' *Public Culture* 14.1 (Winter 2002): 239–73.

Meintjies, Frank. 'Albie Sachs and the Art of Protest.' *Spring is Rebellious: Arguments about Cultural Freedom*. Eds. Ingrid de Kok and Karen Press. Cape Town: Buchu Books, 1990.

Mofokeng, Jerry. 'Theatre for Export: The Commercialization of the Black People's Struggle in South African Export Musicals.' *Theatre and Change in South Africa*. Eds. Geoffrey V. Davis and Anne Fuchs. Amsterdam: Harwood Academic Publishers, 1996.

Morphet, Tony. 'Cultural Imagination and Cultural Settlement: Albie Sachs and Njabulo Ndebele.' *Spring is Rebellious: Arguments about Cultural Freedom*. Eds. Ingrid de Kok and Karen Press. Cape Town: Buchu Books, 1990.

—. 'Taming the Power of Art.' *Scrutiny 2* 7:1 (2002): 61–65.

Mutloatse, Mothobi. *Forced Landing*. Johannesburg: Ravan Press, 1980.

Ndebele, Njabulo. *South African Literature and Culture: – Rediscovery of the Ordinary*. Manchester and New York: Manchester University Press, 1994.

Nkosi, Lewis. 'Postmodernism and Black Writing in South Africa.' *Writing South Africa: Literature, Apartheid, and Democracy, 1970–1995*. Eds. Derek Attridge and Rosemary Jolly. Cambridge: Cambridge University Press, 1998.

Noyes, John. 'The Place of the Human.' *Senses of Culture: South African Cultural Studies*. Eds. Sarah Nuttall and Cheryl-Ann Michael. Cape Town: Oxford University Press, 2000.

Nuttall, Sarah and Michael, Cheryl-Ann. 'Imagining the Present'; 'Autobiographical Acts'. *Senses of Culture: South African Cultural Studies*. Cape Town: Oxford University Press, 2000.

O'Brien, Anthony. 'Literature in Another South Africa: Njabulo Ndebele's Theory of Emergent Culture.' *Diacritics* 22.1 (Spring 1992): 67–85.

Olson, Gary A. and Worsham, Lynn. 'Staging the Politics of Difference: Homi Bhabha's Critical Literacy.' *Race, Rhetoric, and the Postcolonial*. New York: State University of New York Press, 1999.

Parry, Benita. 'Speech and Silence in the Fictions of J.M. Coetzee.' *Writing South Africa: Literature, Apartheid, and Democracy, 1970–1995*. Eds. Derek Attridge and Rosemary Jolly. Cambridge: Cambridge University Press, 1998.

Pechey, Graham. 'Post-Apartheid Narratives.' *Colonial Discourse/Postcolonial Theory*. Eds. Francis Barker et al. Manchester: Manchester University Press, 1994.

—. 'Post-apartheid Reason: Critical Theory in South Africa.' *Current Writing* 10.2 (1998): 3–18.

—. 'The Post-apartheid Sublime: Rediscovering the Ordinary.' *Writing South Africa: Literature, Apartheid, and Democracy, 1970–1995*. Eds. Derek Attridge and Rosemary Jolly. Cambridge: Cambridge University Press, 1998.

Porter, Andrew. 'Effects with Causes.' *Times Literary Supplement* 28 June 2002: 20.

Purkey, Malcolm. 'Tooth and Nail. Rethinking Form for the South African Theatre.' Theatre and Change in South Africa. Eds. Geoffrey V. Davis and Anne Fuchs. Amsterdam: Harwood Academic Publishers, 1996.

Rampolokeng, Lesego. End Beginnings. Rer. 1993.

—. Horns for Hondo. Johannesburg: COSAW, 1990.

—. Talking Rain. Johannesburg: COSAW, 1993.

Rushing, W. Jackson. 'The Sublime is Now: The Early Work of Barnett Newman, Paintings and Drawings 1944–1949'. Art Journal (Spring 1995). http://www.findarticles.com/p/articles/mi_m0425/is_n1_v54/ai_17012120/pg_1.

Ryan, Rory. 'Literary-intellectual Behaviour in South Africa.' Rendering Things Visible: Essays on South African Literary Culture. Ed. Martin Trump. Johannesburg: Ravan Press, 1990.

Sachs, Albie. 'Afterword: The Taste of an Avocado Pear.' Spring is Rebellious: Arguments about Cultural Freedom. Eds. Ingrid de Kok and Karen Press. Cape Town: Buchu Books, 1990.

—. 'Preparing Ourselves for Freedom.' Spring is Rebellious: Arguments About Cultural Freedom. Eds. Ingrid de Kok and Karen Press. Cape Town: Buchu Books, 1990.

Scott, David. 'The Government of Freedom.' Refashioning Futures: Criticism after Postcoloniality. New Jersey: Princeton University Press, 1999.

Sirmans, Franklin. 'William Kentridge: Crowning a Star.' Flash Art (May–June 1998): 74–75.

Sole, Kelwyn. 'The Role of the Writer in a Time of Transition.' Staffrider 11 (1993).

—. 'The Witness of Poetry: Economic Calculation, Civil Society, and the Limits of Everyday Experience in a Liberated South Africa.' Unpublished, 2001.

Sontag, Susan. 'Notes on "Camp".' Against Interpretation. New York: Octagon Books, 1986.

Steadman, Ian. 'Collective Creativity: Theatre for a Post-apartheid Society.' Rendering Things Visible: Essays on South African Literary Culture. Ed. Martin Trump. Johannesburg: Ravan Press, 1990.

Steiner, George. 'A Little Night Music. Correspondence as Collaboration: What Mann and Adorno Owed to Each Other.' Times Literary Supplement 11 Oct. 2002: 3–4.

—. Errata, an Examined Life. New Haven and London: Yale University Press, 1997.

—. Real Presences. London: Faber and Faber, 1989.

Taylor, Jane. 'Taking Stock: The Making of a Bourgeois Life.' Unpublished. Presented at the Winter School in Grahamstown, 2002.

—. Ubu and the Truth Commision. Rondebosch: University of Cape Town Press, 1998.

Van Wyk Smith, Malvern. 'Which Liberated Zone Would That Be?' Current Writing 5.1 (1993): 76–84.

Veit-Wild, Flora. 'Carnival and Hybridity in Marechera and Lesego Rampolokeng.' Emerging Perspectives on Dambudzo Marechera. Eds. Flora Veit-Wild and Anthony Chennells. Trenton NJ and Asmara, Eritrea: Africa World Press, 1999.

—. 'Festivals of Laughter: Syncretism in Southern Africa.' Fusion of Cultures? Cross/Cultures 26. Association for the Study of New Literatures in English – ASNEL PAPER 2 (1996): 27–40.

Vladislavić, Ivan. The Folly. Africasouth New Writing. Cape Town: David Philip, 1993.

—. The Restless Supermarket. Cape Town: David Philip, 2001.

Voss, A. E. 'Reading and Writing in the New South Africa.' Current Writing 4 (1992): 1–10.

Wicomb, Zoe. 'Shame and Identity: The Case of the Coloured in South Africa.' Writing South Africa: Literature, Apartheid, Democracy, 1970–1995. Eds. Derek Attridge and Rosemary Jolly. Cambridge: Cambridge University Press, 1998.

Index